"THERE WERE A LOT MORE THAN THAT" ODSAL 1954

Robert Gate

Published in Great Britain by
RE Gate
Mount Pleasant Cottage
Ripponden Bank
Ripponden
Sowerby Bridge HX6 4JL

ISBN 0 9511190 4 4

Printed by Thornton & Pearson (Printers) Ltd., Bradford

CONTENTS

ACKNOWLEDGEMENTS

I am indebted to many people for assistance in compiling *"There Were A Lot More Than That"*.

I owe particular thanks to Ernie Day, the Warrington Rugby League historian. Nothing has been too much trouble for Ernie, whose help in tracking down and interviewing surviving members of the 1954 Warrington side has been invaluable. Ernie is one of the great unsung men of Rugby League, a former professional player with Halifax, a life-long follower of the Wire, a respected historian of Warrington RLFC and a man who is unfailingly helpful. His contribution to this book has been immense.

My gratitude is also due to the noted Halifax RLFC historian, Andrew Hardcastle, who has kindly proof-read the manuscript.

I am especially indebted to the editors of the Bradford *"Telegraph & Argus"*, the Halifax *"Evening Courier"* and *"The Warrington Guardian"* for permission to reproduce articles and photographic and illustrative material from their newspapers of forty years ago.

Other individuals and organisations who have contributed to the creation of *"There Were A Lot More Than That"* are:

Les Ambler, John R Armitage, Neville Atkinson, Kay Batterbee, Doris Beard, Jack Beaumont, Frances N Bennett, Harold Bennett, Dai Bevan, W Birdsall, Jack Bower, Don Bramley, Derek Bridge (Halifax Reference Library), Roy Broadbent JP, Kath Brooke, Bernard Cain, Emily Carr, CL Cass, Ian Clayton, Tony Collins, Ian Collis, Arthur Clues, WR Cruse, Arthur Daniels, M Darbyshire, Jean Davison, Ken Dean, Trevor Delaney, Mike Dews, Frank Dickinson, Vin Dower, Malcolm Dunn, Albert Fearnley, Hilda Fletcher, Raymond Fletcher *("The Yorkshire Post")*, Trevor Foster, Eric Frodsham, Charles Gate, Myfanwy Gate, William Gate, Ron Gelder, Keith Gilbert, Maynard Glover, Ron Glover, Raymond Graves, Barry Greenman, Stanley Gregory, T Griffiths, David Hanson *("Halifax Evening Courier"* Library), Rodney Hardcastle, EP Harrison, Austin Heathwood, Eric A Hill, Gordon Hill, Keith Hirst, Jim Holroyd, Peter Holroyd, Richard Homer (Bradford *"Telegraph & Argus"* Library), Gordon Horsfall, Fred Huddlestone, Roland Hunter, John Huxley, Sir Bernard Ingham, R Gordon Jackson, FW James, Jock (Warrington), Ron Jones, Stan Kielty, Gordon Kilburn, *"League Express"*, Alan Leigh (Warrington Museum), Stan Lewandowski, James A Lockwood, Albert Lomas, Tommy Lynch, Billy Mather, Stan McCormick, Brenda McNeill, Elvin Meachin, Dr MH Milnes, Ces Mountford, Chris Murgatroyd, John Oakes, *"The Oldham Chronicle"*, *"Open Rugby"*, Chris Park, Gordon Phillips, David Pullan, Les Pyrah, Bernard Rafferty, E Ralph, FD Reynolds, Terence Rice, Dave Roberts, John Roberts, Peter Robinson, Mildred Robshaw, David Rogers (Warrington Library), William G Rowland, Douglas Rowlands, The Rugby Football League, *"The Rugby Leaguer"*, Bob Ryan, Peter Sampson, Derrick Schofield, Alex Service, Roger Shackleton, Alf Sharman, June Sharp, Harry Sheard, Harry Shirley, Harry Smith, Stuart Smith, Geoffrey Spence MBE, Frank Spencer, Jack Stanley, Arnold Stevens, H Sunman, Jack Swales, Brian Taylor, David Thomas, A Thorley, Avona Thorley, John Thorley, Roy Tinsley, Michael Turner, Brian Tyson, Tommy Uttley, Albert Walker, Ann Walsh, Joe Warham, D White, Ted White, Eric Whitehead, Covey Whitham, the late Jack Wilkinson, June Wilkinson, Margaret A Wilson, Harold Winterburn, KJ Woods

Finally, thanks are due to AJ Typesetting, Morley, Leeds, for the efficient way in which they have dealt with the creation of this book.

If anyone has been omitted from these acknowledgements the fault is my own but entirely unintentional.

NOTE: Much of the material included in this book has been derived from scrapbooks and players' photo albums. Consequently the source of such material is not always apparent. If any copyright has been infringed the author apologises unreservedly and invites copyright holders to contact him.

Readers may notice discrepancies and contradictions in various eye-witness accounts in this work. It should be remembered that 40 years is a long time and that memories occasionally play tricks. Unless the facts presented by contributors were demonstrably inaccurate all the eye-witness accounts have been set down almost verbatim. As everyone at the Odsal Replay saw things from a different perspective it is inevitable that memories and opinions sometimes diverge.

INTRODUCTION

The Odsal Replay of 1954 has always held a strange fascination for me. The fact that Halifax, the club I have supported from childhood, was one of the combatants probably had some bearing on this fascination. It is more than mere club loyalty, however. I did not attend my first Thrum Hall match until two years after the replay although my father says he took me to games before I started going on my own. Of course, there have always been tall tales of Odsal 1954 to hear in the Halifax area. If we are to believe some of these tales practically the whole of the Parish of Halifax went to Bradford that May evening and most of them walked a good portion of the way. The referee, naturally enough, was bent, allowed Jim Challinor to score from a forward pass and disallowed two, or was it three, perfectly legitimate Halifax tries.... and, never mind 102,000, everyone knows there were a lot more than that.

Forty years after the event I can look down from my home above Ripponden into the Ryburn Valley and never fail to be amazed that on that evening of 5 May, 1954 whoever lived here before me would have seen a monumental traffic jam stretching far beyond his vision. By all accounts there was a seemingly endless cavalcade of motor vehicles winding slowly and anxiously down over the moors from Oldham and Rochdale. Those towns are 10-12 miles from Ripponden which is six miles from Halifax and from Halifax to Odsal is another good seven miles. Imagine that - a continuous line of traffic snaking from Oldham to Bradford 25 miles across the backbone of England. All this at a time when families with cars were very much the exception rather than the rule.

As a child all this folklore surrounding the Odsal Replay was made more intriguing by my reading habits. In the mid-1950s I used to haunt the children's library in the old Belle Vue mansion. I was seriously into Noddy books and there was a good range of Enid Blyton's other works to choose from. Enid's tales would account for two of the allotted three library tickets but the third ticket was reserved exclusively for Frank Williams' book *Thrum Hall Through Six Reigns and Three Wars* - the only book on Rugby League in the entire library and, as far as I was concerned, the world.

Frank, a Great Britain winger in the celebrated Rorke's Drift Test of 1914 and later Sports Editor of the *Halifax Courier & Guardian*, would no doubt have been gratified to know that I took his book out continuously for the next two years. That book, library-bound in a hard navy blue cover, totally bewitched me. Every fortnight it made the short journey from Belle Vue to our house on Lord Street. It was full of adverts, portraits of past and present Halifax players and officials and the occasional

cup-winners team group. It was, however, the action shots which stuck in my mind. There were only three and they were of the frustratingly indistinct "dotty" type. They were all drawn from the titanic Halifax-Warrington clashes of 1954. One was of Tommy Lynch crossing the Wire line at Odsal, another of Stan McCormick passing majestically in the shadow of the royal box at Wembley and, finally, one of John Thorley about to score the only try at Maine Road. All are reproduced with, I hope, more clarity in this work.

Thus Frank Williams, local folklore and a lifelong study of the game's history have combined to provoke the production of *"There Were A Lot More Than That"*. The only major surprise is the knowledge that no one has previously been moved to chronicle the Odsal Replay. It was, after all, arguably Rugby League's most momentous event. In all conscience it should be regarded as one of British sport's most historic occasions, never mind merely a Rugby League event.

Just what prompted 102,000 (officially), 120,000 (admittedly by the police and other officials) or 150,000 (as likely as not) to descend on Odsal will probably never be understood. It cannot have been the prospect of another game like the 4-4 Wembley bore nor the delights of a modern stadium for even in those days Odsal was hardly palatial. Indeed just a month previously Harry East described Odsal thus:

"an unturfed valley, terraced with the refuse of dustbins and ashpits, a vacant expanse of sloping blackness relieved only by the glinting brightness of tin cans and broken bottles and the yellow ooze of a creeping bed of clay squeezing viscously under the dumped loads of rubbish."

("The Yorkshire Observer", 6 April, 1954)

Some critics trumpeted grandiosely that it was *"the will of the North"*, that people were tired of paying large amounts of money to travel to London where the game was unappreciated, that attendances at Wembley were actually falling after the boom years of the immediate post-war period. Whatever the reasons, the exodus from all the Rugby League-playing areas of the north country that day was of truly biblical proportions and took everyone by surprise.

Of course, there was no real precedent. Challenge Cup Final replays were not everyday affairs. Only the 1910 Leeds-Hull Final had ever resulted in a draw. That year both the final and the replay took place at Fartown with the respective attendances 19,413 and 11,608 so there was no genuine parallel to draw with that. Odsal had been housing very big crowds since before the war but the ground record was a mere 69,898 for the Warrington-Leeds Challenge Cup Semi-final of

1950. The largest crowd in the heartlands of the game had in fact been drawn to a soccer ground and once again Warrington had been a participant. Back in 1949 Maine Road, Manchester had held no fewer than 75,194 for the Championship Final classic when Huddersfield beat the Wire 13-12. That was coincidentally just a week after a Rugby League world record crowd of 95,050 had watched Bradford Northern beat Halifax 12-0 at Wembley.

The crowd for the drawn game at Wembley in 1954 had been 81,841 and the combined total for the two semi-finals was roughly similar at 83,954. Even though there were hopes that the previous Odsal ground record would be challenged and speculation had long been rife as to just how many the stadium could accommodate, few in their wildest fantasies were ready for what happened. On the day of the match *"The Halifax Courier & Guardian"* reported that Odsal officials were prepared to cater for up to 80,000 spectators and that extra crush barriers had been installed. Dai Rees, the manager of Bradford Northern and a former Halifax and test second-rower, said Odsal was *"all set for the biggest crowd ever if need be. My own estimate is that we shall have a crowd of around 60,000"*. On 1 May in the same paper Frank Williams had indeed forecast that the ground record would be broken but had not taken too seriously *"wild estimates"* of the first 100,000 crowd in the North. *"The Warrington Guardian's"* May Day prophecy of 60,000 coincided with Dai Rees's.

Certainly the Rugby Football League cannot have expected anything like a record crowd. Yet the League was usually accurate in its estimations of crowds for major fixtures. They had to be in order to anticipate the number of programmes required. This was worked out on a basis of producing one programme for every three spectators expected and it was generally a good rule of thumb. They were definitely caught out at Odsal. Only 15,000 programmes were printed indicating a projected attendance of around 45,000. Of those, 14,900 were sold realising net proceeds of £310/8/4, the remaining 100 presumably being complimentaries. It is interesting to note that the programme for the Odsal Replay has become one of the most collectable items of Rugby League memorabilia and has been known to fetch a price of £100. The original cost was a mere six pence (2½p). Relatively few programmes of this epic occasion seem to have survived possibly due to the fact that towards the end of the game and after it there was heavy rain and many people used their programmes to cover their heads or even sat on them.

The weather forecast for the match was *"changeable, showers, cooler than normal, fresh winds"* - not exactly encouraging.

Jack Burns, Sports Editor of Bradford's *"Telegraph & Argus"* ran an article on the day of the game under the headline *"Will New Odsal Record Be Set?"* in which he wrote, *"As usual the weather must play a big part in the answering of this query - and one feels that if it is fine this evening it may well be that new figures will be set up. The magic of a Cup Final in the provinces promises to make Bradford the Mecca tonight for many thousands of people from all over the North. These are likely to swell the armies of the rival camps to an attendance of huge proportions. The Rugby League, Bradford Northern, the police and the transport people have made their plans accordingly. The stage is set for a big occasion and a big crowd, and it seems that only bad weather can spoil it."*

The fact that in both Halifax and Warrington early closing day was Thursday (i.e. not Wednesday) should also have mitigated against a big attendance although Halifax's proximity to Odsal would ensure that few would be deflected from attending. It may have misled some forecasters that far fewer trains were scheduled to go from Warrington Bank Quay to Low Moor (Bradford) than had travelled to Wembley ten days earlier. Only six special excursions at 7/6 (37½p) per head were down to run and in the event there was not sufficient demand to fill them. What no one foresaw was the phenomenal utilisation of coach travel. There were 1,239 coaches parked around the stadium area which must have been a good proportion of all the coaches in northern England whilst the highest estimate of cars in the vicinity was round 9,000.

Some notable pundits such as Alfred Drewry (*"The Yorkshire Post"*) and Jack Bentley (*"The Daily Dispatch"*) were sceptical that the ground record would be approached. Both felt the game should have been played on a Saturday and that the kick-off time and difficulties in travelling, especially for Lancashire fans, would keep the attendance down. Certainly the authorities were concerned about the likely chaos. At a meeting of the Rugby League's Cup and Rules Revision Committee held at Odsal on 27 April it was recorded that *"strong representation had been received from the Halifax and Bradford City Transport Departments asking for the kick-off to be put back from 6.30 to 7 pm as they would be unable to cope with the extra crowds during their peak period. It was agreed to kick off at 7 pm and to use floodlighting, if necessary, during the extra time, if any extra time was needed"*. It was also agreed that if a second replay was necessary it would take place at Wigan on Monday, 10 May with a 7 pm kick-off and that NT Railton would act as referee. In view of the events at Odsal one dreads to think what might have happened at Wigan with its capacity of around 44,000.

On the Monday before the replay estimates of 15,000 spectators from Halifax and 12,000 from Warrington were being bandied about. Certainly employers in the two towns were being considerate of their work forces' wishes to attend. Many

Hi-tech 1954. The Halifax team meets the BBC at a pre-Wembley session.

Wembley. Harry Bath and Stan McCormick stop a Halifax attacker.

Warrington firms organised coach trips to the game straight from places of work and flexi-time in both towns became the order of the day even if no one had yet coined the phrase. In Halifax the local bowls league matches were brought forward from Wednesday to Tuesday. The Grammar Schools in various places in the North exhibited their prejudices as the author has received several reminiscences of former pupils having to defy headmasters whose edict was thou shalt not take time off to see Rugby League matches on pain of severe retribution. Boys being boys, the rules were ignored. Of course, the Grammar Schools involved played Rugby Union and experience suggests that had someone in those schools been arranging trips to Rugby Union matches they would have been compulsory, never mind punishable.

A ten-minute shuttle service was operated between Halifax and Low Moor, the nearest station to Odsal, from 4.30 to 5.40. Oddly enough, it was this British Rail service which could have alerted everyone to the immensity of the approaching invasion of Odsal. For days before the game the service had been taking advance bookings which British Rail had said was most unusual for such a short journey.

As kick-off time approached it became apparent that something incredible and inexplicable was occurring. The truly amazing aspect of the Odsal Replay is the realisation that there was no major disaster for here surely was a disaster in the making. Well over 100,000 entered Odsal's immense but potentially lethal bowl that night. Stewarding in those days was rudimentary to say the least. Fans could not be directed into designated areas, the steep slopes and inadequate railway sleeper terracing were potential death traps and there were a mere 150 policemen plus some special constables to control matters. It could not happen today, of course, ringed as we are with crowd safety regulations and restricted capacities. Even today Rugby League supporters are famed for their good behaviour. Forty years ago there were certainly no fears of riotous behaviour from such a gathering but the possibility of calamitous accidents could not have been ruled out.

One of the recurring themes of the interviews with people who were present at Odsal is the admiration for the good nature of the crowd. Most witnesses say that they never felt in any danger even though there were instances of collapsing fences, pitch invasions, crowd surges and tremendous crushes at the exits. However, seventy St. John Ambulance workers drawn from Bradford, Halifax, Pudsey, the Spen Valley and Selby dealt with over 200 incidents - *"bruisings, bumpings and faintings"*, as *"The Yorkshire Post"* referred to them. Fortunately none proved serious and miraculously only two men went to hospital - a 71 year-old who collapsed and a 34 year-old who sprained an ankle. Despite this apparent lack of

danger other people, particularly women experiencing their first big match, spoke of being terrified. Indeed one of the ring-side seat stewards, aged 18 at the time, said he just looked up and never saw anything as frightening in his life and he was used to big games on the ground.

In truth no two people on the ground that night had the same story to tell. Each perspective was unique. Some, perhaps most, were oblivious to dangers, others fearful. Some saw everything, others virtually nothing. Some, not many, journeyed to and from Bradford with hardly a hitch, the majority experienced most of the travelling traumas imaginable. The first fans in the queues arrived at 3.30, an hour and a half before the gates opened, others were still entering the ground after 8 pm.

In hindsight from scores and scores of interviews the impression one gets is that the occasion resembled a battle-field in that no one had an overall view of what occurred. There was no general to marshal affairs. Individuals merely had their own view of things. It appears, however, that two distinct environments developed. On the lower slopes, below the encircling flat pathways there was relative calm and terracing conditions were adequate. It was higher up, above the pathways where there was more disquiet. Spectators were reluctant to move forwards for the nearer they approached the flat area the less they were likely to see. Without effective stewarding spectators literally dug in and would not move. It is not hard to imagine the frustration of latecomers coming face to face, or rather face to backs, with solid ranks of immovable fans.

The fact that this book is being written 40 years after the event is a telling reflection on our game's inability to promote its major achievements for nothing similar has preceded this work. The overwhelming mass of the research has had to centre on interviews and contemporary newspaper reports for no secondary sources appear to exist. It is difficult to imagine an event of such magnitude occurring in any other sport and not being part of the fabric of the nation's sporting folklore. Undoubtedly someone would have chronicled any comparable event in any other sport. In view of the current antipathy of national newspapers toward Rugby League perhaps we should not be too surprised to learn that back in 1954 things were just as bad. For example, whilst the northern editions of such papers as *"The Daily Express"* and *"The Daily Herald"* could find room for news of the Odsal scenes on their front pages, *"The Times"* appeared to be ignorant that a crowd of such gigantic proportions had even assembled in its short, page-four match report. Most of its sports coverage concerned horse racing whilst golf, tennis and athletics all rated more column inches than the small affair at Odsal. In Friday's *"Times"* sculling commanded more space than had the replay report.

It perhaps did not help that the day after Odsal at Iffley Road, Oxford Roger Bannister ran the first

Odsal. Stan McCormick wraps up Arthur Daniels. Gerry Helme moves in to help.

Odsal. Aerial combat as the ball descends.

sub four minute mile to break a physical and psychological barrier that had for so long fascinated the sporting public. Thereafter the sporting press was agog for little else. Ironically the crowd at the Iffley Road meeting was a mere 1,200, one hundredth of the total the police estimated had entered Odsal legally and illegally.

Whilst the major focus of this book is the Odsal Replay the events leading up to and following it have been incorporated into the text for it is doubtful if two teams ever have been or ever will again be engaged in a five match series such as the one which ensued between Halifax and Warrington within the space of five weeks in the April and May of 1954. In the course of those games in London, Bradford, Manchester, Dublin and Belfast more than a quarter of a million people passed through the turnstiles or in some cases through broken down fences.

TIMETABLE - 'FAX AND WIRE 1954

DATE	VENUE	'FAX-WIRE	CROWD
24 April	Empire Stadium, Wembley	4-4	81,841
5 May	Odsal Stadium, Bradford	4-8	102,569
8 May	Maine Road, Manchester	7-8	36,519
27 May	Windsor Park, Belfast	34-15	10,000
28 May	Dalymount Park, Dublin	23-11	15,000

Smiling faces, flat caps and wet heads – a section of the Odsal multitudes

THAT CROWD

The crowd figure returned immediately after the Odsal replay was 102,575. It was that figure which screamed out of the newspaper headlines the following day and is a figure which is sometimes misquoted even today. The official crowd figure was in fact amended to 102,569 by the Rugby Football League a few days later. Just why the discrepancy of a mere six spectators should have arisen has never been explained. Moreover, the figure of 102,575 has never been altered in the League's own attendance books. All reputable sources do, however, accept the 102,569 version. Interestingly, the Wembley attendance was originally given as 81,777 but later amended to 81,841.

"A CAMPAIGN OF HATE AND INTIMIDATION"

On Saturday, 5 April, 1954 the semi-finals of the Challenge Cup were held. At Station Road, Swinton almost 37,000 people watched Warrington defeat Leeds more easily than an 8–4 scoreline suggested. The Wires had had a break on the Fylde Coast prior to the game. Some critics had felt their play was becoming a little stale and that the players needed a tonic. Leeds had been delighted that the game had not been scheduled for Odsal, a venue at which they had not won a cup-tie since the war. Conversely, Warrington's record in cup-ties at Station Road was lamentable. Arthur Clues, the brilliant and fiery Australian second-rower for Leeds, had promised *"to give Bathy the Churchillian sign at the finish"*. It was Harry Bath, his compatriot, who was signalling with his fingers all the way to Wembley, however. Leeds had once again failed to deliver the goods at Swinton despite Warrington's having played with only twelve fit men for nearly all the game.

Wire second-rower Ted White had smashed his fibula but heroically played out the match. Ironically, it was an identical injury to one he had received in a shock League defeat at Hull KR back in August. There would be no Empire Stadium for Ted. Ron Gelder refereed the Swinton semi and when it was announced that he was to officiate at Wembley few Warrington fans grumbled.

Across the Pennines in the other semi at Odsal before just under 47,000 fans Halifax saw off Hunslet 18–3 and a chain of events which rocked the West Riding, if not the whole of Leagueland, was set in train.

Back on 10 October, 1953 Halifax had gone to Headingley and crushed Leeds 40–10 in a sometimes unsavoury game. Eighteen days later Leeds proposed that a "Rough Play Commission" be established. Consequently a somewhat nebulous committee was set up to look into the problem of rough play and never published whatever findings it arrived at.

On the Monday (5 April) following the Odsal semi-final Halifax were to meet Bradford Northern at Thrum Hall. If Halifax won they would retain their Yorkshire League Championship title. It was a local derby and there was a lot at stake. The "Bradford *Telegraph & Argus's*" writer *"Oracle"* previewed the match that day. He described the Halifax forwards thus, *"The pack is one of the best – if not the best ever – that has served the Thrum Hall side"*. In *"Oracle's"* estimation they were *"terrific"*, they were *"brilliant"* and his article bore not a trace of animosity to the blue and whites.

By the 23rd minute Halifax were 8–0 up and clearly going to win even though their reserve centre John Burnett had dislocated his shoulder. At full-time Halifax had won 15–2 and lifted the Yorkshire League Championship again. The following day's *"T & A"* report by *"Oracle"* carried the headline: *"THIS BEAT THE BATTLE OF ODSAL!"*

The report ran,

"The fiery Halifax pack met its master at Thrum Hall last night when Foster and his Bradford Northern forward colleagues refused to be subdued by Ackerley and his men.

. . . The game was, to my mind, even worse than that memorable 'Battle of Odsal' between Great Britain and Australia in 1952.

It was amazing that neither trainer was called on for I have never before seen so much reckless kicking, tripping, obstruction, unnecessary double tackling or individual fights in one game.

The first half was not too bad. It was hard and robust but kept just within the laws of the game . . . The rough stuff became more obvious after the interval, and Mr Coates, the Pudsey referee, was a patient man. He issued many cautions but it was not until five minutes from the end that Tyler and Clarkson, who were swapping punches, were dismissed . . . There was little football for the 11,500 crowd and it is to be hoped there will not be a repetition when the teams meet in the return game at Odsal Stadium next Saturday."

Alfred Drewry's report in *"The Yorkshire Post"* was more graphic. He wrote:

"There were no victory smiles in the tea-room afterwards. Everyone looked uncomfortable; as though they wished they were somewhere else. I certainly wish I had not been at the match. I prefer my boxing in a ring, and with only two contestants at a time. The happenings during the last quarter were a disgrace to the code. The uninhibited fight between Clarkson and Tyler . . . was a clean, honest set-to compared with the sly punching, elbowing, obstructing and general nastiness which during the previous 20 minutes or so had been seen by everyone except, apparently, the referee and touch-judges."

"Oracle", writing in *"Yorkshire Sports"*, the Bradford Saturday pink, commented that the game at Thrum Hall was a *"really nasty exhibition – there should be a special enquiry into it . . . the League Management Committee ought not to allow this match to be best forgotten . . . This wretched match should induce all concerned to redouble their efforts to prevent such blots on the game."* (*"Yorkshire Sports"*, 10 April, 1954).

Within two days of these damning match reports all Hell was let loose as the Halifax players threatened to boycott the return fixture against Bradford

THE NEW H-BOMB

THE President of the United States has named five "fears" produced by his country's hydrogen bomb, but last week's Rugby League H-bomb (H for Halifax) gave rise to "fears" considerably in excess of that number throughout the whole of our game. The stage has now been reached when sportsmen everywhere are demanding to know just what happens when two teams of players meet in a match described as "Rugby League football." No amount of whitewashing will extricate those responsible for the control and government of the sport in this country from the deplorable series of happenings of the past week. The most searching investigation is demanded, together with a firm assurance that effective measures will be taken to prevent any recurrence. **The honour and reputation of English professional Rugby football stands at the lowest level since the code was established nearly sixty years ago.** A superhuman effort will be required to rid the game of its unsavoury reputation, but we are confident that with proper direction sportsmen will once again be proud to acknowledge their association with Rugby League.

For the second time since the war the Halifax club has won its way to the final of the R.L. Challenge Cup. In the Northern Rugby Football League the side is undefeated on its own ground, and have only lost three matches on opponents' pitches. Judging, however, from statements made by the players responsible for this fine achievement, their playing success has been rewarded with a campaign of "hate and intimidation." The fuse has been burning some time but reached and set off the powder barrel when a certain newspaper — not "a little rag of a paper" this time but presumably "a big rag" — alleged that the club were to be "warned by the League." The first team players thereupon decided that if their style of play offended the R.L. authorities they would prefer not to take part in the next League fixture against Bradford Northern, at Odsal Stadium, on April 10th. When the R.L. Cup Committee met in Leeds on April 8th, some of the members who had attended the semi-final between Halifax and Hunslet the previous Saturday expressed dissatisfaction with the way the game was controlled. Finally it was decided to request the referee (Mr. G. S. Phillips, of Widnes) to submit a report, with particular reference to the support — or lack of it — he received from the touch judges. After the exact position had been explained to the Halifax players they decided to call off their strike.

No doubt the majority of R.L. followers wondered whether the Cup Committee had made a mistake over the match on which they required a report. Surely it should have been the League meeting between Halifax and Bradford N. at Thrum Hall on Monday evening, April 5th? We know it is not always safe to place reliance on R.L. reports which appear in some of our contemporaries — the Halifax players are old enough to be aware of that fact by this time — but both "The Yorkshire Observer" and "The Yorkshire Post" are served by Rugby League writers of ability and long experience of our game. Of this match at Thrum Hall, Mr. George M. Thompson, writing in "The Yorkshire Observer," described parts of it as outrivalling some of the worst happenings in the now famous Odsal Test Match (December, 1952). In black type he wrote: "For a club game there must have been the record number of upper-cuts, half-arm tackles, punches, trips, deliberate kicks, and other actions, mostly done shamelessly in front of 10,500 spectators." "The whole affair left a nasty taste," Mr. Thompson added, "and I do not want to see again so much calculated nastiness and deliberate obstruction as came in this game."

Alfred Drewry, in "The Yorkshire Post," was no less disgusted by the Thrum Hall "football-plus." Consider this extract: "The happenings during the last quarter were a disgrace to the code. The uninhibited fight between Clarkson, the Halifax loose forward, and Tyler, the Bradford prop forward, resulted in both being sent off the field five minutes from the end, but that was a clean, honest set-to compared with the sly punching, elbowing, obstructing, and general nastiness which during the previous twenty minutes or so had been seen by everyone except; apparently, the referee and touch judges." In writing as they have done, are both Mr. Thompson and Mr. Drewry guilty of a "hate and intimidation" campaign? Is their reporting a distortion of what actually took place between the leading League club and a near rival? It is understood the Halifax club proposes to take legal opinion on the newspaper report which precipitated the crisis with its players over playing in the return match against Bradford N. The club, and also the R.L. Council, cannot ignore the reports which appeared in the two newspapers named, and which subsequently were the sole topic of conversation in the West Riding. **The allegations made about the conduct of players in the match at Thrum Hall on April 5th must be probed to the full by the R.L. Council. The disciplinary action already taken against the two players who were sent off cannot be regarded as the final word about an affair of this description.**

We have heard a good deal this season about the problem of rough play in Rugby League, and the Management Committee of the Northern Rugby League has undertaken specific inquiries on the subject. It is worth recalling that it was the Leeds club who requested this investigation shortly after they had played Halifax in a League match at Headingley. Commenting on this match, "Rugby League Review" said: "It is a long while since so many stiff-arm tackles took place in one match. The good football displayed by Halifax was unfortunately marred by the other happenings, and instead of the famous 'Headingley roar,' boos were heard during a large part of the game." Will last year's booing be repeated when Halifax and Warrington meet at Wembley on Saturday week? Not much time remains for the R.L. Council to act in this matter and save the game from possibly further shame. A large number of the spectators who will fill the stadium will do so with recent events fresh in their minds. It is a very delicate situation and we trust the Council will let it be known that should anything unworthy of the game take place, the punishment will be drastic. For our part **we are confident both the Halifax and Warrington players can make this Final one which will go a long way towards wiping away the sordid memories of the past weeks. That, and not just to win the match, will be their onerous task on April 24th.**

PROGRAMME FOR EASTER SATURDAY, APRIL 17th

NORTHERN LEAGUE MATCHES — Kick-off 3 p.m.

Ground	Visitors
Odsal Stadium, Bradford	BARROW
Crown Flatt, Dewsbury	WAKEFIELD TRINITY
Bentley Road, Doncaster	ROCHDALE HORNETS
Post Office Road, Featherstone	LEEDS
St. John's Ground, Fartown, Huddersfield	BATLEY
Craven Park, Kingston upon Hull	HALIFAX
Parkside, Hunslet, Leeds	CASTLEFORD
Lawkholme Lane, Keighley	HULL
Kirkhall Lane, Leigh	WIGAN
Watersheddings, Oldham	MANCHESTER BELLE VUE RANGERS
Knowsley Road, St. Helens	WIDNES
Station Road, Swinton	SALFORD
Wilderspool Stadium, Warrington	WHITEHAVEN
Borough Park, Workington	BRAMLEY
Clarence Street, York	LIVERPOOL CITY

NOTE.—All matches subject to cancellation without notice.
B.B.C. Sports Results at 6.25 p.m., followed by "Sports Review" at 6.35 p.m. (to 7 p.m.) with "results and review" of Rugby League games.

RUGBY LEAGUE REVIEW, April 15, 1954—253

"THE DAILY MIRROR DARES!"

ALTHOUGH the R.L. Challenge Cup is safely in Warrington, a very large number of the game's followers are still indignant over the nation-wide allegation made by a so-called R.L. writer against the conduct of Halifax, the Cup runner-up. It will be recalled that following the playing of the semi-final between Halifax and Hunslet, the R.L. Cup and Rules Committee decided to ask the referee in charge of that match — Mr. G. S. Phillips, of Widnes — to submit a special report. Certain members of the Committee who attended the semi-final expressed dissatisfaction at their meeting and the outcome was the decision to ask Mr. Phillips for a report, "with particular reference to the support or lack of it he received from his touch judges." The R.L. secretary later informed the Halifax club that neither the Cup and Rules Committee nor the Disciplinary Committee passed any resolution that the Halifax players should be warned about alleged foul play. The minutes of the two committees, of course, are available and must be accepted as a true record of the respective meetings.

The issue of the "Daily Mirror" for Thursday, April 8th, 1954, published in its sports pages an article by a certain "Joe Humphreys." A four column splash heading announced "Rugby League: Threat to the Wembley Show-piece. 'Stop Rough Play' Warning." Mr. Humphreys certainly left his readers in no doubt over what he was writing about, and his opening paragraph was equally direct. "The Rugby League," he wrote "is to warn one of the Wembley Challenge Cup Final teams about alleged rough play. Officials of the Halifax club, which meets Warrington on April 24th, are to be told this week-end, 'Clean up your game and cut out the foul play. It won't do for the Final.'" The R.L. Disciplinary Committee, stated Mr. Humphreys, were responsible for this "reprimand." Two of the members intended to attend the next Halifax match with the firm resolve to stop their rough play. They are reported in his article as having declared they would "tell the club's officials that they must clean up their game and cut out the rough play." Mr. Humphreys gained the full confidence of the two committee-men, for he informed us they told him the Halifax players were also to be warned about their conduct.

There is nothing ambiguous about the "Daily Mirror" writer's article. The Halifax officials and players were to be warned "to stop their rough play and foul tactics." A responsible committee of the Rugby Football League had decided this action was necessary before the R.L. Challenge Cup Final took place at Wembley. In the whole history of the game there can surely have been no more fateful step decided upon by a body of officials. **But the R.L. secretary, acting on behalf of the R.L. Council, categorically denied that any committee had decided to issue such a warning to the Halifax club.** There is no reason to doubt the truth of the official statement. What has Mr. Humphreys had to say in reply? He used his position as a writer in a mass circulation newspaper to report an alleged decision which as a responsible writer he must have known had never been passed by the committee he named. Moreover, he would appear to have invented the conversation with the two committee-men. **Well may we ask whether there is a word of truth in the entire article, and that it constitutes a grave libel on the officials and players of the Halifax club.**

After reading the "Daily Mirror" article the Halifax first team players were naturally perturbed. We do not propose to discuss whether the action which they subsequently decided upon was the wisest under the circumstances. The Halifax club chairman allowed it to be known that upon receipt of official denial or confirmation of the statements made in the article, legal advice would be sought. The chairman was not long in receiving a reply, but R.L. supporters are still awaiting news of what action is contemplated against the writer and publishers of the offending article. Many readers have reminded us of the legal action taken by the R.L. secretary, with the approval and financial backing of the Rugby Football League, in 1952 against the Editor of "Rugby League Review" and the publishers of the paper. The two cases are not quite similar, for the Editor of "Rugby League Review" did not write or cause to be circulated anything of a false nature.

There is reason for believing, in the light of the Rugby Football League's statement, that the article by Joe Humphreys in the "Daily Mirror," was in the words of the Rugby League's own counsel, "spiteful, malicious, nasty, and twisted." However, counsel cannot claim the "Daily Mirror" is "a little rag of a paper." It is a very powerful and successful business organisation, with financial resources far in excess of "Rugby League Review." We do not know if this knowledge has stayed the hand of the Halifax club, and that even with the backing of the Rugby Football League they decided it was too risky to try conclusions with Mr. Joe Humphreys and the "Daily Mirror." Whatever decision the Halifax directors and the Rugby Football League have now reached, it does not alter the fact that the article was written and received widespread publication.

It is easy for any writer to be mis-informed on a particular point, but the "Daily Mirror" article permits of no such admission. Until it was repudiated by R.L. headquarters it had the hall-mark of an authoritative and official pro-nouncement. We suggest that was the one reason why the "Daily Mirror" editor allowed it to be published, and that Joe Humphreys, whoever he may be, is the man who should be placed in the dock. It may be too late at this stage to refer the whole matter to the Press Council, but that course should certainly have been taken by the Rugby Football League after the article had been brought to their notice by the Halifax club. **Rugby League football is anxious to obtain the maximum mention in the mass circulation papers, but nothing is to be gained through the publishing of fictitious statements which precipitate a crisis among players, creates bad feeling between clubs, and damages the reputation of the sport in the eyes of the whole nation.**

Whitehaven Player Fined. John Patrick McGuinness, 23-year-old labourer and Whitehaven R.L. player, fined £5 and ordered to pay £5 5s. costs at Maryport Court. He was charged with having struck a girl on the nose after a dance on April 8th. Superintendent Threlkeld after stating that McGuinness was a professional R.L. player, commented, "It may be that he is used to giving similar blows when tackled by male companions, but this was a female." The chairman told McGuinness that he was very fortunate he had not been sent to prison. — Friday, May 14th.

Darwin Arrival. Arrival of 'plane with English R.L. tourists at Darwin, after flying through a bad storm. Sydney reached during the evening. — Monday, May 17th.

Not Cricket! Committee stage of the Finance Bill in the House of Commons. Series of amendments designed to exempt all sports from payment of entertainments duty defeated. Another amendment which provided that in the case of Association or Rugby League matches, and boxing, the amount of duty payable in respect of any fixture should be reduced by £100 in every case where the total receipts for admission did not exceed £2,000, was rejected by 247 votes to 237. — Tuesday, May 18th.

£4,500 Offer Refused. Wigan's offer of £4,500 to turn professional declined by Terry Davies, Swansea R.U. full-back. Davies played for Wales against England, Ireland, Scotland, and France, in 1953, while in the Royal Marines. He is now working as a clerk for a firm of contractors. Fine goal-kicker. Wigan club declined to make any comment on the reported offer but the secretary stated that the fee of £4,500 was "very wild." —May 18th.

Opening Victory. English R.L. tourists defeated Western Division, at Bathurst by 29 points to 11. First match of tour. — Wednesday, May 19th.

Asked to Join. Blackpool club approached Kia Rika, Halifax Maori utility reserve back, with offer to sign. Rika joined Halifax in December, 1947, having previously played for the Thrum Hallers during season 1945-46 while serving with the New Zealand Forces. Halifax have now granted Rika a free transfer. — May 19th.

Odsal, Cup semi-final. Halifax players rush to congratulate try-scorer Arthur Daniels as Hunslet are beaten 18-3. Referee George Phillips (far right) was asked to prepare a report on the conduct of his touch-judges after this game.

Swinton, Cup semi-final. Brian Bevan sprints through the Leeds defence.

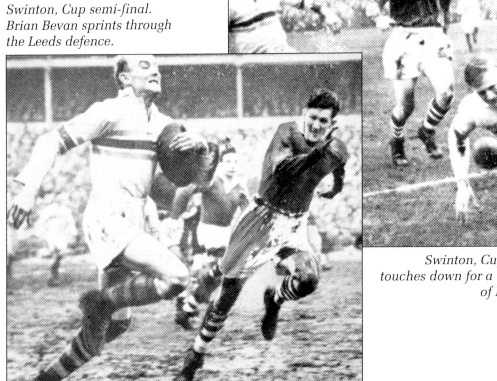

Swinton, Cup semi-final. Jim Challinor touches down for a Wire try in their 8–4 defeat of Leeds. Bevan is in support.

at Odsal. An article by Joe Humphreys had appeared in the *"Daily Mirror"* on Thursday, 8 April. In it Mr Humphreys said, *"The Rugby League is to warn one of the Challenge Cup Final teams about alleged rough play. Officials of the Halifax Club . . . are to be told this weekend, 'Clean up your game and cut out the foul play. It won't do for the final'."*

Joe Humphreys' source for the proposed censure of the Halifax team was allegedly the Rugby League Disciplinary Committee which had met prior to the *"Mirror's"* article. This was flatly denied by League Secretary, Bill Fallowfield who pointed out that the Disciplinary Committee merely dealt with players who were dismissed or were reported by referees. It was not within its jurisdiction to make pronouncements such as had appeared in the press.

Matters were exacerbated and confused after the Rugby League Cup Committee met on 8 April when some members had expressed disquiet at the handling of the Halifax-Hunslet semi-final. At that meeting it was decided to ask the match referee, George Phillips, to prepare a report on the conduct of his touch-judges, who were obviously felt by some committee members to have not fulfilled their duties.

On Friday, 9 April *"The Halifax Courier & Guardian"* front page was full of talk about player strikes and legal action. The players were reported to have had a meeting the previous evening following training. Appropriately enough, it lasted as long as a match – 80 minutes. One of the players was reported to have said, *"We were thunderstruck, appalled by this allegation that league officials were concerned about our conduct as a team."*

The Halifax players were reported to have made the following three points in interviews with club officials:

(1) *A campaign of 'hate and intimidation' is being developed against the Thrum Hall players and that this has been intensified since the RL cup semi-final success against Hunslet.*

(2) *Even experienced players find it difficult to give of their best if they have the feeling they are suspected of unfair conduct.*

(3) *Continuance of the 'hate campaign' might affect the playing form of younger, less experienced members of the team, particularly in the Cup Final at Wembley and in the vital league games of the next two weeks.*

The upshot was that the Halifax players unanimously agreed to strike and not play the Bradford Northern fixture on 10 April.

Bill Hughes, the Halifax Secretary, told the *"Courier"* that anxious fans were phoning in at the rate of 40 per hour pleading with the club to get the RFL to intervene. Frank Williams wrote, *"I cannot understand this uncalled-for attack on the way the Halifax forwards go about their work. Throughout 1953–54 the forwards have played to a plan, and with every man trained to a high pitch of efficiency.*

They play vigorously, but rarely, unless provoked to retaliation, has there been need for a referee to reprimand a Halifax player. The away matches against St. Helens and Wigan were two of the most vigorous football displays anyone could wish to see, yet there were no cautions and the trainers of either side had no cause to enter the field of play. There have been powerful packs in the past. Douglas Clark, Bob Taylor and other great players not only enjoyed their football but put every ounce of energy into it, and no one cried out about them. The Halifax club and players have been unjustly singled out."

Halifax vice-captain, Stan Kielty said, *"These insinuations and allegations are plainly ridiculous. Some of us had thought certain people were trying to put us off our game, but what has been said in the last day or two is too serious to overlook. I am sorry to upset our supporters but they will understand no team can go out on to the field and play normally with the feeling that every action of every player is under scrutiny. It just won't do."*

Frank Dawson, the coach, merely said, *"There is a good deal of bunkum talk – part of it a case of sour grapes from certain people."*

Eventually tempers subsided and Halifax fulfilled their fixture at Bradford on 10 April. Two members of the Disciplinary Committee, WH Hughes (Salford) and Hector Rawson (Hunslet) were present at the match which drew Northern's biggest league crowd of the season (19,370). Halifax won 15–7 and it was remarked that the experiment of playing with a white ball caused more bother than the players. Ironically enough, George Phillips was again the referee. On the one occasion he admonished Albert Fearnley he was roundly booed!

Peace appeared to have broken out by 17 April when the writer of *"Halifax Hints"* in *"Yorkshire Sports"* commented, *"Could anyone wish for a cleaner game than that seen at Odsal? Plus a little extra fire, it was a display typical of Halifax. It is incredible that this particular side has had to bear the brunt of criticism, for they are athletes who work together as a team – and they love their work. To vouch for the irreproachable manner in which they have reached the top they have testimonials from Wigan, St. Helens, Leeds, Huddersfield, Keighley and from every Rugby League centre where Halifax have provided the opposition."*

An article by *"Veteran"* in *"Yorkshire Sports"* (10 April) was equally fulsome in its tone. Quite amazingly in the selections for the 1954 Australasian tour which were made before the semi-finals only one Halifax and two Warrington players were deemed good enough. This from the two teams who finished first and second in the table and dominated the season! Imagine the outcry in 1994 if Wigan and, say, Bradford Northern were so treated! *"Veteran"* wrote, *"The selectors could have made their task in relation to forwards a simple one.*

Postcard of Odsal's largest pre-war crowd. The Challenge Cup Semi-final of 1939 drew a crowd of 64,453 to see Halifax beat Leeds 10–4.

The largest crowd for a Rugby League game in the North prior to the Odsal replay assembled at Maine Road in 1949. 75,194 witnessed Warrington's 13–12 Championship Final defeat by Huddersfield. Here Gerry Helme feeds a scrum.

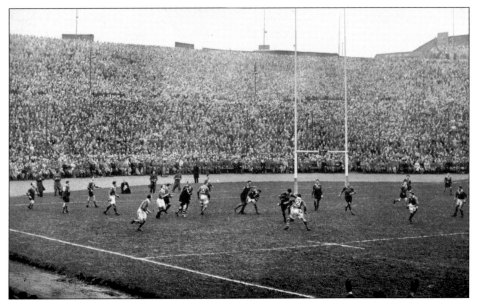

Before 1954 Odsal's record crowd stood at 69,898 for the Leeds–Warrington Cup semifinal of 1950. Above we see Leeds penned in their '25' at the Rooley Lane end. Warrington won 16–4.

They could have picked the Halifax pack en bloc and if the Australians had ideas about continuing the famous Battle of Odsal they would, in this event, have had second thoughts. 'Rough' does not connote 'foul' and the Secretary of the League himself has said Rugby is rough. For the sake of staving off criticism I prefer the word 'robust'. Certainly the Hunslet spectators at Odsal (in the semi-final) were bitterly resentful of the toughness, roughness or robustness of the blue and white forwards, call this attribute of theirs what you may. Yet Hunslet will admit, I hope, that the Halifax side had far more than vigour – that they had pace and intelligence and that in three of four Halifax tries they co-operated in brilliant, sweeping movements that began in the Halifax half."

All storms blow themselves out, of course. Frank Williams perhaps encapsulated the problem which beset Halifax in his book *"Thrum Hall Through Six Reigns and Three Wars"*. He wrote, *"It is my belief that the brilliant work of the team in 1953–54 had got on the nerves of some people. To complain about the play of the Halifax team was, in my opinion, fantastic. They were certainly robust, but Rugby is a naturally keen game, and Halifax possessed such brilliant team spirit that their play was concentrated and looked more determined in its execution . . . The psychological effect of the outpourings of a certain misguided writer, I am certain, left its mark on the efforts of the Halifax players. Their play in the final games was at least 25 per cent less enthusiastic than before the uncalled for criticism, which must have had a demoralising effect on the Halifax players and referees."*

Had this passage of events taken place in the sleazy tabloid world of the 1990s one dreads to think what colourful tales would have hit the front pages. Looking back on it after 40 years it seems a bit like a storm in a teacup. However, the reaction of disgust of some of the Halifax players transcends the passage of time. They were deeply offended, still are. In truth, if memories of some of the players hold good, it may well have been whispering campaigns and the newspaper placards which caused more offence than the articles of Joe Humphreys and *"Oracle"* (Roland Tinker). Some players recall placards which screamed *"Halifax Thugs"* or even *"Halifax Animals"* which were certainly well over the top for the 1950s and, equally certainly, more lurid than the actual articles themselves.

Yet it should be remembered that the world of Rugby League in the 1950s was very much on its guard. In 1948–49 the average attendance at League fixtures stood at 11,500 and around 6,000,000 fans paid through the turnstiles. The figures for the market-led, bound-for-the-super-league, cloth-cap-banning version of Rugby League in the satellite age are an average per game of 3,499 from an aggregate 1,679,897 (1993–94 season). From 1949–50

until 1952–53 the attendances had fallen each season. In the latter season the average crowd had fallen to 7,381 and the aggregate to 3,985,712. The 1953–54 season, however, provided a blip in the downward trend. Attendances actually rose to an average of 7,409 from an aggregate 4,008,083. Bradford Northern, Halifax, Huddersfield, Leeds, Warrington and Wigan all drew over 200,000 to their home league fixtures and St. Helens, the number one crowd-pullers, attracted 301,000 to their home games and over half a million to their complete league programme.

The League were therefore understandably keen to keep attendance levels up. One of the main contributory factors to declining crowds was thought to be the stifling effect of the play-the-ball rule but what was most feared was the taint of rough play. The League had good cause to be worried about it. The previous season had been a horror. The 1952 Kangaroos had been involved in some brutal games culminating in the third test at Bradford which became infamous as *"The Battle of Odsal"*. With falling attendances at Wembley, there had been a renewed call for the Cup Final to be brought back to its homelands. All the League's worst fears had been realised in the Challenge Cup Final of 1953 when Huddersfield and St. Helens, particularly the latter, had sullied the game's image in a sometimes unedifying and violent spectacle.

Visons of a repeat performance by Halifax and Warrington proved a mirage. In fact the three games at Wembley, Odsal and Maine Road were fought out in exemplary fashion.

Warrington's preparations for Wembley were less controversial. In fact the furore over the Pennines seemed to go practically unnoticed in Warrington. There was only a solitary passing mention of the Halifax brouhaha in the Warrington press. Their problems were more mundane but possibly more worrying. Ted White had already been ruled out of Wembley with his broken fibula whilst his second-row partner Syd Phillips, son of George Phillips, the referee, was also crocked with a broken collar-bone sustained in a 21-5 victory at Widnes on Good Friday, 16 April. It was far from a good Friday for the Wire as skipper Ally Naughton sustained a bruised calf. Ally played the following day in a 43-7 home thrashing of Whitehaven but aggravated the injury and failed to finish the game. Ally would not play again until the end of season games in Ireland. Eric Frodsham took over the captaincy.

Ron Ryder, the former test centre, rocked the boat a bit on 9 April by requesting a transfer and was listed at £1,500. Young Jim Challinor and Naughton had been keeping him out of the first team and he thought a change might help. Otherwise the Wire kept things ticking over nicely. In the three weeks between the semi-final and Wembley they drew at Oldham and won games against Belle Vue Rangers, Widnes, Whitehaven and Leigh. Their victories enabled them to lift the

Lancashire League Championship, four points clear of St. Helens. Apart from their injury problems the only queries centred on whether to play Frank Wright, the former Fylde and Lancashire RU player, or the vastly experienced Ike Fishwick at hooker. Wright had been playing League for less than a season and there were worries that Alvin Ackerley, Halifax's hooker, might clean up possession. Frank got the nod. There were also suggestions that Stan McCormick and Challinor should exchange positions but coach Ces Mountford stuck with Stan on the wing and Jim at centre.

One Warringtonian who was having difficulties was the playwright Norman Holland, then living in London, who appealed through the local press for seating tickets for himself and Boris Karloff! At the other end of the social scale 53 year-old miner and Wire fanatic, Alfred Townsend was walking to Wembley, as he had done in 1950. There was certainly Cup fever in the town although the *"Warrington Guardian"* was quick to point out that *"Warrington is not merely a town club but belongs to folk over a wide area, even as far as North Wales."*

Halifax had no real injury worries in the lead up to the Cup Final but like Warrington they had five games to negotiate before the big game. They despatched Bradford Northern twice and won at Wakefield Trinity and Hull KR but sent the reserve team to the Boulevard for the fixture against Hull which was scheduled for five days before Wembley. The reserves performed creditably in losing 15-7 to Hull.

All was now set for the showdown at Wembley. Fifty years previously Halifax and Warrington had met in the Challenge Cup Final of 1904 at Salford. On that occasion the Tykes, already the Cup-holders, had retained the trophy with an 8-3 victory. Although no one contemplated a drawn final in 1954 perhaps they should have. History showed the last three Challenge Cup-ties between the two clubs had in fact ended in drawn games in 1923 (3-3), 1936 (2-2) and 1938 (4-4). Of course, only a fool would anticipate a fourth consecutive tie!

HALIFAX FOR THE CUP?

INJURIES HANDICAP WARRINGTON

"STARS" WHO SHOULD SHINE

By "D'ARTAGNAN"

WELL, who's it to be at Wembley? Halifax or Warrington — Yorkshire or Lancashire? Can the "Wire" bring glory to the County Palatine, or will Halifax see to it that the Rugby League Challenge Cup returns to the eastern side of the Pennines?

Judged purely on the basis of what is popularly accepted as "Cup-tie style," Halifax will, I fancy, be for most people outside the Warrington area the favourites for the trophy. Yet, a team which contains such incalculable factors as Brian Bevan and Stan McCormick, not to mention two of the tour half-backs, cannot be lightly dismissed from the reckoning.

This "Roses" Cup Final could be a thriller, even though it may not provide the feast of open football which so many of us would like to see in a Wembley Final. Several of the players have previously played at Wembley, so that, in their case at least, a little of the edge should be taken off the nerves which have affected the contestants and spoiled the quality of the play in some past Finals.

SOURCE OF STRENGTH

Halifax will doubtless pin their faith in their forward power. That power has brought them into hot water with many critics but it has paved the way for many of their victories. Also it has helped, despite frequent comments that Halifax are in a false position in the Northern Rugby League, to maintain their position near the head of the table for the last year or two.

Can Warrington hold those Halifax forwards and make the play which will bring their match-winning backs into action? That is probably the question upon which the result of this Final revolves.

RIPE EXPERIENCE

A glance at the teams shows that there are plenty of experienced men on both sides. Halifax full-back Tyssul Griffiths was considered by many people to be a "back-number" at the time of his transfer to Thrum Hall some sixteen months ago, but he has proved a good investment. After service with Hunslet he was one of the men who gave Doncaster such a successful first season.

Arthur Daniels is a long standing favourite with the Halifax crowd, as well

ARTHUR H. DANIELS
(Halifax)

he might be, seeing that he has been their leading try-scorer for so many

years, has toured Australasia, has played in Test football, and made many appearances for his native Wales.

Tommy Lynch, being a New Zealander, will probably feel that special thrill which is popularly attributed to players from the other side of the world when they step out on to the Wembley turf. A brilliant centre on his day, he has this last year or two helped to maintain Daniels' reputation as a free-scoring wing.

Peter Todd, Lynch's centre partner in the absence of the injured Creeney, has proved to be one of the most useful players on the club's books, taking up any position in the backs as required. A Huddersfield lad, and son of a former Fartown three-quarter, Todd joined Huddersfield as a youngster and had a spell at Salford before going to Thrum Hall. Dai Bevan, after a slow start with his new club, has already shown his worth and is coming back into the form which gained him International and Test honours while at Wigan.

INTERNATIONAL HALF-BACKS

The Halifax halves, Ken Dean and Stan Kielty, have been a regular choice for Yorkshire this last season or so, and both are Internationals. Kielty's crafty play around the scrum has had more than a little to do with the Halifax success story. No one connected with the "blue and whites" agrees with the tour selectors that there are two better scrum halves in the game!

In the forwards, Halifax have so often reigned supreme this season. John Thorley has developed into an international, while Jack Wilkinson has indeed had a rapid rise to fame. Alvin Ackerley

(Continued Overleaf)

HALIFAX FOR THE CUP ?

(Continued from Front Page)

(captain of the side) has long been regarded as one of the game's most effective hookers and forms yet another bone of contention which Halifax supporters have to pick with the tour selectors.

FORMIDABLE PACK

Bradford product Albert Fearnley played for Rochdale Hornets and Oldham before signing for Halifax, and he has another former Hornet alongside him in Derrick Schofield. The latter was a useful goal-kicker in his Rochdale days, but owing to Griffiths' ability in this direction he has not had many chances at Thrum Hall.

At loose forward, Des Clarkson was happy to break his semi-final "jinx." Even then he nearly missed his chance of playing at Wembley for he got sent off and suspended. Fortunately for him the suspension ends in time to allow him

DESMOND CLARKSON
(Halifax)

to play at Wembley. Clarkson (who previously played with Hunslet, Leigh, and Leeds) completes an 80-minute pack that has the attributes of solidity and mobility in attack and defence. It is the serious belief of many Halifax people that this pack could, with advantage, have been chosen for the tour as a complete unit.

GALAXY OF TALENT

Warrington full-back, Eric Frodsham, although not having the experience behind him that his opposite number has, comes off a football family and has steadily improved his play as Warrington have increased their challenge for a place in the Rugby League sun. Griffiths may carry the older head, but Frodsham should be quicker than his rival.

Brian Bevan and Stan McCormick remain a danger to any side when the ball is in their hands, and it will be the primary duty of the Warrington inside men to see that it gets there. Jim Challinor, after a run on the wing, seems to be settling down nicely in the middle

BRIAN BEVAN
(Warrington)

alongside Albert Naughton, who has made a rapid recovery from the knee injury which prevented him from making a serious bid for a place on the 'plane to Australia. Both Challinor and Naughton are aware of the potential menace to the opposition which they

STAN McCORMICK
(Warrington)

have alongside them, and Challinor used it very cleverly to get an important early try against Leeds in the Semi-final at Swinton.

At half-back, the "Wire" have Ray Price and Gerry Helme, the tour selectors' choice as one of the half-back pairs for "Down Under." Price, strong and forceful, has justified manager Ces Mountford's hopes in him, while Helme has all the accumulated knowledge and wisdom that can be gathered in years

GERRY J. HELME
(Warrington)

of scrum half play. The Helme — Kielty duel should be a very interesting one!

UNFORTUNATE MISHAPS

Many people will not consider the Warrington forwards to be the equal of their Halifax counterpart, especially when under-strength, yet I for one would not underrate a pack which contains men like Harry Bath, Bob Ryan, and Dan Naughton. Perhaps Warrington have not been too happy about their forwards just recently — they recently restored "Ike" Fishwick to first team duty after a long lay-off — but make no mistake about it, the "Wire" pack will be geared up for the job on hand! It will be an important question for Warrington to decide whether to include Fishwick for his hooking experience or Frank Wright who is such a power in the loose.

Harry Bath, of course, provides a double danger in that he can win a match with goal kicks apart from the power of his forward rushes. Bad luck for Ted White, whose leg injury looks like costing him his place in the team. Gerry Lowe, who came in as a deputy in the 1950 Final, is likely to deputise. Sid Phillips also had an unlucky break on Good Friday, when he fractured his collar-bone, and will not now be able to tread the footsteps of his referee father, who had control of last year's Wembley Final.

Who'll win? Well, if I were a betting man, which I'm not, I'd have my humble "tanner" on Halifax. But Warrington are fully capable of playing the better football — and Wembley doesn't often let the undeserving side get away with the spoils!

Cup Final Referee

Mr. Ronald Gelder, of Lupset, Wakefield, will referee this year's Final. Mr. Gelder, who is aged thirty-three years and a technical representative, passed his referee's examination in 1944. In his first season as a Grade 1 official he had charge of the Yorkshire Challenge Cup Final between Huddersfield and Castleford on November 4th, 1950.

At Wembley Mr. Gelder will use the whistle bequeathed him by his friend, the late Lawrie Thorpe, the Wakefield referee who collapsed and died while refereeing the Whitehaven v. Barrow match last Boxing Day.

Mr. Gelder is married with two children.

Wembley. The Warrington players give the stadium the "once-over".

"On our way to Wembley!" Halifax fans in Trafalgar Square on the morning of the Cup Final.

WEMBLEY

"Warrington Examiner" Friday, 30 April, 1954

81,777 SPECTATORS AT WEMBLEY RUGBY CUP FINAL, BUT THEY SAW NO TROPHY!

Fixture crowding and tired players give poor game

By CRITICUS

NEARLY 82,000 PEOPLE, MOSTLY FROM WARRINGTON AND HALIFAX, WENT TO WEMBLEY ON SATURDAY FOR THE RUGBY LEAGUE CHALLENGE CUP FINAL, AND RETURNED WITHOUT HAVING SEEN A CUP OR A MEDAL!
IT WAS A DRAMATIC ANTI-CLIMAX TO A POOR GAME, IN WHICH WARRINGTON AND HALIFAX DREW 4-4, AND MUST MEET IN THE REPLAY AT BRADFORD AT 6.30 NEXT WEDNESDAY.

That the final fell below expectations was not altogether the fault of the players. The Rugby League legislators must take some of the blame for fixing such an important match within less than a week of a heavy Easter programme, a state of affairs now further complicated by the League Championship semi-final, the cup replay, and the Championship Final within the next few days.

A strange thing about last Saturday's game was that Warrington could do nothing right in the first half when they had a liberal supply of the ball. They did much better in the second period when they were out-scrummaged, but could not find a way through a sound defence. In a dramatic finish, Halifax nearly won the match with a penalty kick which passed inches outside the upright.

Call it staleness, "Wembley nerves", or what you will, the fact remains that Warrington can hardly play as badly again.

That is why the thousands of supporters who made the long journey have talked not so much about Saturday's final as about the coming replay, in which they confidently expect Warrington to show vast improvement, and win. But that's a story that can wait.

After the teams had walked out on to this vast Wembley arena to be introduced to the Earl of Derby, President of the League, I looked at them through my field glasses. Halifax looked much more composed, several Warrington players appearing really anxious.

This was borne out by the early play. Right from the kick-off, Halifax entrenched themselves in opposing territory, and but for brief raids, remained there for the greater part of the opening forty minutes. They "found" one another better with their passes, and they handled with much more certainty.

CHAPTER OF MISTAKES

Warrington could do little right. When they heeled from the first scrum, Helme had to make two grabs for the ball. Heathwood lost it in a tackle. Lowe

was guilty of a similar error, and so it continued, a chapter of mistakes to the interval.

Warrington were doing quite well in a department where it had been feared they might be outplayed - in the scrums - but near equality here was thrown to the winds by these constant mistakes. Even when a player took a ball, he invariably lost it when he went to ground, and Halifax were not slow to profit.

An uncertainty at half-back was apparent throughout the first half. Helme was requiring too many attempts to pick up at the scrum. When he did pass first time, Price was dropping the ball as if it was hot.

BATH'S GRAND KICK

During Warrington counter-attacks Bath raised our hopes with a grand kick from near halfway which dropped only a yard beneath the cross-bar, Griffiths having been similarly unsuccessful for Halifax.

But he made no mistake when Lowe was penalised for offside in the fifteenth minute. Directly afterwards the referee erred (not for the first time) when he not only failed to see an obstruction on Price after he had kicked through, but penalised Lowe in the ensuing play-the-ball.

Still Halifax continued to hold territorial advantage, and when Lowe burst from the scrum too soon and was rightly penalised for offside, Griffiths made it 4-0 for the Yorkshiremen.

CHANCES MISSED

When Warrington did develop a move, it invariably ended with a dropped pass or somebody kicking badly when the obvious policy was to "stick".

Bath was just outside with two penalty kicks, and Griffiths had no better fortune. There was a thrill when Dan Naughton stole a pass and ran hard for the line, being stopped only a couple of yards short.

From a play-the-ball Halifax were penalised and Bath tip-tapped the ball and threw it into the middle. The movement came over to the right where Helme served Price, coming in on the burst, but he dropped the ball and a chance had gone.

Wembley. Alvin Ackerley and Eric Frodsham lead out their teams. Chairmen C.E. Horsfall and F.Davies precede the captains.

Lord Derby shakes hands with Halifax scrum-half Stan Kielty. To Kielty's left is Ken Dean. On his right are John Thorley and Jack Wilkinson.

Warrington made one more despairing effort with a well-conceived movement on the left, but Frodsham, after joining in to make the extra man, inexplicably turned the ball inside and the effort fizzled out, while men in support on the left waited for the pass that never came.

STEADIER RE-START

It was a somewhat steadier Warrington when the second half began. Halifax had some anxious moments but they defended calmly and efficiently. Kielty removed the danger with a kick upfield but Bevan came through from his own quarters, and his speed carried him forty yards before he served Ryan, who was accounted for.

But from the attacking position which had been gained, Halifax were penalised eleven minutes after the resumption, and Bath kicked the goal. The game was again wide open.

Frodsham immediately gave us all the jitters when after falling back to field a long kick, and with Bevan in support, he kicked weakly right into the hands of Dai Bevan, and the Warrington line was in danger.

The forwards relieved, and again Bath narrowly failed at goal after Kielty had been penalised for wrongly feeding the scrum (which he did far too frequently). Then Fearnley was offside, and again Bath had no luck with his kick.

Heathwood ran very well down the wing, and gained considerable ground after knocking an opponent out of his path, but McCormick had "gone wandering" and there was no support.

Just as quickly came a thrill at the Warrington end, where Dean broke through and kicked over the line but Bevan not only saved but came racing away in inimitable fashion to find touch at half-way.

THE SLOW HANDCLAP

Halifax had now adopted the policy of "what we have, we hold". The forwards, keeping the ball among themselves, were content to be tackled and play it back, and it brought from the Warrington section of the crowd the slow handclap (a thing which Wembley surely has never heard before in a match of such importance).

Time was passing, and although Warrington were having the better of matters, there was nothing tangible to show - and that was what they badly needed.

THIRTEEN MINUTES

But with thirteen minutes to go Kielty was again faulted in feeding the scrum, and to the accompaniment of a great roar of cheering Bath safely steered the ball between the uprights.

Now Warrington threw in all they possessed and Halifax wilted. Frank Wright dashed through from loose play, used a dummy and a hand-off. He was stopped five yards short but when he played the ball it was passed quickly across to the right and produced the heaven-sent, match-winning chance. But with the defence hopelessly outnumbered, and with three colleagues in support, Ryan knocked on.

Lynch cleared with a fine touch-line run and Halifax were again on the attack but Helme came through in dazzling style, only to go a little too far before parting, and he was accounted for.

It was now the Warrington attack versus the Halifax defence, and Dan Naughton burst through and kicked to the corner, but again the Yorkshiremen refused to capitulate.

DRAMATIC TWO MINUTES

Wilkinson led a Halifax raid and when Helme was penalised with only two minutes to go, Griffiths carefully prepared his kick at goal, which could decide the match.

It was a good kick and the Yorkshiremen cheered themselves hoarse in joyful anticipation, but the ball veered a little and passed just outside the upright.

So the game ended all-square - a game which will not be looked back upon with much pleasure. It was hard, keen, and fought out in sportsmanlike manner but with none of the thrills of top-class Rugby such as in the meeting of Warrington and Huddersfield at the same venue.

Halifax lived up to their reputation, in that after gaining the lead, they tried to retain it by keeping the ball close and it nearly proved their undoing.

Warrington, even with their second half improvement, never captured that free-moving style which we know they possess. But it was in the first half that they missed their way, for Wright and his colleagues managed to get a very good share of possession, and a Warrington back division at only half their best could have done the rest.

CAPTAIN MISSED

But Helme was completely out of touch and Price never found his true form, and, of course, when the main cog of a machine is not functioning properly, there is little hope for the rest of it.

Whether a fit Albert Naughton would have proved the solution with his steadying influence and his close-to-the-line bursts can only be a matter for conjecture.

Let it be said at once that young Stevens by no means let his side down, and although once or twice out of position, he tackled splendidly on the whole. But on attack he lacked just that little experience which counts such a lot in these games, and a similar remark may be applied to some extent to Challinor. He ran hard and defended resolutely but was never able to bring just that bit out of Bevan which might have counted for so much.

One must remember, of course, that the young Warrington centre was opposed by Todd, one of the fiercest tacklers in the game, and that the Halifax cover defence was exceptionally good.

Bevan did all that a player could do without having the opportunity to produce his great wizardry on the wing, and McCormick on the other flank was safely held by speedman Daniels, although he frequently ran across field trying to bring Bevan more into the game.

*Wire on the attack.
Frodsham fends off
Dean. Daniels
shadows Price.*

*Wire on the defence.
Halifax centre Lynch is
swamped by McCormick,
Lowe and Helme. Bath is
in the background.*

ENCOURAGING FACTOR

There were times when Frodsham, like some of his colleagues, was nervous and indecisive, and several times he kicked badly. The forwards were well beaten for possession in the second half, when to have got more of the ball might have proved a match-winner.

But one encouraging factor was that they proved just as good as the opposing "terrible six" in the loose, every man pulling his weight and giving just as much as he took. Wright's fine work in the open was perhaps the biggest surprise but all did well.

I thought Clarkson the best Halifax player, constructive in attack, and always to the fore when his side were under pressure. Lynch was a forceful attacking centre, but Dean and Kielty should have made better use of the ball in the second half.

Griffiths gave nothing away at full-back and the wingers, like those of Warrington, were invariably cancelled out before they had a real chance to get into their stride.

STRANGE DECISIONS

To sum up, Halifax were dour and sound, while Warrington, if one takes the match right through, never operated smoothly enough to master a strong defence.

Referee Gelder missed one or two obvious knocks-on, and, I thought, a glaring offside which resulted in Frodsham being tackled in possession in the first half. Many people also thought he erred in penalising Helme and awarding Halifax the kick which almost won them the match.

Result:
Warrington   2-0-4
Halifax   2-0-4

WARRINGTON: Frodsham; B Bevan, Challinor, Stevens, McCormick; Price, Helme; Lowe, Wright, Naughton, Bath, Heathwood, Ryan.
HALIFAX: Griffiths; Daniels, Lynch, Todd, D Bevan; Dean, Kielty; Thorley, Ackerley, Wilkinson, Fearnley, Schofield, Clarkson
REFEREE: Mr. R. Gelder (Wakefield)

"STANDING AT THE GATE",

with Ian Guard

"Warrington Guardian", 1 MAY, 1954

It all started, I think, with Friday's bombshell that Ally Naughton was unfit to play. Nothing tangible, of course, but there was something in the air - you could feel it.

Cheerful enough were the thousands as they poured into London: rattles, cheers, cracks at the Cockneys, a brisk whip-round for an eyeful of the sights. But this invasion of the capital didn't strike me as whole-hearted, confident. Perhaps it was apprehension (at the type of game for which Halifax is notorious) growing as the stadium grew nearer.

The same kind of reservation pervaded the Halifax contingent. Perhaps they knew what was coming. Whatever the cause cup fever was missing or had abated considerably. I detected it even in the community singing.

Not until midway in the second half did 11,000 Warringtonians really let themselves go. First with the slow handclap at the exasperating tight tactics of Halifax, then as a mighty spur to the "Wire's" closing onslaught.

But I suspect it was more in desperation than because the game, even at that stage, justified it. A refusal to be denied those abandoned cheers which are one of the main attractions of a cup final.

The final whistle - and anti-climax was so great it almost stunned.

Twenty-five minutes later the great stadium was deserted except for the odd straggler unable to believe it was all over, a few Pressmen pounding out the disappointment on typewriters and a party of workmen with a crane uprooting the goal-posts. Significant?

Which poses the problem; was it worth it? Listen to a tired fan as he flopped into his seat at Euston at mid-night. *If anyone mentions Wembley to me"*, he gasped, *"I'll scream - for twelve months anyway!"*

Yes, it's there. Despite disappointment they would not have missed it - and they'll be there next year if Warrington is fortunate enough to go. And so will I!

But we don't want to see a repetition of this game at future finals. The code's showpiece of the year deserves better.

And now: on to Odsal and a result - the right one!

ODSAL BOUND

4.30 Match ends
Presentation of the Trophy and Medals
THE NATIONAL ANTHEM

The above is the schedule for the end of the Challenge Cup Final of 1954 as laid down in the official programme. Under the team lay-outs on the opposite page was printed *"If the match is a draw after 80 minutes play, no extra time will be played"*.

There was no elaboration anywhere else in the programme as to what was to happen if the game was drawn. Nor did anyone at Wembley appear to know what to do when the game drew, literally, to its close. It had, of course, been decided at a meeting of the Cup and Rules Revision Committee held at Chapeltown Road on 8 April, that any replay would take place at Odsal. It had even been decided that the price of tickets would be 25 shillings, 10/6, six shillings and three shillings. However, no one had deemed any of that information worthy of inclusion in the Wembley programme, let alone the date of any replay.

It was therefore little wonder that players, spectators and officials were at a loss as to what was to happen next when Ron Gelder blew the final whistle at the Challenge Cup Final of 1954. There was total anti-climax. No one had won the Cup, no one could tell the fans and players where or when they would next have to gather to decide the issue.

In the Halifax *"Green Final"* of 1 May, Frank Williams complained, *"The Rugby League slipped up badly at Wembley. When it was fairly obvious that the match would end in a draw, arrangements should have been made by someone for the replay announcement. The Press and the 80,000 spectators were in a complete 'fog'...... All they got from the loudspeaker announcer was 'The game will now take place on another ground'. This bare fact only made matters worse, and the confusion only brought contradictions from various sources. Obviously the first drawn game at Wembley caught the Rugby League officials on the wrong foot. But the announcement on the loudspeaker did not show the Rugby League up in a good light."*

The replay could not be played the following Saturday as that was set aside for the Championship Semi-finals whilst the Saturday after that (8 May) was to see the staging of the Championship Final itself. Logic suggested that the replay should take place on Saturday, 15 May but instead the authorities decided on a Wednesday evening replay (5 May) between the Championship semis and the Championship Final.

Halifax still had to play Keighley at Thrum Hall in their final league match on the Monday following Wembley - the day they travelled back from London! Over 13,000 turned up to watch the Thrum Hallers pile off the bus and beat Keighley 17-3 to clinch top spot in the League table with Warrington in second place one point behind.

The following Saturday Halifax defeated Workington Town 18-7 and Warrington vanquished St. Helens 11-0 in the Top Four Play-offs to set up, as it were, a replay of the replay. History was created as for the first time the clubs finishing first and second in the League would contest both the Challenge Cup and Championship Finals. At the conclusion of the semis Halifax and Warrington were presented with the medals for winning their respective County League Championships. Unfortunately, Halifax found they had been given the Lancashire League medals and Warrington had received the Yorkshire League medals! The Rugby League's indiscretions were limitless! It was arranged for the two sets of medals to be exchanged at the Odsal Replay.

The Wire management elected to take their players to a hotel at Ilkley for a few days preceding Odsal. They did no training there but had team meetings and talks from coach, Ces Mountford. It was reported that they would not even see a rugby ball until they took to the pitch at Odsal. On the Tuesday they went walking in the morning and visited Odsal in the afternoon to examine the pitch. A final team talk on the day of the game and the Wire moved out of their hotel and crossed the moors to Bradford.

In complete contrast the Halifax players carried on as if it were just another game. Most of them worked on the day of the Odsal Replay.

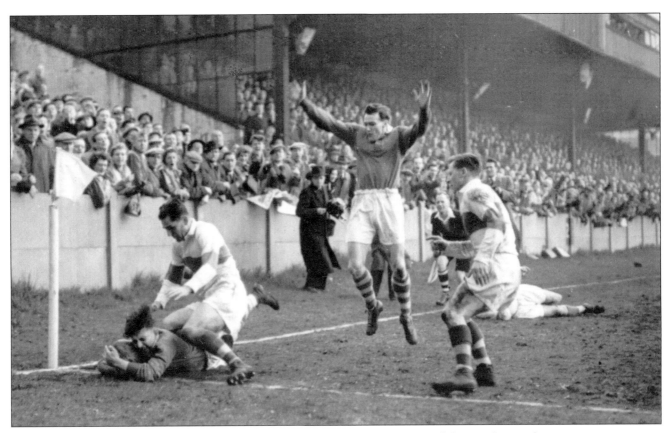

*Thrum Hall, Championship semi-final. Tommy Lynch leaps skywards
as young Billy Mather scores against Workington Town.*

*The one which did not get away! Jack Wilkinson and Albert Fearnley chair Halifax captain Alvin Ackerley
who holds on to the Yorkshire League Championship Cup. The trophy was presented at the conclusion of
Halifax's victory over Workington Town in the semi-final of the Rugby League Championship.*

Edition, Halifax Daily Courier and Guardian), Saturday, May
KEN ADAMS'S SKETCHBOOK
"Final" Freddie AT THE ODSAL "STAMPEDE"!
SO MANY FANS SWARMED INTO THE ODSAL BOWL ON WEDNESDAY THAT IT LOOKED AS THOUGH
THE TEAMS WOULD HAVE TO STAY IN THEIR QUARTERS & CUT THE CARDS FOR THE CUP!
CUT ALVIN! PITCH IS UNDER PEOPLE!
BY KICK-OFF TIME A SEAT ON A TELEGRAPH POLE WAS A LUXURY AND—
THOUSANDS ON THE FRINGE HAD TO KEEP A SHARP EAR TO FOLLOW THE GAME
I'LL TELL 'IM!
HOW DO THEY STAND?
AND THOUSANDS MORE COUNTED THEMSELVES FORTUNATE TO JUST SEE ONE CORNER OF THE PITCH
IMAGINE STOOPING TO THAT!!
IF THA WATCHES BETWEEN YON LUGS THA'LL SEE BALL,—IF THERE'S A PENALTY,—IF THEY KEEP STILL
AND AS TO THE MATCH ITSELF,—THOUSANDS VOTED IT THE BIGGEST THRILLER THEY NEVER SAW!
WOT A GAME!—AT LEAST, SO I HEARD
WELL THERE IT IS,—(AS THE NURSE SAID TO THE PROUD FATHER),—GERRY HELME HEREWITH
AND DAME FORTUNE SNATCHED THE CUP THAT SO NEARLY TOUCHED DOWN ON THRUM HALL'S SIDEBOARD
AND ALTHOUGH THE FIRST WARRINGTON TRY CAME FROM A FORWARD PASS TO CHALLINOR (AS WE SAW IT)
EE, I'M THAT FORWARD I'M CHEEKY
& DERRICK SCHOFIELD SHOWED BRIAN BEVAN THAT A HEAVYWEIGHT COULD RUN FAST TOO
NOWT WENT RIGHT!! FOR HALIFAX
KEEP TO THE LEFT MATES!
PART 2 OF THE TOP TWO SERIAL TOOK PLACE TO-DAY & HERE'S HOPING THE BALL RAN FOR US FOR A FAIR SHARE!
WHO ME?
CHAMPIONSHIP

Aerial view of the Odsal Replay (courtesy "Telegraph & Argus"). Note the areas where there are no people. These were the flat pathways. In postcards of the crowd published later the "empty" areas were "touched up" to make the ground appear completely covered.

ODSAL

"Halifax Daily Courier and Guardian" (Football Edition),
Wednesday, 5 May, 1954

WARRINGTON WIN THE CUP
Thrum Hall men concede early try
HALIFAX BELOW PAR IN REPLAYED FINAL AT BRADFORD

By FRANK WILLIAMS

An early try by Challinor gave Warrington an incalculable advantage in the replayed R.L. Cup Final with Halifax at Odsal to-night.

The Thrum Hall men began the game in fine style and the match developed into a real dingdonger. The Warrington defence looked well-nigh impregnable, though Halifax had a try disallowed for a forward pass.

Halifax had plenty of the ball and launched many attacks and Warrington were at full stretch to save their line many times.

Griffiths kicked a goal for Halifax after Bath had missed some penalty chances for Warrington but a goal soon after the interval put Halifax three in arrears again.

The ground, despite the rain, and they had had a good deal in Bradford, was in good condition. But at 6.30 p.m., when the ground looked well filled - the estimate had been about 60,000 - light rain began to fall.

There were two changes in the teams compared with those which played at Wembley. Halifax had Mather at left centre in place of the injured Todd, while in the Warrington team Ryder came in at left centre for Stevens.

A further Griffiths goal was offset by a Helme try.

HALIFAX

	Griffiths		
Daniels	Lynch	Mather	D Bevan
	Dean	Kielty	
	Clarkson		
	Fearnley	Schofield	
Thorley	Ackerley (capt)		Wilkinson

Naughton		Wright		Lowe
	Bath	Heathwood		
	Ryan			
	Price	Helme		
McCormick	Ryder	Challinor	B Bevan	
	Frodsham(capt)			

WARRINGTON

Referee: R Gelder (Wakefield)
Touch Judges: KW Bland (Blackpool),
WL Desmond (Leeds)

Warrington won the toss and Kielty started for Halifax. The ball went direct into touch and the first scrummage was formed at halfway. Warrington heeled and Price kicked to Griffiths who responded with a good run, but he was obstructed.

The Halifax forwards, however, took up the running and Halifax were the first to become aggressive. Bevan made a good run off the left wing. Halifax were throwing the ball about freely.

Kielty was once in a position when it looked as if he was going to try a shot at goal, but his view was obstructed, and he had to run round to support his three-quarters instead.

McCormick subsequently got in a rather lucky kick to touch just outside the Halifax "25" but a penalty to Halifax for hands in the scrummage against Warrington enabled Clarkson to find touch five yards inside the Warrington half.

WARRINGTON AHEAD

The tackling was keen and accurate but with Halifax throwing the ball about at every opportunity, there were a few slips and once Brian Bevan looked like taking advantage of such a failure while later Challinor got away in similar fashion and it was Warrington who were now enjoying the better of the play.

Halifax backs and forwards tried hard to find an opening but Warrington's defence was equally as good as that of Halifax. It was a tendency of the Halifax men to play the open game that was giving Warrington their chances. Dropped passes and sometimes indiscreet transfers were quickly pounced upon by the Lancastrians.

The Halifax spectators and team had a set-back when after eight minutes play a good move by Warrington ended in CHALLINOR scoring. Bath broke away cleverly and he gave a pass which looked as if it was well forward to Lowe and he handed on to Challinor, who went over at the corner. Bath failed to improve.

Straight away Halifax went to the attack through a grand effort by Clarkson but Daniels failed to accept a pass although he was too close to the touch-line to make much progress.

THRILL-PACKED ACT

The two Bevans clash, the tackler being Bevan, of Halifax.

About to fall to a Warrington tackle, Clarkson (Halifax) prepares to fling a pass to Schofield, at the same challenge.

Here, Warrington's winger (Bevan) wins a race for the line and kicks dead before Schofield, the Halifax forward, can get his hands on the ball to touch down.

Griffiths, the Halifax full-back is tackled in possession when attempting to clear his line.

McCormick (Warrington) gets across to stop Mather, the Halifax centre.

ther Warrington

Wing threequarter McCormick takes a pass from colleague Naughton in the R.L. Cup final at Odsal Stadium.

Scene outside Odsal Stadium showing late arrivals pouring into the ground. The well-filled terraces can clearly be seen. On patrol is a mounted policeman. The queues began to form at 3.20 p.m., the last few were going in at half-time. Over 8,000 vehicles were parked in the vicinity of the stadium, including over 1,200 buses.

r (Warrington), supported by Bevan, kicks ahead as Mather (Halifax) comes in to tackle.

SCHOFIELD MOVE

Racing to the other end, Helme was prominent with a good run but Bevan, who tried to come across from his wing, found no loophole and Halifax were quickly back on the attack through a brilliant run by Schofield, who had the misfortune to become entangled with an opponent's legs when he looked as if he was clean through.

Halifax were now having the better of the play, and they were tackling well but they could not find that vital opening.

Griffiths twice shaped as if he would drop-kick for goal but his attempts were bad.

A brilliant kick by Bath forced Halifax back again to their own "25". The Warrington defence was very accurate, their covering being masterly. The forwards were having a rare set-to. Offside against Halifax for play-the-ball gave Bath a chance to increase the Warrington lead but his kick went just wide although it was a good one from long range.

SPOTTING

It was a terrific cup-tie and Warrington had a grand chance of increasing their lead, but Bath was again at fault with a penalty shot from practically in front of the posts and 35 yards out. He again sent wide.

Lynch and Daniels tried hard to beat down a very solid defence but they were always mastered. Ryder was keeping a very close watch on Lynch. The Halifax passing, owing to the close spotting of the opposition often lost ground, while Dean at fly-half was finding a difficulty in retaining his foothold.

Halifax were just moving up to the attack again when Wilkinson was penalised for incorrectly playing the ball and Bath took a penalty shot from two yards inside his own half. He teed the ball up and he had the wind in his favour but the ball fell just under the bar.

Helme was using the touch-line well with some adroit kicking, and it was this player who forced Halifax on the defensive again. So far Warrington had had the better of the deal, and only rarely had Halifax offered a threat to the Warrington line.

REAL THRILL

Although the Halifax forwards began to get more of the ball, the backs could not work an opening likely to cause anxiety.

A real thrill came when Challinor fed Brian Bevan. His namesake, however, made no mistake about the tackle.

Griffiths at full-back was allowing the ball to bounce and he was losing ground as a result. Halifax caused a great thrill for their followers when Schofield broke through magnificently and put in a kick and was only just beaten for the touch by Brian Bevan. It was a great effort which thoroughly deserved a try.

The next minute Halifax were on the move again and Lynch went over from a pass by Daniels but was recalled for a forward pass.

Warrington were now having to stand up to some battering by Halifax, and some grand passing and a fine move by Dean, supported brilliantly by Lynch and Daniels, nearly brought a try, Daniels being pushed into touch a yard from the Warrington line.

To relieve the pressure of the crowd, the spectators were being allowed inside the enclosure. In some cases they were in close proximity to the touch-line. Hundreds were on the dead ball line.

It must be the first time in the history of the Odsal ground that people have encroached so near the goal posts. It must have been done as a safeguard owing to the crush behind the barriers, and they were still being allowed in by the police during the interval.

Halifax were making strenuous efforts to wipe off that three points arrears and the Warrington defence was having a very trying time.

Offside against Warrington gave GRIFFITHS a chance to reduce the arrears from close in and he kicked the goal. This came after 38 minutes' play. Half-time:

Halifax	1-0-2
Warrington	0-1-3

The first thrill of the second half was when Price got through and gave to Brian Bevan but Griffiths tackled the flyer in great style. This effort gave Warrington the initiative. Helme increased the advantage with a run of over 40 yards.

CHASING

Halifax were now having to do some chasing. McCormick tried a drop kick at goal but he was wide. Halifax had a narrow escape when Warrington, throwing the ball about magnificently, enabled Brian Bevan to run diagonally but Heathwood, who received the pass from his winger, was tackled on the corner flag by Griffiths.

Warrington were now moving the ball about very cleverly, whereas the Halifax tackling was inclined to be a little shaky.

Warrington were on top and they were using the ball better than Halifax. When Mather attempted to put in a short kick for Daniels it was a bad one. There was always a danger when Brian Bevan was placed in possession but Dai Bevan once brought him down well.

The Halifax passing was at times disappointing and the backs lacked penetration. It needed a penalty kick, well taken by Clarkson, to get Halifax out of difficulties.

A well-planned move by the Halifax backs should have brought better results but Daniels failed to take a pass from Lynch when things looked very bright for Halifax, who were now making Warrington defend for all they were worth.

McCormick had a bit of luck when Lynch put in a kick intended for Daniels, his hand striking the ball when, had it gone through, Daniels would have been well placed.

Warrington got into an advantageous position through some passing but a pass was definitely forward and this gave Bevan a chance to make considerable ground.

THE WINNING TRY

Wire scrum-half Gerry Helme scored the decisive points of the Odsal Replay.

Top: *Helme breaks clear of the Halifax defence.*

Centre: *He bounces across the line to score.*

Bottom: *This shot says it all – Helme grins broadly as Challinor picks him up. Symbolically Halifax, in the shape of Ken Dean, are brought to their knees.*

Previously Kielty had attempted to drop a goal but was short. The Halifax passing was slow compared with that of Warrington.

After 16 minutes in the second half Warrington went further ahead as a result of a penalty goal kicked by BATH. This was awarded because of off-side at play-the-ball.

Halifax appeared to tire at times but it was their passing which left much to be desired. The supporting tactics also lacked the usual initiative.

Halifax, however, did not despair and good work by Daniels on the right might have brought better results had he not been obstructed by McCormick. GRIFFITHS, from a most difficult angle, and 28 yards out, kicked a magnificent goal.

ONLY A POINT

This was a spark to Halifax and they set about retrieving the one-point arrears but the Warrington cover was very accurate.

Still with only a point between the teams there was always a chance. The Warrington backs drew their rivals far better than did Halifax, and this provided them with more opportunity. Griffiths had a long range shot but was short.

Though Halifax were getting the ball 2-1 it was Warrington who showed up the better in back play. Frodsham at full-back for Warrington was playing a really good game, his fielding of the ball being outstanding.

TOP SPEED TRY

After 27 minutes in the second half HELME got a magnificent try for Warrington which deserved to win any match. He ran from 40 yards out at a terrific speed to score at the corner. Bath failed at goal.

The Halifax tackling throughout the match had not been as good as usual and it was a mistackle that enabled Helme to start on his long run to the Halifax line.

Price, who had played a fine game throughout, was injured and had to be carried off. Warrington always drew their man cleverly before parting with the ball.

Halifax made a last desperate effort but it looked as if they were fighting a losing battle. Price had returned to play. Good work by Thorley looked promising for Halifax while Daniels put in a short kick but could not regain possession.

On another occasion Clarkson tried to go through under the posts but lost possession of the ball and also lost Halifax valuable ground. A chance presented itself when Mather was placed in possession on the left but he kicked badly.

The failure of the Halifax backs to function properly and their slowness in manoeuvre had been the main weakness.

The margin was only four points. The Halifax backs could not complain about lack of possession but their efforts had not had the polish of the Warrington set.

DISALLOWED

There was a real thrill a couple of minutes from the finish when from a kick by Kielty, Daniels seemed to score a try. But the referee disallowed the try apparently owing to Daniels failing to ground the ball.

The better team won.

Result:

HALIFAX	2-0-4
WARRINGTON	1-2-8

"Halifax Daily Courier and Guardian"
(Football Edition),
Wednesday, 5 May, 1954

TO-NIGHT'S WAS A CROWD WITH A DIFFERENCE

It was a cup-final crowd with a difference - so different from Wembley's - a cup-final crowd the like of which England has never seen these last 20-30 years. For replays are so very, very rare.

It was a Yorkshire crowd mainly, and that was one very striking difference from Wembley. It was a Yorkshire crowd rather than a Thrum Hall crowd, for there were perhaps three favours with the gay white rose emblem for every one in the blue and white.

There were here, so the experts said, perhaps one in eight of Halifax's people, against one in ten from Warrington. But there were Bradford's thousands too and a couple of train loads from Leeds, half a hundred coaches and a train from Keighley, a train from Wakefield, even some coaches from Hull.

Oddly, Lancashire's members of the crowd had most of the handbells, the rattles and even an odd bugle. Or it may not have been so very odd after all. For Warrington's fans came here on a half-day off; Halifax's and Bradford's and the fans from Leeds came rushing here after a day's work.

* * * *

But the stadium had the magic - the magic of the cup. It was the immensity, the sheer immensity of the crowd that made this occasion - five thousand a few minutes after the opening of the gates, a full two hours before the match, going up to 20,000 by 5.45 p.m.. Not, they said, quite the crowd that had been expected at this time - the weather was unfavourable - but still an immense crowd by ordinary Rugby League standards.

Then, from 5.45 onwards, came the real army, Halifax's - and Lancashire's - throngs swarming in, a dozen abreast with cars and coaches moving nose to tail along the roads through Shelf.

There were police by the score at the ready as the great processions of the fans inched across the junction of the roads at Odsal Top to join the lengthening queues moving ever so slowly into the stadium. There were foot police every twenty yards, with squads more held in reserve just across the road from the stadium itself; there were radio men, police equipped with walkie-talkie sets, radio cars and motor-cyclists; and the mounted police were there with their white horses and black horses and the great dappled black and white, Bradford's pride.

* * * *

Traffic arrangements were working very well indeed between 5.30 and 6 with about the expected crowd now inside the ground. Buses were dropping their loads some 300 yards away from the stadium itself, so that the roads immediately about the ground were given over almost entirely to private cars and the unending columns of men and women moving along five of the main roads converging on Odsal.

The street vendors were not doing so well. *"Just ordinary"*, said one hawker of rosettes and favours. That remark pointed another difference from the Wembley cup-final crowd.

It was not so colourful to-night. Nor was it so cheerful. *"Cheer up, lads, you haven't lost yet,"* a man sporting primrose and white streamers from a "topper" of garish yellow called out to the waiting queues when he jumped off a St. Helens bus.

The crowd laughed for about 15 seconds, then moved silently on towards the gates .... a Yorkshire crowd, a solemn Yorkshire crowd, almost as dour as the day itself.

* * * *

TRAFFIC STREAM WAS MILES LONG
Superintendant W. Griffiths, Halifax Deputy Chief Constable, laid down his microphone, took off his glasses and mopped his brow. *"That's it, boys,"* he said. *"It's all but over now."*

For two hours he had been at his two-way radio set, directing cup traffic through the town - traffic at times so dense that there was a continuous nose-to-tail stream from Odsal Top to Sowerby Bridge.

"But it all went without a hitch," he confided afterwards. *"Nothing went wrong at all."*

The traffic started rolling about 5 o'clock and by six had reached its peak. Early indications suggested that many more than the originally forecast 16,000 Halifax supporters were Odsal-bound.

There were seven police cars on duty in the borough before the match. And 24 policemen on point duty - assisted by a dozen "specials" - kept the traffic rolling.

FEW HOLD-UPS
Crucial point was Northgate and North Bridge. Here traffic from Lancashire, Huddersfield and Halifax converged into a bottleneck. But there were few hold-ups. By 5.15 vehicles were going up New Bank at the rate of 45 a minute. It was not until half past six that this exodus subsided.

When one car stalled in the middle of Broad Street, three policemen were on the spot within seconds to wheel it aside. Traffic was held up for less than 30 seconds. Special buses and trains were filled to capacity. Buses to Odsal Top were leaving at the rate of one a minute.

And when everyone had left, the streets were deserted. After seven hardly a car was to be seen in the town. Only a few regular - and empty - Halifax Passenger Transport buses passed along Northgate.

("Oldham Chronicle")

HEAVIEST TRAFFIC JAM BLOCKED OLDHAM ROADS FOR NEARLY THREE HOURS

The heaviest traffic jam in Oldham's history blocked the town's main roads for nearly three hours on Wednesday afternoon as motor-coaches, cars and motor-cycles carried thousands of Warrington rugby supporters to Odsal Stadium, Bradford, for the replay of the Rugby League Challenge Cup.

The Chief Constable, Mr. W.E. Schofield, said today that it was the worst traffic problem Oldham has ever encountered; yet there were no accidents to vehicles or pedestrians

The traffic stream began as a trickle shortly after 4 pm. Half-an-hour later it had reached huge proportions, and at one time it was estimated that there was a continuous line of vehicles from Bower Lane, Chadderton, to Odsal Stadium, Bradford.

As the traffic increased in volume it clashed with rush-hour buses and transport in the town centre, and thousands of local workpeople on their way home were delayed.

RING ROAD NEEDED
The Chief Constable told the *"Chronicle"*: *"The problem arises because there is no ring road around Oldham. All traffic on its way to Yorkshire has to pass through Mumps. At tea-time yesterday the situation was complicated because workpeople's buses were leaving the depot just at that point. All this points, of course, to the provision of a ring road to obviate the bottleneck conditions at Mumps Bridge."*

Extra police strength was needed to cope with the traffic block, which was kept moving at a reasonable pace through the town centre.

The traffic on its way to Bradford was then directed along Ripponden Road to make its way to the stadium by a different route from the Halifax contingent. Bradford and Huddersfield police authorities had requested the Oldham Force to do this.

By 6.30 the rush was over. On the way back the situation was not repeated, partly because of some traffic travelling by a different route, and because there was, of course, no rush-hour transport.

NO ROWDYISM
At Odsal one of the biggest crowds ever to see a football match in the country - 102,575 - saw Warrington win by 8-4.

Brighter comment by Oldham's Chief Constable:

"Fortunately we had no scenes of rowdyism in the town later when people stopped here on their way back."

It took 40 minutes on the outward journey to travel one mile at Brighouse. Nearer the ground it was a case of bumper to bumper, and there was an inch by inch approach.

In between the noise of revving engines one bystander commented to motorists: *"If you're in a hurry, get out and walk!"*

Some coaches did not arrive at the ground until half-time. Many which left Oldham at 5.15 pm approached Odsal 20 minutes after the kick-off.

COACH HEMMED IN

One coach-load arrived so late that the passengers did not consider it worthwhile to get into the ground. Their coach was hemmed in and they had to wait for the match to end and the crowd to disperse before they could make their way home.

It was just as bad on the return journey. The *"Oldham Chronicle"* car was blocked in the ground's lower car park for two hours before escaping - and there was a long queue left behind.

It was a happy Red Rose crowd that made its way home - Warrington had brought the Cup back to Lancashire.

GERRY HELME WONDER TRY LIFTS THE CUP

OVER HE GOES .-. . grim-faced, determined Gerry Helme, Warrington scrum half. It's the winning try. Open-mouthed, grasping that ball firmly, Helme dives over the line . . . and the Rugby League Cup goes to Lancashire.

UP HE COMES . . . staggering under boisterous back-slapping, the stranglehold of joy applied by a happy Warrington fan, the congratulations of smiling team-mates . . . and off goes the Warrington hero to the mighty roar of Odsal's 103,000 crowd.

What courage! And what a crowd!

By DAVID NICHOLLS: Warrington 8pts, Halifax 4pts

GERRY HELME, 5ft. 5ins. and 10st. 12lb. of football courage and skill, Great Britain and England player, climaxed an unforgettable evening in the Odsal Bowl at Bradford with a fantastic try that won the Rugby League Challenge Cup for Warrington.

The mighty roar of 103,000 fans, swelled in crescendo across the packed terraces, and rolled out across the Yorkshire moors as Helme, starting inside his own half, passed groping, frustrated men on his way to the line.

He veered away to the left, turned back inside, found two customers for a dummy, turned outside again, ducked and scuttled in at the corner under a barrage of tacklers.

What a try! It put Warrington 8-4 in front with 13 minutes to go; it drove Halifax back to defeat when they were controlling the scrums and threatening to take charge. It won Warrington their second Challenge Cup in five seasons.

I have known modest, likeable little Gerry Helme, a fitter by trade, since his early days at Warrington, through the good times and the bad, through England and Test honours. But I have never seen him score a better try.

Relentless

Congratulations Gerry for getting your Lance Todd Memorial Trophy as the best player in the final—the first man to win it twice.

Poor Halifax. Helme set them back on their heels just when their relentless forward power was beginning to tell. But all praise for the way they fought—to the last gasp.

Their failings were in the inside backs where they were too often passing standing still and the sluggish handling of the forwards in the loose. But Daniels (twice) and Schofield were oh! so near to tries.

The Warrington tackling was terrific against a two to one possession beating in the scrums. And when they had the ball there were more ideas in their backs.

Helme, Price, Bevan, Challinor, Bath and Wright were the big men for Warrington.

Breathless

Schofield and Wilkinson did some tremendous work in the Halifax pack and there was danger in the Lynch-Daniels wing.

A game memorable for the ruthless tackling, the courage of both teams and this mighty Odsal, packed with breathless fans. Here is the time table of events.

Eight minutes : Bath set Price moving from play-the-ball and a reverse pass left Lowe in the clear. He made 20 yards before throwing a high pass to Challinor who got over for a try at the corner. Bath's touchline kick was just wide of the posts.

Ten minutes : Schofield was clear down the right touchline but he tripped and the chance was lost.

Sixteen minutes: Bath grazed the post again with a 45 yards penalty.

Nineteen minutes: After some fierce tackling in midfield, Halifax were penalised again, but Bath half kicked the ground and was well wide.

Twenty-five minutes: Bath tried another penalty from five yards inside his own half and was only just short under the bar.

Thirty-five minutes: Halifax drove home an attack for the first time. Schofield broke from his own half and kicked. Bevan just won the race to make the ball dead.

Thirty-six minutes: Lynch was over on the right but was pulled back for a forward pass—a near thing but not so near as the next minute when Schofield broke to the right and Frodsham and McCormick just got Daniels into touch.

Thirty-nine minutes: It had to come. Warrington got offside under their own posts and Griffiths kicked a simple penalty goal to make it 3-2 at half time.

Confusion

Forty-four minutes: Brian Bevan threw confusion into the Halifax defence with a weaving run to the left but Heathwood lacked the pace to finish it and was hurled into the corner flag.

Fifty minutes: Halifax were controlling the set scrums now and Warrington had to tackle like demons to keep them out.

Fifty-six minutes: Kielty got offside and Bath kicked a penalty from 45 yards to make it 5—2.

Sixty minutes: McCormick obstructed Daniels and Griffiths kicked an angle goal from 35 yards

Sixty-seven minutes : Helme's try of tries.

Seventy-five minutes : Halifax were hurling all into attack but Clarkson lost the ball under the posts.

Eighty minutes : Halifax made a last desperate effort with a high penalty punt. Daniels got the ball but was held on his back over the line by Frodsham and McCormick *Phew ! What a finish !*

Warrington won a fine RL Cup final

Halifax's forwards checked

By ALFRED DREWRY

HALIFAX 4 pts., WARRINGTON 8

Warrington won the most memorable Rugby League Cup final of all on their merits. Before an Odsal Stadium crowd officially returned at 102,575—the biggest football match attendance anywhere in England outside Wembley since 1923— they showed up Halifax's limitations as they have never been exposed before during this triumphant season.

Triumphant? Well, Halifax have finished at the head of the League table and won the Yorkshire League Championship, but they met their match last night in a tremendously exciting game and will do so again in Saturday's League Championship final if Warrington play as they did at Odsal.

Halifax had a 2 to 1 advantage in possession from the scrums (14-7 in the first half and 15-8 in the second) and they were awarded 17 penalties against Warrington's eight. But Warrington's superior use of the ball in the open was so marked that despite all those penalty awards Griffiths had only two shots at goal and only during a spell of five minutes towards the end of the first half and again during a desperate late onslaught did Halifax seem likely to score a try.

Better methods

Halifax's forward challenge was taken fairly and squarely on the broad shoulders of Bath, Danny Naughton, Heathwood, Ryan and Lowe. Schofield broke away once and very nearly scored a solo try from halfway, but Warrington saw that the slip was not repeated. In loose play Warrington showed the better method. They handled smoothly, fell into position like clockwork and stretched the Halifax cover to its limits—and beyond—by faster running.

Frodsham picked the right moments to join his threequarters from the full-back position and Ryder and Challinor were able to provide running space for their wingers. One brilliant run by Bevan which split the Halifax middle nearly brought a try to Heathwood. Despite their restricted scope, Helme and Price at half-back never allowed Kielty and Dean to dictate the course of the match and Helme indeed made himself the man of the match with a brilliant second-half try.

Halifax looked slow in the backs but I suspect that they played little if at all below their best. Their lack of speed in handling and running— judged by the very highest standards, that is—has been screened hitherto by their tremendous forward power. In this match the screen was brushed aside and the faults exposed. The intricate manoeuvres of Kielty and Dean failed to make openings in the middle and Lynch and Mather, the centres, were never dangerous because the passing generally was not quick enough.

Warrington, who make a habit of shock starts in their big matches at Odsal, struck the first blow after eight minutes. Bath moved across with the ball towards the right wing and as the defence went with him to cover Brian Bevan, Bath slipped the ball inside to Lowe. Lowe went through a gap as wide as a barn door. His final wide pass to Challinor seemed to be blown forward by the wind but the referee, Mr. R. Gelder was well up with the play and had no hesitation in pointing for a try when Challinor crashed over at the corner.

Shrewd touch finding by Bath, Frodsham and Helme delayed any effective counter until just before the interval. In a spell of three minutes Bevan beat Schofield by inches to a ball over the line; Lynch crossed the line only to be brought back because he had given a forward pass to Daniels at the start of the move; and Daniels was stopped at the corner after a cut through by Dean— his only one of the match. This assault culminated in Griffiths kicking an easy penalty goal for offside at the play the ball and at half time it was 3-2.

Helme opened the second half with a glorious 40-yard run which made one think that Halifax were tiring but the next score did not come for 16 minutes. It was a 36-yard penalty goal by Bath with his fifth attempt at goal. Griffiths made it 5-4 with an equally good shot but 13 minutes from the end Helme crowned a magnificent display with a try which he will remember for the rest of his days.

Last minute thrill

He began as he did with his earlier effort at halfway by swerving out to the left touchline at terrific speed.

Gerry Helme, Warrington's scrum half, who next week goes to Australia with the Rugby League tour team, became the first player to win the Lance Todd Trophy for the second time with an outstanding performance in last night's Cup replay at Odsal. A panel of journalists by a clear majority made Helme the man of the match. Helme also won the trophy when Warrington beat Widnes in the 1950 final at Wembley.

This time Helme went on, sold a monumental dummy, was knocked over by Griffiths's tackle three yards short and rolled over and over across the line. Every one but the Halifax players knew that Halifax were beaten but they very nearly snatched the Cup out of the fire in the last minute.

Kielty put in a high kick over the line from a close-in scrum. Daniels leaping high took it and fell in a smother of tackles. Halifax players claimed a try and many spectators in the vicinity thought that Daniels had scored, but the referee ruled that he had failed to ground the ball. A spectacular finish to a splendid match. Mr. C. W. Robinson (York), chairman of the RL Council, presented the trophy to Frodsham, the Warrington captain. Teams:—

HALIFAX.—Griffiths; Daniels, Lynch, Mather, Bevan; Dean, Kielty; Thorley, Ackerley, Wilkinson, Fearnley, Schofield, Clarkson

WARRINGTON. — Frodsham; Bevan, Challinor, Ryder, McCormick; Price, Helme; D. Naughton, Wright, Lowe, Bath, Heathwood, Ryan.

REFEREE.—Mr. R. Gelder (Wakefield).

Brilliant Helme try turned tide to victory

A BIRD'S-eye view of Huddersfield Road, from Odsal Top down towards Low Moor, where scores of coaches which had brought in Rugby League fans from far and near for the R.L. Challenge Cup final replay at Odsal Stadium, parked until the match was over.

WARRINGTON ...... 8 points, HALIFAX .... 4.

A 102,575 CROWD, a world record for a Rugby League game (receipts £18,650), saw Warrington most worthily beat Halifax to win by 8 points to 4 in last night's final replay at Odsal Stadium, Bradford.

This was more than 30,000 above the previous Odsal best and 20,798 more than at Wembley for the first match.

It was a match worthy of such a multitude—and it means the Rugby League will have to consider what has been regarded as formality—the renewal of the Wembley contract just expired. Odsal's claim must be recognised.

It is the greatest fillip the Rugby League game has had and it must also emphasise Odsal's case for a League Championship final, which has made Manchester City's Soccer ground its home.

The second half was one long thrill. Halifax were always fighting a rearguard battle, and gallantly they fought it. But they weren't in Warrington's class.

They couldn't do the things with the ball that Warrington did. And their crackajack pack, sound though it was, was not one whit better than Warrington's set of six.

Great try

The issue turned on one of the best tries that Gerry Helme, Warrington's scrum-half, who was their Wembley hero in 1950, has scored. He was on the ball like a swooping hawk as it came from a scrum.

Two Halifax players bought a dummy and away went Gerry, finally to double somersault over the line for a try, which made it 8-4 for Warrington after Halifax had been striving desperately to get in front.

No wonder Helme won the Lance Todd Trophy for the

By ALLAN CAVE

best player afield, as he did in 1950.

Helme and his co-half-back Price ruled the middle. Their bursts tore furiously into Halifax, for whom Dean and Kielty could reply in no such terms.

Halifax started to use the forward steamroller way, but when they found this no use they changed to the more open game. And at that they were not in the same street as Warrington.

But Halifax will always argue that they scored in the last minute, when Daniels caught Kielty's kick and dropped over the line. His colleagues hugged him, but referee Gelder ruled no try, signalling that the ball had not been grounded.

Brian Bevan alone gave the crowd their money's worth, although Halifax's Dai Bevan saw to it that he did not score. The less famous Bevan tackled the other with rare gusto and efficiency.

It was indeed a game of gusto. Once Warrington got into their stride Halifax did not look their victory part.

Splendid

Warrington's backs were splendid, with the Price-Helme half-back combination, which is going to Australia next week, out on its own.

No Warrington forward was better than Bath, but it was the collective sustained striving which won this Warrington pack its marks. Halifax misfired in their back division cylinder and their forwards were tame.

Warrington scored first, in the eighth minute, when Challinor took a suspiciously looking for-

ward pass from Lowe, but Halifax cut this to a point when Griffiths kicked a goal.

That was the way matters stayed at half-time, though Schofield made one tremendous save only to be overtaken by Brian Bevan, who came out of the blue.

As in the first half, Halifax ran away with the scrums, yet despite Ackerley's winning hooking ways Kielty could not get his backs going.

Bevan thrills

When Warrington got going they were dangerous. Brian Bevan gave the crowd two quick thrills. Challinor got him away each time.

On the first occasion he chased 50 yards diagonally, but Dai Bevan followed him and got him just in time. And the Halifax Bevan did it on the Warrington ace again.

But Warrington put two points on to their lead after a quarter of an hour when Bath landed a goal with his most difficult shot.

Halifax cut the gap to a minimum in five more minutes. Daniels was obstructed 40 yards out and wide. Clarkson prepared for a tip and run, but Skipper Ackerley insisted that Griffiths should kick at goal. And Griffiths kicked the goal.

It was grim for a while afterwards, but with Warrington beginning to see more of the ball Helme started to engineer some telling moves. Then he broke through for his dazzling try.

Price hurt

Ten minutes to go and Price was taken off hurt. But he came back quickly.

All those last minutes were spent in the Warrington half, many of them actually inside the Warrington 25.

Wilkinson twice got near, but weight of numbers held him down. Then it was Clarkson, but he lost the ball.

Mather had a chance to send Dai Bevan in from ten yards, but he chose the short kick and kicked too hard. Finally the Daniels incident.

Whitehaven job for Emery

Neville Emery, former Australian R U international, signed by Whitehaven two years ago, has been appointed player-coach to the Cumberland R L Club.

Yesterday's racing results

The crowd surges forward . . . the barriers break . . . and the police rush to form a cordon while ambulance attendants stand by for casualties. This is Cup fever . . and a Y.E. News cameraman was on the spot to get this dramatic picture during the R.L. Cup Final replay between Halifax and Warrington, which drew a record R.L. crowd of 102,575 to Odsal Stadium, Bradford. As the spectators mill round newsreel cameramen record the scenes.

MILESTONE IN THE HISTORY OF THE GAME

By ARTHUR HADDOCK

BIG talking point in sporting circles to-day is the record R.L. crowd of 102,575 which descended upon Odsal Stadium for the R.L. Cup final replay between Halifax and Warrington.

It has raised anew the question whether the final, which apart from one occasion—in 1932 — has been taken to Wembley ever since 1929, should be brought back permanently to the North of England.

The remarkable thing is that this six figure Odsal crowd was attained in adverse circumstances.

First, the final at Wembley on April 28 was one of the dullest on record and a poor advertisement for the replay.

Second, the kick off time of 7 p.m. was thought to be a most inconvenient one for the majority of the fans who wanted to see the replay.

Third, it was a rainy day, and several hours before the kick-off time, a drizzle set in.

Despite all this people poured into the ground from all parts of Yorkshire, Lancashire and Cumberland.

Even the most optimistic R.L. official was taken by surprise; and the attendance surpassed everybody's estimate.

Jubilantly the Bradford Northern chairman, Mr Harry Hornby, said after announcing the attendance: "I am a very happy man. I always knew that Odsal possibilities were tremendous. We have achieved that 100,000 crowd in the North, and it will always be a milestone in the history of the game.

"If only the Bradford Corporation and the Rugby League were to get together and build up Odsal think what could be achieved."

Odsal at present is only partly developed, and because of this, not all the people who went last night saw the game.

Many told me such was the crowd that they returned to their cars to listen to the broadcast on the game.

People were still entering the ground long after the kick-off such was the late descent of people trying to gain admittance.

BETTER SIDE

With an 8-4 victory Warrington won the Cup—and I imagine that few among the vast crowd would question their right to the trophy.

They were the faster and better side throughout, and despite the fine tackling of the Thrum Hallers, were able to create room in which to work.

Their speed advantage not only enabled Warrington to be the superior attacking side, but it was also used to good purpose in defence, the Halifax raids being invariably well covered.

CLAIMS DISALLOWED

It is true that the "breaks" went against Halifax. There was, for instance, a suspicion that the final pass was forward when Challinor scored Warrington's first try, and the Yorkshire club had two claims disallowed.

These were when Lynch crossed (a forward pass was ruled) in the first half, and when Daniels grabbed the ball in the closing stages after a high kick by Kielty (on this occasion it was ruled that he did not ground the ball).

And they were a bit unlucky when Schofield was accidentally tripped after breaking through.

Yet making all allowance for these there can be no doubt that Warrington were the better team and nowhere was their superiority more pronounced than at halfback.

Helme, man-of-the-match and the Lance Todd trophy winner, achieved penetration which no one else quite achieved—not even the quicksilver Brian Bevan—and overshadowed Kielty as much as Price outplayed Dean.

These two tourists were the Warrington heroes, but it must be emphasised that Warrington's pack, although beaten two-to-one in the scrums. did a manful job in the loose

SPLENDID TACKLING

They stopped the Thrum Hall pack from dominating the game and the vaunted Halifax cover was found wanting when Helme in particular shot through brilliantly three times. selling dummies left and right.

Schofield was the best Halifax forward, and, behind. Dai Bevan did the best job with his splendid tackling of his namesake

Footnote: The previous best attendance figure for a Rugby League Cup final was 95,000 at Wembley in 1949 and 1950 This year's Wembley figure was 81,777 In 1913 there was a crowd of 120,028 at the F A Cup final at Crystal Palace and in 1948, 133,570 saw Rangers play Morton in a Scottish Cup final replay at Hampden Park

try of the match

Helme, the Warrington scrum-half, goes over the Halifax line after a brilliant run from the half-way line in which he dummied his way past a bewildered Halifax defence.

THIS WAS THE ODSAL "FULL HOUSE"—RECORD 102,575

Warrington worthy winners

(By JACK BURNS, "T. and A." Sports Editor)

A WORLD record Rugby League crowd of 102,575 at Odsal Stadium last night saw Warrington take the Challenge Cup into Lancashire by beating Halifax 8—4 in the replayed final.

And all those people who like their Rugby to be of the open variety must agree that justice was done.

Can Halifax turn the tables when the pair meet again in Manchester on Saturday—this time in the championship decider? Not unless their backs can make better use of greater possession than was the case last night.

In the English periods the ball was kept tight—and one is not inclined to be unduly critical of that on so tense an occasion—but there were many when, especially in the second half when the ball was given air, and practically all of the really spectacular stuff came from Warrington.

Halifax hammer in vain

Halifax's attempts at progress by passing were neither as frequent nor successful as those of the Lancashire team. Indeed, one of the most dangerous breaks-through by a Halifax player came from second row forward Schofield, who burst ahead near the halfway line, kicked forward and followed up so well that even the speedy Brian Bevan had to hustle to kick the ball dead just in time.

Despite their Ackerley-gained advantage in the scrums, Halifax hard though they battled—and it was a stern, terrific tussle all the way—rarely looked like revealing the penetrative qualities of men like Warrington's Bevan and Ratcliffe.

The latter, it "brought down the house," and crowned a grand performance which earned for him the Lance Todd trophy for the second time in his career.

He had a great-hearted partner in Price—this half-back pair should do well during the forthcoming tour of Australia—and another Warrington back who did tremendous work was McCormick, roaming all over, tackling hard and kicking shrewdly.

The winners had no better forward in the loose than Bath, who landed a penalty goal to augment the tries of Challinor and Helme.

Halifax's powerful back was again their biggest potential match-winner, but, always Warrington managed to keep this battering ram short of their line.

Kielty, Dean and the determined Daniels also gave the Lancastrians some anxious moments, but the finish touch was not there. Brighouse scored two penalty goals, but his handling of the ball was not as clean and sound as that of the other full-back, Frodsham.

THE AFTERMATH

("Warrington Examiner", 7 May, 1954)

WARRINGTON WAS SINGING AFTER THE VICTORY

Even "Monty", Warrington's famous railway carthorse, had primroses peeping coyly from behind his long silken ears on Thursday morning; not to mention the primrose and blue ribbons decorating his mane and tail.

The "Wires" had pulled it off! The Wembley whines and worries were forgotten. Warrington was a deliriously happy town of people walking on air and exchanging *"told-you-so's"* with their neighbours.

What should have been "hangover" day after the big match was a gala day. Cup fever, instead of abating, was mounting to League Championship hysteria.

The populace, to a man behind those 13 Herculean heroes in the primrose and blue jerseys, was drinking the joys of one victory, and eagerly looking forward to a carousal after the next!

There's no doubt, of course, about the outcome of the Maine Road match. Not a man or woman in this cup-happy town would dare predict defeat for the all-conquering 13.

Win or lose, they are all set for the triumphant tour from the Town Hall to-morrow night. Securing of the League double will only heighten the enthusiasm; nothing will diminish it. The mood's there and it will remain until the crowds have had the chance of lionising their heroes with the cup.

THEY WORK BETTER?

A popular belief among local industrialists is that production rises in the factories following victory by the "Wires". Be that a fact, Warrington's output since Wednesday must be sending the Red faces in the Kremlin green with envy.

And there may be something in it. Local firms reported almost full attendance on Thursday morning, backed by 100% increase in morale. "You'd think every other man was Bing Crosby, the way they are singing and humming," said one spokesman.

At Rylands Brothers, Ltd., the *"Examiner"* was told: *"We have not lost any production over the match. The men who wanted to go made up the time beforehand and there have been no reports of exceptional absenteeism."*

Dr. W.L. Kent, of the British Aluminium Company, said a handful of men on night-shift failed to turn in, but the following morning it was work as usual for nearly every employee. The management has an agreement with the Works Council that employees only have concessions for semi-finals and finals.

Naturally, just lately, the men have taken advantage of the agreement. *"But last month our target was exceeded and we are hoping for the same thing this month,"* said Dr. Kent.

At Joseph Crosfield and Sons and at Electro Hydraulics few men failed to turn in the following morning and the same was true of most firms in the town.

Warrington on Wednesday was a town of strange contrasts. In the early afternoon and tea-time bumper-to-bumper traffic jostled and jockeyed through the main streets. Coach-loads of rattle-waving, singing, shouting supporters exchanged banter with equally excited pedestrians. The trek to Bradford was on.

The scene in Bridge Street at 8 pm: An evening sun glinted down on rain-washed, deserted pavements; a brilliant rainbow spanned clouds that were ganging up in the distance. It might have been Sunday morning.

Two raincoated policemen tramped a slow beat along the shops. They, a few Americans, and one or two girls, were the only souls on the wet, glistening street.

Warrington had gone to Bradford. If not physically, then in spirit practically every man, woman and child in the town was in the Odsal Stadium.

Those who had stayed at home were glued to wireless sets, terrified of missing one word of the commentators who could never hope to satisfy, fully, their hungry listeners. In cinemas, too, where the score was flashed on to the screen at intervals, the Marilyn Monroes and Rock Hudsons fought a losing battle for the interest of their fans. Every time the score showed the "Wires" ahead, a cheer broke from the audience and in at least one cinema when the victory was announced, there was almost a riot. Hats, programmes and tickets were thrown into the air, and it was several minutes before they settled back into their seats.

Only when the match ended was the Sunday morning silence of the streets shattered. People appeared from nowhere and public houses, which had been practically deserted, were suddenly busy with celebrators.

CHAOS AT BRADFORD

It later transpired that many of the stay-at-homes were able to give a better description of the match, after hearing it on the radio, than those who went to Bradford.

For one of the greatest highlights of Warrington Rugby Football Club's illustrious career, will go down as one of the greatest fiascos among its followers.

Many hundreds of those who left the town with tickets, happily looking forward to the match,

The Warrington defence excelled at Odsal. Here they bundle Arthur Daniels into touch at the flag.

Odsal, 5 May 1954. "To the victors the spoils". Warrington celebrate their great triumph.

never even saw the Odsal turf. Held up in traffic-jams, which really tightened at Oldham, many arrived after half-time and were unable to get a glimpse of the play.

Typical was the experience of Mr. H. Rose of Hallfields Road, Orford, who organised three coach-loads of supporters at Crosfield. *"There were 105 of us altogether. Not 20 managed to get inside the ground,"* he said bitterly. *"Most of them went into nearby pubs and listened to the radio. I managed to get on the ground in time for Gerry Helme's try, and I was mad enough. I don't know how all those felt who never even saw a bit of the play. Most of them held 12s 6d stand tickets."*

Leaving Warrington at 3.45 pm, the three coaches took five hours to make the journey. *"If anyone talks to me about bringing the cup-finals North, I'll tell 'em where to go,"* said Mr. Rose. *"It was organised chaos."*

Another coach-load which left Crosfield's was organised by Mr. G. Dickenson, of Brighton Road, Warrington. *"It was shocking,"* he said. *"When we did eventually reach Bradford, we had to park our coach two miles from the ground. Local coaches which had arrived much earlier were parked right outside the stadium."*

But both he and Mr. Rose are going to Maine Road tomorrow!

One coach which did not reach Bradford until after half-time carried the Deputy Mayor of Warrington (Councillor Percy Martin), Aldermen D. Plinston, H. Harding and J. Morris, several councillors and council officials.

Even the Mayor, Councillor W. Taylor, was late. And accompanying him was the chairman of the Warrington Club, Mr. Fred Davies. They arrived at the match just in time to see Challinor score Warrington's first try. Said the Mayor yesterday: *"The trouble was that no-one expected a record crowd of 102,000. If they are going to play the final at Odsal in future years, something will have to be done as far as traffic arrangements are concerned. Diversions and one-way street systems will have to be introduced to avoid such chaos again, or people will just not take the chance of going."*

The Mayor described the "crawl" from Brighouse to Bradford. *"I thought we'd never make it,"* he said. *"And Mr. Davies came with me because he thought we would be on time!"*

But the Mayor's parting shot perhaps represented the feelings of many. *"It was worth it,"* he said, *"if only to see Gerry Helme score that try. And those fading minutes when it looked as though Halifax could bring off a victory. How I sighed with relief when the final whistle blew."*

Such were the security measures in the dressing rooms after the match that even the Mayor was unable to congratulate the players. *"It will have to wait until Saturday. And then I'll be able to congratulate them on winning the championship as well,"* he said.

JUBILATION - IRRITATION - FRUSTRATION VICTORY SOOTHED OUTRAGED FANS AT CUP-CRAZY ODSAL

("Warrington Guardian", 8 May, 1954)

The town is delirious with Cup-fever. With the Rugby League Challenge Cup in the bag, jubilant crowds will be pouring into Manchester today (Saturday) for the third mighty clash with Halifax - this time for the League Championship Cup at Maine Road.

A world record Rugby League crowd saw the Warrington team smash its way to unforgettable victory at Odsal Stadium, Bradford, on Wednesday. But for thousands of Cup-crazy fans the glitter of the cherished prize was dimmed, and only victory softened the blow for hordes of outraged Warringtonians.

Trapped in the writhing streams of traffic on the approach roads to Bradford, at least 3,000 of more than 10,000 primrose and blue supporters who went did not see the game.

Others managed to storm on to the ground after half-time for a limited peep at the play. Stand ticket holders battled their way to their seats only to find them taken.

Hundreds experienced the irony of listening to the second half BBC broadcast on their coaches' radios outside the ground. And many more whose coaches had no radios packed cafes and hotels to listen in - mingling with Halifax supporters and other disgruntled followers of the code.

102,575

Even the coach carrying members and officials of the Town Council failed to reach the ground until 7.30. All the party had tickets but none reached their seats!

Bumper to bumper for sometimes more than six miles, coaches and cars crawled their laborious way. Frustrated fans tumbled out of them miles from the ground striving desperately to salvage a glimpse of the game.

Police and organisers, unprepared for this record crowd of 102,575, were powerless. Spectators forced the barriers and squatted on the speedway track. Many clambered on to the roof of the stand and loudspeakers warned them the structure was not considered safe to hold the extra weight.

It was a repetition of the first FA Cup Final at Wembley in 1923 when an estimated 120,000 stormed the stadium.

Droves of disgusted fans turned away tearing up stand tickets. Others kept them and are seeking means to recover their money.

As more and more poured through the turnstiles with half the game over they were warned of conditions inside the ground and told they went in at their own risk. One Wire fan paid three shillings ten minutes from the end - and saw nothing.

STRANDED

The final whistle blew but all was not yet over. For many it was more difficult to get out of the mêlée than it had been to get in and scores were left stranded in Bradford.

Fans searched in blustering rain and darkness for the coaches they had left miles up the road. But, among the hundreds there, the task was difficult and in a number of cases unsuccessful. Many returned in the early hours of Thursday in different coaches from those they had left in.

These and other fantastic scenes are to be the subject of official complaints at high level.

Mr. Fred Davies, chairman of the Warrington Club, pulled no punches in his criticism. *"Rank bad organisation at the Bradford ground,"* he told the *"Guardian"* the following morning.

Apart from the price of stand tickets which he considered far too high, Mr. Davies is concerned about many of those who not only failed to get to their seats but could not get in the ground at all.

And his comments on Odsal's being the "Wembley" of the North in the future is echoed by thousands who journeyed to Bradford.

"I am dead against it," he said. *"There is only one main road leading to the ground and the ground itself is unsuitable."* He added, in fairness, that a Wembley draw was unexpected and only a week-and-a-half remained for preparation for the replay.

COMPLAINTS POUR IN

Meanwhile the *"Guardian"* office telephones have been alive with complaints from irate supporters over what they describe as the *"disgraceful chaos"* at Odsal.

Mr. F. Timmins, 78, Orford Lane, who organised two coaches - most of his passengers had ringside tickets - said: *"We started at 4 pm and got there for half-time. I was lucky. I could see as far as the 25-yard line."*

Mr. W.V. Smith, Smithfield House, Paddington, who arrived after a four hour journey 20 minutes after the start and unable to use his 10s 6d stand ticket said: *"If this is bringing the Cup Final to the North, let's keep it at Wembley."*

So many complaints have been put to Mr. S. Jacobs (Labour agent) that he is taking up the matter with the Member for the borough (Dr. H.B.W. Morgan) and intends to submit a resolution deploring the organisation at Bradford at the next meeting of the Trades Council.

Supporters who went by rail from Bank Quay Station tell a different story. Bookings were disappointing, an official said, but passengers on the last "special" leaving at 3.54 pm were on the ground by 6.30. All were home before midnight.

MAINE ROAD

"Halifax Daily Courier and Guardian Green Final"
Saturday, 8 May, 1954

WARRINGTON GET THE "DOUBLE" WITH R.L. CHAMPIONSHIP

But Halifax came so near to winning thrilling game: Bath goals snatch victory

HALIFAX 2-1-7   **WARRINGTON 4-0-8**

By FRANK WILLIAMS

In the Northern League Championship game at Maine Road this afternoon, Halifax started in fine style in their bid to avenge Wednesday's Cup Final defeat by Warrington at Odsal. This third meeting of the teams in a fortnight found the Halifax men, to whom Todd returned at left centre, in a different mood. They opened the scoring in the third minute and for long periods of an exciting first half they had the mastery.

Thorley opened the Halifax scoring with a try which Griffiths converted. Subsequently, Halifax were held several times when nearly over and Warrington, at this period, had much for which to thank a fine defence.

A feature of this half was the manner in which Dai Bevan, the Halifax winger, held his fast-running Warrington namesake.

Bath kicked two goals for Warrington, and Griffiths got one for Halifax, to make the interval score 7-4.

In a thrill-packed second half, in which the excitement persisted to the end, Warrington snatched the victory, however, by a one-point margin, thanks to two more penalty goals by Bath.

The teams were presented to the Earl of Derby, President of the Rugby League. Halifax were led out by Mr. C.E. Horsfall, the club's chairman.

HALIFAX: Griffiths; Daniels, Lynch, Todd, D Bevan; Dean, Kielty; Thorley, Ackerley, Wilkinson, Fearnley, Schofield, Clarkson

WARRINGTON: Frodsham; B Bevan, Challinor, Ryder, McCormick; Price, Helme; Naughton, Wright, Lowe, Bath, Heathwood, Ryan

REFEREE: A. Hill (Dewsbury)

TOUCH JUDGES: A.E. Durkin (Dewsbury), H. Hyde (Manchester)

THREE-MINUTE TRY

Ackerley won the toss and decided to play with the breeze at his back. Naughton started the game.

Brian Bevan was early in the picture, receiving a pass from McCormick, who had run round from the left wing. McCormick was injured in the tackle which followed and had to have assistance from the trainer. Bevan was brought down without making any substantial gain. He had run round towards the left wing.

On the resumption Tommy Lynch was prominent with a grand tackle of Ryder and this gave Halifax the first attacking position. Halifax's tackling was much tighter than in previous games against Warrington.

There was a great shout for Halifax when, after three minutes, Kielty stole the ball from Frodsham and handed on to Thorley a yard from the line. THORLEY went over for a fine try, which GRIFFITHS improved.

This was a really good start for Halifax and it put them on their mettle, but Warrington were quick to respond and took play into the Halifax half before Kielty drove them back with a kick which Bevan failed to field. Dai Bevan, racing up, prevented Frodsham from getting in a reply.

GOOD MOVE

Halifax were not reluctant to throw the ball about and a good movement on the right finished with Dean kicking into touch ten yards from the Warrington line.

There was a good move between Kielty and Daniels but the effort was pulled up owing to a forward pass. Then Helme broke away brilliantly and gained fully 30 yards before passing to McCormick who passed the ball back inside. But Helme was quickly smothered. Following passing, Dai Bevan put in a good kick but unfortunately the ball rolled into touch after he had beaten Brian Bevan.

Both Todd and Lynch were tackling superbly, and Ryder and Challinor were having little chance to get their wings into operation.

MAGNIFICENT GOAL

A dropped ball by Dean provided Warrington with an opportunity and Heathwood gained fully 15 yards as a result. Halifax were penalised for offside at play-the-ball and Bath took the kick from two yards inside the Halifax half. His effort, however, was a poor one.

BATH had another chance a minute later owing to Kielty being penalised for incorrectly feeding the

Maine Road. Halifax prop John Thorley surges on to Stan Kielty's pass to score the only try of the Championship Final and Halifax's sole try in the three finals.

Maine Road. A classic action shot of Brian Bevan.
Halifax winger Dai Bevan is up to the job, however. Kielty moves into view.

Maine Road. Ron Ryder and Stan McCormick head off Tommy Lynch

Maine Road. Dai Bevan makes a spectacular tackle on Brian Bevan. Tuss Griffiths looks on.

scrummage. He kicked a magnificent goal from 30 yards out and from a difficult angle.

On the resumption Challinor got Brian Bevan away but Dai Bevan, keeping his man to the touch-line, brought off a fine tackle before the Warrington man had got properly into his stride.

Kielty threw a bad pass to Dean who was fortunate in covering the ball in time to prevent trouble. Later, however, Dean and Kielty worked the standing pass successfully and Todd raced away to give to Dai Bevan, who put in a fine kick to touch a couple of yards from the Warrington line.

Halifax were getting the ball well but Warrington, like their rivals, were using the ball to advantage in the open. Kielty, from 20 yards out, attempted a drop-kick at goal but the ball failed to rise.

IN CLEVER STYLE

The Halifax close tackling was much better today. There was danger when the Warrington backs got moving and Dai Bevan was left with two men, Challinor and Brian Bevan. But the Halifax man summed up the situation cleverly to bring down Challinor in style.

There was some exciting play in midfield and Frodsham was lucky in saving from a kick by Daniels, the ball deceiving Clarkson when he was favourably placed.

Then followed another thrill for the crowd when Brian Bevan took an inside pass from Challinor to beat several men until he was stopped at the centre by Fearnley.

Warrington were penalised near half-way but Griffiths' kick was a bad one. Kielty had very bad luck with Halifax still attacking when he knocked on in intercepting a pass from Helme, who earlier had made a grand effort to break through.

Halifax maintained the advantage and brilliant work between Lynch and Daniels resulted in Lynch being pulled down a yard from the Warrington line. The next minute Halifax were again nearly over, Kielty failing by a foot to score. They were two narrow escapes for Warrington.

AN EASY GOAL

Halifax were doing all the pressing at this period and the Warrington defence was kept on the stretch. We were watching a different Halifax from Wednesday. The team work was much better and the tackling much closer.

Warrington were doing everything possible to get Brian Bevan on the move and a wide-flung pass by Heathwood got him away, but Dai Bevan again made a great tackle to stop his progress.

After 23 minutes, however, Schofield was penalised for offside and BATH kicked an easy goal. These points came against the run of play as Halifax, for fully 10 minutes, had kept Warrington on the defensive. They had been unlucky on one or two occasions in not scoring.

Helme once again came into the limelight with a quick thrust down the middle but he did not get far. On the run of play to date, Halifax should have been more points in front. They went straight into the attack again but Warrington's defence was very solid.

Lynch and Daniels tried to work an opening on the right wing but Frodsham held Daniels. Wright was temporarily injured but resumed after attention and then Warrington were penalised through Bath getting offside.

GRIFFITHS kicked a grand goal from 40 yards out. This score came after 27 minutes' play.

FINE DEFENCE OF DAI BEVAN

It was a good game with both sides throwing the ball about well. Kielty got through with a smart run and Dean the next minute ran magnificently before passing to Daniels, who made a magnificent effort to cross at the corner. He was pulled down a yard from the Warrington line. It was an effort that deserved a try.

Clarkson, the next minute, was again held short in an effort to burst through. Warrington were again having the worst of the deal and, with the Halifax backs playing much better than on Wednesday, Warrington were finding it difficult to keep their rivals at bay.

On every possible opportunity Warrington tried to get Brian Bevan away and another wide pass got him on the run but Dai Bevan was his master. The Halifax man's defence was one of the features of the game. Dean knocked on, unfortunately, a pass by Kielty when he might have made substantial progress but still Halifax had a slight advantage. Again Dai Bevan stopped his more famous rival with a grand tackle.

WARRINGTON STRUGGLING

Warrington were struggling for most of the time and they had to thank some very fine defensive work and covering for keeping their line intact. Halifax were again forcing the pace and, when Frodsham misfielded on his own line, things looked black for the Lancastrians. Some robust scrummaging took place within a couple of yards of the Warrington line.

Continual pressure by Halifax kept Warrington on tenterhooks and the way Halifax hurled themselves into the fray must have been a delight to their followers. It was more like the real Halifax.

Kielty and Dean, despite the fine work of Helme, were having a good game and it was Kielty again who put Halifax on the attack with a good kick to touch. Offside twice relieved Warrington from continual pressure.

Warrington tried every move possible but they found the Halifax defence safe and in tip-top form.

Obstruction on Bevan lost Halifax a lot of ground. When Halifax were penalised Bath took a shot at goal from 40 yards out - almost at the precise spot from which he kicked his first goal. This time Bath was wide with his attempt.

Half-time

Halifax	2-1-7
Warrington	2-0-4

50

Outstanding features of the first half were the work of the two Halifax half-backs, Dean and Kielty, and Dai Bevan's grand tackling.

A dropped pass by Lynch gave Warrington an advantage but they did not gain much ground. It was obvious Warrington were out to use the wind and Frodsham immediately got in a long kick, but Griffiths responded cleverly and, with the Halifax forwards following up well, Warrington were quickly in trouble, Frodsham being tackled a couple of yards from his own line.

In an effort to bring relief, Frodsham attempted a kick which landed directly into touch and back went the scrummage to the Warrington line. Halifax tried passing from the scrummage but Ryder quickly pounced upon Lynch.

Halifax lost ground with some passing but the cover was there to prevent any real trouble. Lowe was penalised for an infringement but the short kick did not gain much ground. The Halifax tactical play today was much better and the change of play from one wing to another, as well as the short kicking by Kielty, got Warrington guessing on more than one occasion.

GRAZED UPRIGHT

With Halifax still pressing, Helme was penalised for incorrectly feeding the scrummage and Griffiths took a shot at goal from 30 yards out, almost on the spot from where Bath had kicked his first goal. Griffiths, however, grazed the upright with his kick.

A big kick by Bath on the resumption won Warrington some ground. The defences on both sides were very accurate. There was a thrill for the Halifax spectators when Lynch went sailing along the right touchline in great style, but his inside pass to Daniels was a bad one, or Warrington would have been placed in desperate straits.

Though playing against the wind, Halifax had had nearly all the play so far this half. In fact the Lancastrians had not got into the Halifax "25" since the interval.

LEAD NARROWED

Frodsham eventually brought welcome relief to Warrington. The Lancastrians were doing more kicking than in the first half, and by these tactics they eventually got into the Halifax "25".

Kielty was penalised on his own "25" for incorrectly feeding the scrummage and, after 12 minutes in the second half, BATH kicked his third goal to put Warrington within a point of their rivals. This was a spur to Warrington, who immediately forced Halifax on the defensive. Throwing the ball about with deliberation, Warrington caused the Halifax defence a good deal of running about.

Halifax were penalised just outside their own "25" but Bath failed to kick the goal, the ball passing wide of the upright as the Halifax spectators sighed with relief.

The wind was of advantage to Warrington, who were using the ball well. There was a grand save by Griffiths after Bath had kicked through. Griffiths ran fully 30 yards before being pulled down inside the Warrington half. It was a hectic struggle and there were thrills in plenty.

Clarkson hit the upright with a penalty kick, but it was below the cross-bar. Against the wind, however, it was a very fine attempt at long range.

The covering and tackling of both teams continued to be magnificent. Warrington were all out to snatch victory but whenever they tried passing the Halifax cover was always there in readiness.

A grand kick by Price was well taken by Dai Bevan, who saved ground by keeping the ball out of touch. The pace was still a cracker. Todd got in a good run.

There was a thrill for Warrington supporters when Helme manoeuvred cleverly and then gave to Ryder, who went through the middle brilliantly, but he was pulled down by Schofield when he looked all over a scorer.

After 24 minutes and against the run of play, BATH put his side a point in front with his fourth penalty goal. The position was an easy one.

There was a great run by Griffiths to put Halifax on the attack, but Warrington were now playing with greater determination and they defended magnificently. Lynch made a grand run but Halifax could not find an opening.

THRILLS ABOUND

Grand work by Helme, who was supported by McCormick, nearly brought disaster to Halifax. McCormick kicked across to Brian Bevan on the wing, who took the ball in full flight, but the Australian was adjudged offside and was recalled.

Thrills now abounded with Halifax putting in all they could. Kielty was a foot short with a drop kick at goal. Halifax were putting up a great fight to regain the lead. They were throwing the ball about, but the closely-packed defence of Warrington was keeping Halifax out.

With the minutes going by it was thrilling to watch the way Halifax struggled. Warrington were keeping the ball close and Kielty had another dropped goal attempt but it was smothered.

Price had a chance of sending Ryan away on the right in a late attack by Warrington but he held on too long and was tackled. When Halifax responded Frodsham was lucky in taking a bouncing ball as Dean was kicking through.

The goal-kicking of Bath had decided the issue.

A minute from time, Griffiths had a shot at goal from a penalty, but as at Wembley he was a few inches wide in his attempt.

Halifax had lost by one point. They were most unlucky losers.

Halifax today had every right to be proud of its team, who had put up a magnificent struggle. They had had the major share of the play and, but for a magnificent defence by Warrington, they must have won.

RESULT:
WARRINGTON   4-0-8
HALIFAX   1-2-7

George Crawford on Australia's Test Possibles

RUGBY LEAGUE REVIEW

THE INTERNATIONAL RUGBY LEAGUE FOOTBALL WEEKLY

Vol. 8 No. 290   MAY 13, 1954   EIGHTPENCE

WHAT WE THINK

THE WILL OF THE NORTH
Magnificent Return Home of Final
PROBLEMS REVEALED BY REPLAY

By THE EDITOR (Stanley Chadwick)

WEDNESDAY evening, May 5th, 1954, will long be remembered by sportsmen in the North of England. The largest crowd ever to watch a mid-week football match in this country and the highest attendance at any match in England apart from London, gathered at Odsal Stadium, Bradford, for the replayed Cup Final between Warrington and Halifax. 102,575 people who paid for admission following a tortuous and shocking road journey to the ground, demonstrated to the rulers of the Rugby Football League in a clear and unmistakable manner that they desired the final for the game's major trophy to be played in their midst.

In the whole history of British sport there has never before been such a clear-cut decision on the part of the followers of a particular sport. The Rugby Football League can no longer run counter to the wishes of the whole game, and with the completion of the existing Wembley contract the way is clear for the immense task of equipping Odsal Stadium to accommodate the largest assemblage in the world.

OUR SUPPORT

Since the inception of "Rugby League Review" almost eight years ago, we have never once relaxed our efforts for the R.L. Challenge Cup Final to be played in the North — at Odsal. We have on numerous occasions urged the parties concerned in the development of the ground — Bradford Northern (tenants), City of Bradford Corporation (owners), and the Rugby Football League (organisers of the Cup Final), to get together and push on with the work of making the stadium a first-class sports arena, alike for players and spectators.

We are only too well aware that the difficulties of obtaining building licences, shortages of materials and suitable labour, has slowed down this work. It is a fact, however, that more could have been undertaken if the determination had been evident, especially on the part of the Rugby Football League, of making Odsal the ideal venue for the Final. Many of the very dangerous scenes and complaints from patrons of their inability to watch the play of the two teams, would have been avoided if urgent attention had been given to providing more amenities for spectators.

OFFICIAL APPROVAL

Full responsibility for any failing on the part of Odsal Stadium to provide those who paid to watch the match with a clear view of the play rests with the R.L. Council. Before allocating the replay to this ground it is reasonable to presume they took the necessary steps to ascertain that the existing facilities were equal to the strain of the large crowd certain to be present.

The official programme for this year's R.L. Challenge Cup Final at Wembley contained the assurance that all R.L. grounds are "maintained and kept in good repair at great expense solely for the comfort of the spectator." That is a plain guarantee that any member of the public paying for admission to a ground under the auspices of the Rugby Football League will be afforded a full view of the match throughout its progress, and will not be subject to personal injury while in the act of entering or leaving such ground.

Wisely the Rugby League makes no promises about the quality of the entertainment provided at the different grounds. After the dismal display in the drawn match at Wembley it might have been thought few would have wished to be present at another such match, and on an evening far from promising as regards the weather. We are firmly convinced that a majority of those who made the journey to Odsal on May 5th, 1954, did so in an effort to convince the R.L. Council that they desired the R.L. Challenge Cup Final henceforth to be played in the North, and on this particular enclosure.

ROAD CRAWL

While the Rugby Football League must be held responsible for spectator conditions inside Odsal Stadium, the blame for the chaotic traffic congestion on the roads leading to the ground must be ascribed to a section of the county's police force. We think it will be agreed that the Bradford force handled the road traffic exceedingly well within the city boundaries. The bad hold-up was the traffic passing through Brighouse from Lancashire and Huddersfield.

It took over an hour to travel a mile on the main road from Huddersfield to
(Continued Overleaf)

THE WILL OF THE NORTH
(Continued from Front Page)

Brighouse. At an important road junction in the latter town a female member of the police force was on duty. While appreciating the road traffic was exceptional, there was no justification for the shocking hold-ups which took place on this stretch of road leading into Brighouse. The West Riding Constabulary had ample time to devise plans to prevent any congestion of this description, and in consequence of their failure hundreds of people did not arrive at the ground until long after the kick-off.

ANSWERS, PLEASE

Reference to the kick-off invites the query why the match was allowed to commence five minutes before the advertised time? Lord Derby (president) was announced to present the Cup to the winning team at Wembley, and it is pertinent to ask why he was not in his place to perform this function at Odsal? The Lord Mayor and Mayoress of Bradford were the guests of the Rugby Football League at the replayed final, and it would surely have been a graceful gesture to have invited his worship to perform this ceremony in the absence of the League president.

The day following the record Odsal crowd the R.L. secretary was reported as stating that the ground could not yet be considered as the permanent home of the Cup Final. The chairman of the R.L. Council also observed that the question has never been discussed of changing the venue of the final. The only reply to such a statement is get it put down on the agenda for the very next meeting.

" THE THRILL OF A LIFETIME "

Writing in last week's issue before the replay, we ventured to suggest that R.L. Challenge Cup Finals played on proper R.L. grounds would not disappoint spectators. The first half of the replay had its dull moments, but the second half was a thriller all the way. Brian Bevan's length of the field crossing with the ball and Gerry Helme's marvellous beating of man after man to score at the corner, will long be remembered.

If we can be sure immediate attention will be given to the shortcomings of Odsal Stadium, with proper control of road traffic converging on Bradford for the 1955 R.L. Challenge Cup Final, we shall be happy to forget some of the painful episodes in the greatest day in the history of our game.

The North has welcomed back its Final with a roar which reverberated throughout the land, and never again will those who truly love the game be deprived of the satisfaction of attending the last match of the Cup Competition. As Edmund Burke once declared " In all forms of Government the people is the true legislator," and the R.L. Council must be reminded of this simple truth for future R.L. Challenge Cup Finals.

RUGBY LEAGUE REVIEW

THE INTERNATIONAL
RUGBY LEAGUE FOOTBALL
WEEKLY

Editor - - Stanley Chadwick
Assistant Editors
Vincent Firth, A. N. Gaulton,
Gerald Grayson.
Australia:
George Crawford (" Sydney Daily Telegraph "), R. B. Noble.
New Zealand: G. N. Nuttall.

Founded 1946 in the town of Huddersfield, Birthplace of the Game. Eighth Year Continuous Publication. Contents Copyright.

Editorial and Advertising Offices: The Venturers Press, Ltd., 38, Byram Arcade, Huddersfield, Yorks., England.

Subscription Rates (post free): 13 copies 8s. 8d.; 26 copies 17s. 4d.; 52 copies £1 14s. 8d.

Printed in Great Britain by A. T. Green & Co., Carr Lane, Slaithwaite, Yorks.

BLACKPOOL ELECTED

AT an extraordinary general meeting of the Northern Rugby Football League held in Manchester on Thursday, May 6th, the application of Blackpool for membership was accepted. Twenty-five clubs voted in favour, and five abstained from voting.

For next season there will be fifteen clubs in the Yorkshire and Lancashire League. The bottom club in the Yorkshire League (sixteen clubs) will not play in either League but will have an equal number of fixtures with clubs from both counties.

Bramley and Doncaster offered to balance the Lancashire League (Bramley has played in the Lacashire League for the past two seasons).

Workington Town Capture. William Wookey, 18-year-old Furness R.U. centre. The fee paid was " considerable." — May 6th.

Whitehaven Appointment. Neville Emery, who joined the club two years ago from Sydney R.U. club, appointed player-coach. — Wednesday, May 5th.

FROM OUR FILES

R.L. CUP FINAL FOR THE NORTH

IN the past there has been much glib talk of making Odsal " the supersports arena of the North," and too little attention to translating this into adequate covered stand and seating accommodation, comfortable terracing, and other amenities of a modern sports stadium . . . and we also call upon both Northern and the City Engineer's Department to take off their coats to the job of putting the stadium into shipshape . . . — February, 1947.

WE want our challenge Cup Final to be played on our own hearth and to be able to attend with the minimum of trouble and expense. — June, 1947.

THE R.L. Challenge Cup Competition has its roots in the North and the opportunity of witnessing the final tussle should be made available to all those who have followed the fortunes of their favourites through the succeeding rounds. — May, 1949.

ODSAL Stadium must in future be the venue of every big R.L. match, the Challenge Cup Final not excepted. Here is a ground easily accessible to the game's supporters in the North and already capable of holding vast crowds. — May 26th, 1950.

IF the 1952 Final serves no other purpose, it has shown our game can no longer afford the luxury of a London final. We shall lose nothing by playing the final in the North, while new and old friends will help to fill our coffers and the whole game reaps a full reward. — April 24th, 1952.

THE 1955 Final in the diamond jubilee season of R.L. football should be played in the true home of the game — the North. There is adequate time to prepare Odsal Stadium for the holding of a 100,000 crowd .. . The R.L. Council can afford to provide financial assistance for the improvement of Odsal Stadium instead of making a yearly contribution to the dividends of a London company. — March 11th, 1954.

Northern League Final
THE RECORDS UP TO DATE

Twenty of the clubs to finish at the head of the League table have won the Championship in the thirty-eight finals played.

Fifteen clubs occupying second position in the League table have won the Championship Final.

The Championship has been won on 22 occasions by Lancashire clubs. There have been 20 " Battles of the Roses."

The Northern Rugby Football League Championship Final
COMPARATIVE TABLE OF ATTENDANCES AND RECEIPTS FOR THE NINE POST-WAR FINALS

	1953-54	1952-53	1951-52	1950-51	1949-50	1948-49	1947-48	1946-47	1945-46
Attendances	36,519	51,083	48,684	61,618	65,065	†75,194	69,143	40,599	67,136
Receipts	£9,077	£11,502 16 6	£8,215 6s.	£10,993 7s.	*£11,500	£11,073	£9,791 12 6	£5,894 12 6	£8,386 13s.

† Record Attendance for Final   * Record Receipts for Final

OVER THE SEA TO IRELAND

The Rugby Football League was approached by the Marist Fathers of Milltown to stage a match in Dublin with a view to raising funds for a new church. The original idea was to invite Wigan and Warrington to play at Dalymount Park, the home of Bohemians FC. However, the end of season rivalry between Halifax and Warrington clearly fired their imagination and the Marist Fathers declared they wanted nothing less than yet another game between the Cup and Championship finalists. A £600 guarantee was put up by the organisers for the Dublin game. In the event the gate realised £1,378 despite heavy rain which threatened to spoil the day. The principal organisers were Marist Father Corcoran and Jim O'Meara.

The Secretary of the Rugby Football League, Bill Fallowfield was enthusiastic enough about the project to arrange an additional fixture for Belfast's Windsor Park on the day prior to the Dublin game. He had, apparently, Northern Irish connections having spent time there with the RAF during the war.

The famous Australian journalist and Rugby League expansionist, Harry Sunderland donated "The Dublin Copper Kettle" as a prize for the winners of the Dublin game. The Halifax players, who won the match 23-11, each received a miniature kettle embossed with a shamrock.

Warrington's half-backs Ray Price and Gerry Helme and Halifax prop forward Jack Wilkinson missed the Irish trip as they were touring Australasia with the 1954 Lions. Wire captain Ally Naughton and Ted White, both cruelly robbed by injury of appearances in the major finals, played in the Irish games as did reserves Alan Brocklehurst, Roy Glover and Bill Sheridan. Additions to the Halifax squad were Irish centre Martin Creeney, who had also been ruled out of the big games by injury, Brian Vierod, Len Olsen, Les Pearce and Ray Illingworth.

Warrington's players had originally been promised a trip to France at the season's close and by all accounts treated the replacement jaunt to Ireland as more of a pleasure than a chore. Halifax, possibly smarting from their disappointments at Wembley, Odsal and Maine Road, were reported to have taken the games in a more serious vein.

For those who believe modern players engage in too many games, it is salutary to note that before the Irish venture Halifax had played in 48 competitive fixtures and Warrington in 49.

Warrington prepare to fly to Ireland. Eric Frodsham, Jack Hamblett and Ally Naughton carry the cups.

15,000 Dubliners roused by storming R.L. exhibition

HALIFAX AGAIN BEAT WARRINGTON

(By Harry Sunderland)

HALIFAX scored another triumph last night when in Dublin they led Warrington 11-5 at half-time and finally won 23-11. The match was a successful venture for the Marist Fathers who sponsored the match in aid of the New Mill Town Church fund.

They had guaranteed the Halifax and Warrington clubs £300 each for expenses on top of their own match expenses, and a gate of £1,378 will pay all this and leave a profit for the church funds.

The match had some brilliant features and the "Irish Press" this morning head their story—"The leaguers came, saw and conquered," and says, "This code is certainly an all-action one with the ball always circulating freely right across the field, demanding a terrific pace and stamina." The only bad feature of the match was the poor goal-kicking. Griffiths even missed some in front of the posts, and Warrington had similar errors, trying three goal-kickers to only achieve success on one occasion.

The Halifax combination of Todd and Vierod was very successful, Vierod scoring two tries. The try by Thorley was magnificent, eight men handling the ball before the touch-down. The seven Halifax tries (only one of which was converted by Griffiths) were cored by Vierod (2), Daniels, Lynch, Dean Kielty and Thorley (one each). For Warrington, Frodsham kicked one penalty goal and unconverted tries were scored by Bevan, Naughton and Wright.

The Halifax players will all receive a miniature copper kettle adorned with a shamrock, and a larger copper kettle which I have given will become an annual trophy for Rugby League teams invited to play in Dublin.

TOURISTS BEATEN AGAIN

Sydney, Saturday.

THE Great Britain Rugby League touring team suffered the second defeat of their tour here to-day when Sydney beat them by 32 points to 25.

A crowd of 50,000 saw Sydney gain an early lead of seven points but the British side rallied so well that by half-time the score stood at 14 points each.

Lewis Jones, the Leeds back who played on the left wing in place of Castle (Barrow) scored 13 of the British team's total of 25 points.

He landed five goals and scored a try after a splendid run by Valentine.

Boston, Williams, Valentine and Henderson also scored tries.

The British team's first defeat was by 11-10 against Newcastle a week ago.

Great Britain's team was: Cunliffe (Wigan); Boston (Wigan), Greenall (St. Helens), Ashcroft (Wigan), Lewis Jones (Leeds); Williams (Hunslet) capt., Helme War—

More open play than in whole Irish season

(By Our Dublin Correspondent)

THE crowd of 15,000 Dubliners left Dalymount Park, elated with the feast of Rugby served up by Halifax (who might well have won by a more substantial margin) and Warrington. They saw more open football and slick passing than they would normally expect in a whole season of Irish club Rugby. There is no doubt about it, Halifax deserved their triumph, and but for indifferent goal-kicking it would have been even more pronounced.

While the much-publicised Brian Bevan, who in scoring a try brought his total for the season up to 69, got in some scorching runs on the Warrington wing, the finest winger on the field was Arthur Daniels, of Halifax. The try he scored was a beauty. He "jinked" his way past at least three Warrington defenders in a 40-yard run. And Vierod on the other wing brought the crowd to its feet with some dazzling runs.

In Ken Dean and Stan Kielty Halifax had a pair of "cracker-jacks"—attacking halfbacks who outshine the opposing pair.

SLOW STARTERS

But where Halifax scored over their rivals was in the passing of their forwards. Des Clarkson was ever boring his way through the gaps, and starting off movements which caused the Warrington defenders a load of trouble. Len Olsen was always in the thick of the fray, using his weight to bullock his way through the opposition.

Illingworth was another forward to shine, though the outstanding forward on the field was Ted White, of Warrington. He took a deal of holding, with his bustle through the smallest gap.

Warrington were five points up in 20 minutes, Eric Frodsham landing a goal, and Wright going over for a try. Then Halifax, slow to warm up, got going, and it was their game right to the end. Daniels roused the crowd with a magnificent run to score Halifax's first try, and then Vierod went away at top speed to record a second Halifax try.

Halifax were on top to the interval and John Thorley brought off a really glorious passing movement in which at least eight players handled the ball, and clinched it with a try which Griffiths converted, to leave Halifax leading at half-time by 11 points to five.

UPPER HAND

After weathering a series of hot attacks for about 10 minutes after the change of ends, when Brian Bevan dazzled with a 40-yard run which put him between the posts and reduced Halifax's lead three points, the Yorkshiremen got the upper hand and never relaxed their grip. Dean and Kielty went over for a couple of tries in a space of two minutes, and later Vierod scored a second try. Albert Naughton replied with a try for Warrington, but Halifax were on the attack at the end and before the

Wire Captain, Ally Naughton, who missed the finals but played in Ireland

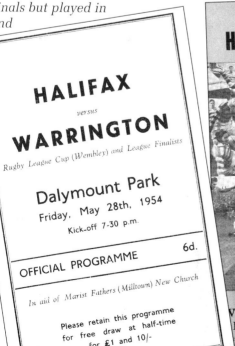

Five thrilling years, but there's one big disappointment

TWO Wembley Cup Finals, one Cup Final replay, three Rugby League Championship Finals, and a couple of Yorkshire Cup Finals for good measure . . . yes, I have been places in my seasons with Halifax. And yet . . . and yet . . . I'm disappointed.

Five good years, thrilling years, years of high endeavour by everyone at Thrum Hall—high endeavour and much of brilliant accomplishment, too. And yet there's something missing.

Anyone who has followed Thrum Hall during the last few years will know as well as I do just why there's that feeling of disappointment. We didn't get the R.L. Challenge Cup, the greatest prize of them all.

And yet, you know, although skipper Alvin Ackerley was never able to show the Challenge Cup to the Thrum Hall crowds we did, in my opinion, win a Cup Final. We won it that evening on May 5, 1954, when we met Warrington at Odsal Stadium, Bradford, in the replayed final.

Do you remember that Odsal replay? I'll never forget it. The immense crowd, for one thing, the biggest ever for a Rugby League game certainly in this country; and the occasion, the meeting of the season's premier sides after the first-ever Wembley draw.

We went into the game pretty certain that we could pull it off despite the bitterness of the Wembley disappointment. What a shock for us (and for most of the crowd) when Warrington got in first—that first try in a big game is, nearly always, half the battle. Well—it's pretty important. In fact, I believe Halifax would have won the Rugby League Challenge Cup this year at Wembley had we scored first and not St. Helens.

o o o o

However—back to Odsal and that wonderful, thrilling, so disappointing evening of May, 1954. Young Challinor got that all-important first try after an astute opening move by Harry Bath, the Australian, who passed to Lowe (some people thought that pass well forward, by the way) who, in turn gave to Challinor.

But did Challinor really score? Some people have their doubts. I have no doubts at all. He didn't. It was a good run, a splendid attempt, and it very nearly came off. But he never grounded the ball. He was tackled almost on the line went down—and the ball went loose.

Several of us saw it and we had (and have) no doubt at all: Challinor did not score.
Still, the referee ruled a try. Warrington were ahead.

Ten minutes later I went over the line and touched down for what I felt then and still feel now was a try; a perfectly genuine try. I'm as sure of that fact as of anything I have ever experienced in this game.

Arthur Daniels gave me the pass. It was a good one—a Daniels' pass and I need say no more. But the referee ruled a forward pass, disallowed the try and called me back.

How did it happen? I can only surmise the referee was temporarily unsighted. Anyway, that was the decision and the referee's word is the final word.

So we went to the interval one point behind—you may remember Griffiths kicked a penalty goal, a good shot, just before the whistle went for half-time.

o o o o

Then, the second half. First, Harry Bath kicked a penalty goal. Griffiths kicked a penalty goal.

Then, Helme, the dazzling Helme, went over after a wonderful 40-yard run. But we were still in the game—and then came the second perfectly good Halifax try to be disallowed by the referee.
Arthur Daniels, my partner in so many matches, was the one to suffer this time. He went clean over from a kick by Kielty. But the referee ruled that he had failed to ground the ball before he was hustled back across the line.
I think I know better. Arthur did go over. Arthur did ground the ball. Then, ball and Arthur were rolled over and over and back again, back over the line by one of the Warrington players, McCormick, I think.

Arthur Daniels has always been emphatic that he did genuinely touch down over the line. So am I. I remember, quite distinctly, that he was not rolled over until he had first slithered down to the ground . . . he actually finished up on his hands and knees.

But the referee ruled that he had not touched down. And, of course, it is the referee's decision that counts. So the Challenge Cup and the cup-winners' medals went to Frodsham and his men of Warrington that night.

We lost (officially) by eight points to four. Always in my own mind I have made it we really won by 10 points to five, even discarding the possibility either of or both the disallowed tries might have been converted.

Certainly, I think Griffiths would have been able to convert Daniels's try. For Griffiths, earlier on, had kicked a really magnificent goal from a point almost in line with the Daniels touch down.

It was the biggest disappointment of my career with the Thrum Hall club. I would not have felt it so much had we really been beaten. But we've always felt that we won. And there's the rub.
Of course, you might argue that any beaten team—particularly in

Later in this series Tom Lynch will tell of the inside drama of two famous Cup games . . . of a goal-kick that could have won a match and of a goal-kick that did win a match.

He will tell of his own saddest moment on the field; of a player who won a Cup Final; the story of how the Thrum Hall players once threatened to go on strike; about the Cup team . . .

He will also answer some questions the fans are putting. Why is it Halifax lose so many of the biggest games? Why is it Halifax, in recent years, have just missed so many trophies?

One of Lynch's finest tries. Up in the corner Lynch is over—against his own countrymen. Lynch scored near the end of the Halifax-New Zealanders match on September 17, 1955 . . . and Halifax won.

a match of the importance of that at Odsal—can try to make it out it really won. I suppose so. But I've always held very firmly to the opinion we really did win that replay. I often wonder what the spectators thought about that match.

From the purely personal point of view of course, I've no doubt at all that had that Odsal try of mine been allowed and the three points credited to Halifax (and it might have been five—Griffiths was in good form) I suppose I should have accounted it to-day the best try of my life.

Where is the player, I wonder, who has not sometimes dreamed his dreams of scoring a try in a Cup Final? We're only human, after all, although people sometimes seem to forget it!

o o o o

The try that did give me the greatest satisfaction during my years with Halifax? Well, I was really delighted with the very first of all in my first match, way back on a snowy day in 1952. But I'll be going back to the early days later on in the series.

As it is, I think the try that gave me more satisfaction than any other came my way a year or so ago when I was playing against the New Zealanders touring team up at Thrum Hall.

I wonder if you were one of the crowd who roared disappointment when I dropped the ball and saw Sorenson tear in to snap it up and dash on and on and over our line to score a try?

That try gave the lead to the New Zealanders. It wouldn't have been so bad, my dropping the ball I mean, if our opponents had been the Australians or Bradford Northern or Oldham or Warrington—anybody but my own countrymen.

Of course, I don't suppose anybody thought I had really let Sorenson through on purpose. But I decided that I really must make amends. And in that very match.

I pulled out about everything I had got but it wasn't until pretty late on in the game that I got a nice pass (from Derrick Schofield, I think) and went over. . . . I was more pleased with that try, I think, than any other I have ever scored, certainly during my time with the Halifax club.

The scene is the Odsal Stadium. The date, May, 1954. The occasion, the Challenge Cup Final replay between Halifax and Warrington. Tom Lynch is over the line, making for the posts, the Warrington defence beaten. Then . . . he is recalled for a forward pass.

❏ I was on leave from National Service then. We lived in Bolton Brow. I went with my dad to the game and we got there in good time although I don't remember how we got there. I remember there was plenty of space even though there were 102,000 there. We seemed to have plenty of elbow room and it wasn't like squashed sardines where we were although it might have been in other parts.

Brian Tyson

❏ I was working in a solicitor's office, waiting to go in the army. I was about 17. My dad got up a coach party from Midgehole Dyeworks. We left about three o'clock even though it was a seven o'clock kick-off. I remember Gerry Helme scoring the winning try, little bugger. Grinned all over his face.

Roger Shackleton

❏ It was my first real experience of a big occasion at a Rugby League match. I was 12 and a group of about half-a-dozen of us went from school. Alan Kaye, one of the lads, organised the trip from Dewsbury. The bus went from the Long Causeway. It was a Yorkshire Woollen bus. I can still remember the ticket. It was purple. For some reason it went via Cleckheaton and parked up somewhere around Low Moor which meant we had miles to walk. We got in all right and ended up at the right of the tatty stand. I could see about 2' 6" of the pitch between people's heads. I didn't see any of the tries. I didn't see any of the moves. In fact I don't even remember the score. I don't remember being conscious of being in danger. It wouldn't be allowed now.

Rodney Hardcastle

❏ I went with my father. We left Huddersfield about 4 o'clock. It was all right at first until we hit Bradley Bar and from there the traffic was solid to Odsal. We got off the bus and walked from Bailiff Bridge. It was amazing. All the people who lived on the route came out of their houses to watch the crowd and the traffic. They had never seen anything like it. We had just got in the ground when a gate was pushed in. It was chaotic. All these people just burst in. Many a thousand got in free. Neither me nor my father were tall and I didn't see much of the game at all. I ended up in a car park listening to the radio commentary with a few other people. I remember I got split up from my dad and I had to scrounge the bus fare home.

David Thomas

❏ Many years ago I was clearing out some cupboards in an effort to contribute some clothes to our local church jumble sale and I came across the maternity corset my wife had endured during the last months of her pregnancy with our son born in April 1953.

The memories came flooding back - not of the birth, but of the debt of gratitude that I owed to that tattered corset. I was suffering from a slipped disc when Warrington qualified to figure in the Challenge Cup Final of 1954 and, although I queued and got my ticket, I didn't relish the thought of making the trip to Wembley in my condition on what would be a very long and tiring day.

Then my wife, realising my despair, bless her, suggested that I wear her old maternity corset and, after the giggles from my two young daughters had subsided, I crept upstairs to try it on and then, glory be, instant relief. Yes, I got to Wembley - and in fairly good shape - but the game is best forgotten, with both sets of supporters in limbo, foregoing the pleasure of celebrating a win, or drowning their sorrows of a defeat with the game ending in a dreary draw.

The replay at Odsal though was something else, a moment in sporting history and an unforgettable experience. It was all so unpredictable with perhaps an attendance of 70,000 expected in view of the disappointing exhibition at Wembley, but, for some inexplicable reason, almost double that number of people descended on Odsal almost within a couple of hours.

Four of us from Warrington were working in Oldham at the time and we "borrowed" a van to travel to Odsal, safe in the knowledge that we were already halfway there from Warrington but we were shocked to find that on leaving work about 5 pm we became bogged down in Oldham town centre when the normal rush hour traffic converged on the convoy of traffic coming from all over Lancashire. After crawling for mile after mile we eventually arrived about a couple of miles from Odsal Top and decided to abandon the van and walk the rest of the way. I was in no fit state for that but there was no alternative with the kick-off only fifteen minutes away. We made it though and joined the thousands of fans rushing around like lemmings trying to find a turnstile.

Let me here give thanks to whoever organised the police control because they must have been faced with a terrible problem with so little time to prepare for it, as were the numbers of St. John Ambulance people who were treating a few fainting cases. Our little party had now been split and there were just two of us who eventually found ourselves inside the ground but, as yet, nowhere near the terraces. We were virtually swept along until we surfaced high up in the corner opposite to where Gerry Helme scored the vital try. I didn't see him do so and I don't remember seeing much else of the game. We were more concerned with survival on

"Wire" Back: Wright, Challinor, Bevan, McCormick, Ryan, Phillips.
Front: Helme, White, Frodsham, A. Naughton, Price, Bath, D. Naughton.

"Fax" Back: Fearnley, Wilkinson, Thorley, Schofield, Griffiths, Bevan, Clarkson.
Front: Daniels, Kielty, Ackerley, Todd, Dean, Lynch.

the sleeper and ash terraces that offered so little protection.

It was simply too many people being in the wrong place at the wrong time. It really was a miracle that no one was killed or for that matter no serious injuries resulted from that night, especially when later tragedies occurred at Heysel and Hillsborough in much better locations.

To finish my story, we eventually arrived back at our van to find our two mates waiting for us, together with six lads from Warrington who had lost their coach and had no idea where they had last seen it. So we got back to Warrington at 2 am, weary and worn, with me hardly able to drag one leg after the other but thankful for that battered old corset that had made it all possible.

Ernie Day

❏ I worked at Metropolitan-Vickers Trafford Park and my mates and I arranged a coach to go to Bradford. The gaffer allowed us to leave work fifteen minutes early. We left Trafford Park at 4.45 pm and were still in Oldham at 5.45 pm. When we started going over the tops there was a long, long trail of vehicles from Warrington to Bradford with quite a lot of steamers stopped on the roadside. We eventually arrived about a mile from the ground and left the coach because the driver could not get any nearer. There were thousands of others doing the same. When we got to Odsal there were people standing on buildings and toilets, all hoping to see something inside.

The turnstile we found was open but not taking payment. There was a large queue waiting to go in so we went further along and found many gaps that had been made in the fence. After going round trying to find a viewpoint I managed to find one. From the terracing the pitch looked the size of a pavement flag. The second half was already in progress but at least I was able to see the winning try.

Coming out of the ground was quite an experience. My feet never touched the ground for a hundred yards. When we came down to earth we could not find the coach and so decided to go for a drink. Well, this was easier said than done. The pubs that had beer had no room or glasses and the others had run dry. We could not find anywhere to eat either. When we eventually found the coach we had lost the only two Yorkshiremen with us. The day after we found they had more gumption than us for when they could not get to the ground they came home by train. We arrived back in Oldham to find the pubs and even the chippies shut.

The one good thing this trip sorted out was the argument why the Rugby League Cup Final was held at Wembley instead of in the north.

H Sunman

❏ I got to Odsal about half past five and was near the front on the lower slopes. Round where I stood it never really got full and it seemed the same all around the lower slopes. They never packed people in properly at Odsal. I was staggered after the match when they announced the attendance. They could have got a lot more in but people wouldn't move down. I remember after the game I had to walk all the way home to Thornton. There was just no chance of catching a bus. The traffic was absolutely incredible. It was amazing how there was never any trouble at those big games at Odsal. You never felt afraid. There were no barriers - just old sleepers which broke when you trod on them.

I remember we knew a chap called Geoffrey Varley who used to stand near us. He was about 6' 1" and twenty stones. He wanted to stand where he usually stood behind the posts but arrived late. He managed to force his way right from the back to the front though. At one point about five Warrington supporters tried to stop him pushing through. He told them he was either going through them or over them. They let him through!

I have been a Bradford Northern supporter for over 50 years and the only big match I have missed at Odsal was the 1949 semi-final between Halifax and Huddersfield because I was at Swinton watching Northern beat Barrow in the other semi. We used to be able to tell how many people were in the ground and sometimes the attendances they announced used to make us laugh. They would say there were 11,000 in when we knew it was nearer 20,000. I think the most remarkable crowd for a game at Odsal was the 69,000 they got for the third round cup-tie against Huddersfield in 1953. Imagine, 69,000 for a club game!

Jack Bower

❏ I have been following Bradford Northern since 1947 and I'm 84 now. I used to organise the coaches for Northern. For the replay I had a seat in the New Stand on the front row near half-way. So I had a good view. It is the crowd I remember. How it swayed and waved. It was a wonderful experience. I remember Harry Hornby, the Bradford Chairman, going up and down the stand telling everybody how big the crowd was. He was excited. I remember a newspaper man kidding me on before the game that there would only be a couple of hundred folk there! The day after I went in to work and bragged about being there. I was proud to have been there. I used to stand at the top of Odsal sometimes and wonder why so many people would go to watch men throwing and kicking a ball about. They should have done something with Odsal a long time ago. They are still talking about it.

Emily Carr

❏ My father Hubert Chapell and his brother James went to the game. They both played rugby, my father for Brighouse Rangers - I think they were a Rugby Union team then - and his brother for Batley. They went to Odsal from Huddersfield and got there late when the ground was full. They picked up a St. John Ambulance stretcher and the crowd let them through right down to the pitch. They had a ring-side view! Anyway, that's the story that's always being told in my family.

Jean Davison

❏ I got there early and stood near where the players came onto the field. There was plenty of room there. There was a young woman there and she was really frightened. I said, *"stick with me and you'll be all right"*. Nothing happened, of course. I think Daniels and Lynch scored fair tries but that was only my opinion. The referee said they didn't and that's all that mattered. Helme and Price were the difference between the sides. They won it for Warrington.

Anon

❏ In those days I was a long distance driver delivering in the Birmingham area. Anyway, nothing was going to stop me going to the game. I left Wolverhampton about two o'clock. Everything was OK until I got to Wakefield and then it was one long jam to Odsal. I left the wagon on Rooley Lane and ran the rest of the way. I got in just after the kick-off and spent the next 90 minutes running round the top of the ground jumping up and down to catch a glimpse of the game. The only time I saw the ball was when someone kicked it into the air. I was fourteen stones, fit and had done a bit of wrestling and I tried everything to get through the crowd, even shoulder charging, I'm ashamed to say, but I just could not get through the crush. There were a lot more than 102,000 there. They were still pouring in behind me. None of them will have seen anything.

Harry Smith

❏ I have been on Halifax Town Council for over forty years now. Back in 1954 I had only been a councillor for a year. On the night of the replay there was a town council meeting and it opened my eyes about council proceedings. The Mayor, Alderman Harold Pickles opened the meeting and said, *"We know what's in front of us"*. All the items on the agenda were then passed without a word against any of them. It was just a matter of agreed, agreed, agreed! When the meeting ended we trooped out to the waiting bus. We would never have got to Odsal in time if we had not been picked up by two police outriders between Shelf and Odsal. They escorted us down the wrong side of the road all the way to the ground because we were an official party and our seats were all booked. I remember I sat next to Councillor Harry Ludlam.

Of course, I was disappointed with the result. I am 74 now and I have supported Halifax all my life. My interest started at Battinson Road School. Halifax used to give complimentary tickets to pupils who did well. That's what got me going.

Eric Whitehead

❏ On May 5th, 1954 my pal and I were two sixteen-year-olds. At that time I lived on Netherlands Avenue, three-quarters of a mile from the stadium. Although we were more ardent speedway supporters we enjoyed the thrill of mixing with the large crowds converging on Odsal for the big Rugby League games.

May 5th was a fine, sunny Spring evening and the large crowd began descending on Odsal from early tea-time. In those days nine out of ten supporters travelled to games by coach. As at all big games the scene for two miles on all roads leading from the stadium was of rows of coaches, nose to tail on both sides of the road. You can imagine the dangerous situations created as in the avenue where I lived, should there have been a serious incident such as a house fire, the fire brigade would have stood no chance of getting through.

One of the scenes that stands out most in my mind is of my pal and I standing in Huddersfield Road by the caravan sales centre. There were "unofficial" programme sellers in evidence. My pal and I stood by advising supporters where they could buy an official programme. We received thanks from them and the promise of a thick ear from the touts!

We entered the stadium late in the game after the exit gates had been opened. The scene was magical and awesome. I had been in the stadium on many occasions when there had been large crowds but this was different, especially to a sixteen-year-old. A scene of black as most supporters had arrived for the game straight from work in the day-time, standing shoulder to shoulder with less than inches between them. Remember, they were standing on steep slopes of packed-down ashes and old railway sleepers. When you consider the stadium disasters of recent years - I was in the stand during the Bradford City disaster - it is a tribute to the crowds of those days, their standard of fair play and general behaviour. All that was needed that day was a small surge from the back and the consequences are unimaginable.

I still have the original postcard produced to commemorate the occasion - an aerial view of the stadium during the game.

David Pullan

❏ I was just short of my eighth birthday at the time. We lived down Raymond Street, between Mayo Avenue and Parkside Road, opposite Heron's Mill. This particular tea-time coaches began to be parked down our street. For all the big games at Odsal - before or since - our street had never been affected. Of course, for the Final Replay both sets of supporters had travelled and not many had cars then. My father attended the game. I will never forget all those coaches parking down our street and the passengers pouring out of them and rushing up the street. I never saw the buses leave. The match would end well past my bed-time.

John R Armitage

❏ Three of us went by bus from Lowerhouses to Bradford and then out to Odsal. I had never seen queues like it. We stayed in the ground for about an hour but never saw a thing. We were big lads but there was no way we could get further in or down. I just shouted when the others shouted. After an hour we just left. No one started chanting or raving for their money back. They just accepted it as part of life. It was amazing no one got injured.

Roy Tinsley

❏ I am 67 now but I went with my father to Odsal in 1954. He had a seating ticket and I had a ground ticket but we were late getting to the ground as our coach was stopped a mile and a half from Odsal. I had followed Warrington all the way through the Cup rounds but I hardly saw any of the replay. On the way there we saw men actually running across the roofs of cars. It wasn't vandalism, just pure enthusiasm to get in.

What I remember most is the crowd pushing at the fence to get in, they were so desperate to see the game. Most of them had tickets but couldn't get through the turnstiles quickly enough. Anyway, all of a sudden someone shouted really loudly, *"Don't push it. Pull it"*. And they did. It came crashing down and I'll never forget the sight of a lone policeman and a groundsman helpless with their arms in the air.

I ended up at the side of a stand and being only 5' 7" I could hardly see anything. I ended up asking people what was happening most of the time. I did see Gerry go over for his try though. It was at the opposite end to where I was. I remember we stopped on the way back and bought a bag of meat pies because we knew we would be very late back. We never saw any trouble at all.

Vin Dower

❏ I went to Odsal but I didn't really want to. I remember it so clearly though because it was the first of three important events. The game was on May 5th, I was 21 on 13th May and I got married on 3rd July. I actually hate Rugby League and sport in general but I was courting and my future husband, Ron, was a Warrington fan. I worked at CWS Printers and the firm organised a coach trip to Odsal. You were only eligible to go if you worked for them but you could take someone else with you and Ron was obviously the one. I remember coming out at the end of the game, slowly shuffling along, shoulder to shoulder holding onto my umbrella. When we did get out I only had the umbrella handle and all the buttons on the front of my coat had disappeared!

Maynard Glover

❏ If Maynard had not got me the ticket for her works trip I would have missed the game. I had been away with the Territorial Army when the Wembley Final was played and heard it on a little transistor. My boss said I could go to the replay. We missed the first seven or eight minutes and would have missed a lot more if a mounted policeman had not directed us to an empty turnstile which had just opened. We wormed our way down to a place where we could see and I can actually say that we did see all the action. I remember seeing Gerry Helme dive under someone's arm to score. He practically went down on his knees for that try. I once went to Swinton to see Warrington play St. Helens in a Lancashire Cup Final and I only saw the ball twice when someone kicked up-and-unders so that night at Odsal I didn't do so bad. I remember people running round and round the flat bit half-way up the slopes all through the match.

My future father-in-law, Maynard's dad, went to the game on another coach and he couldn't see anything. He ended up listening to it on the radio in a pub. It took us ages to find our coach after the game. It was about three-quarters of a mile away. We didn't get back until well after mid-night and, of course, I had to take Maynard home. Her father was fuming, playing hell. He said, *"She doesn't even like football and she saw the match while I have to sit in a bloody pub listening to the wireless"*.

Ron Glover

❏ I was involved in getting a report of the match to one of the national newspapers in a rather unusual way. Press facilities at Odsal in those days were rather primitive, to say the least. There was none of the high technology in communications so available nowadays. I had just started covering the occasional local Rugby Union and cricket matches for Crabtree's, the press agency in Bradford, and I was asked to act as messenger for one of the national press reporters at the match.

There were very few 'phones in the press box itself because GPO Telephones had either been unable to provide sufficient 'phones in the time available or there was simply not room for them. It was therefore arranged to make use of the telephone in the newsagent's shop at the top of Manchester Road - long since demolished - and it was my job to take the "copy" up to the shop where a colleague was sitting by the 'phone to transmit it to the office of this particular newspaper.

You can imagine my thoughts as the crowd built up as to how in heaven I was going to get through it from the stand to the exit of the ground. Somehow I did! There was a sloping pathway that led from the old changing rooms to the stand, and I was able to fight my way up and down this considerably narrowed path about six times during the match. As you can imagine, I saw little of the game but I like to think my efforts enabled many people to read about it next day.

Geoffrey Spence M.B.E.

Odsal still far from "Wembley of the North"

CHIEF talking point in Bradford today was the Rugby League Cup final replay at Odsal Stadium, and in particular the crowd figures of 102,575—a record figure far in excess of what officials had anticipated.

It was a great night for most of that crowd.

There were, however, complaints from many who could not see all the game. Hundreds left the ground on this account, some others inside caught only glimpses of the play, and the obvious conclusion is that much has to be done at the stadium before it can be considered as the "Wembley of the North."

The police dealt with the biggest inflow of traffic ever experienced in the city, and there were few complaints of the way in which it was handled.

A number of buses, however, did not reach the ground until some time after the start, and eventually the "gates" of the stadium were thrown open and people could leave or enter as they pleased.

At Odsal Top the traffic—pedestrians and vehicles—was controlled by Supt. N. D. Bennett from a walkie-talkie van on the roundabout. The Chief Constable (Mr. H. S. Price) and the Assistant Chief (Mr. Harry Ambler) watched the operations. Many policemen walked round the stadium carrying walkie-talkie apparatus.

The statement from Bradford City Police headquarters today was: "So far as the police were concerned, the arrangements were satisfactory."

By 10 p.m. all traffic had been dispersed from the Odsal area.

POLICE PRAISED

Mr. S. G. Wardley, the city's engineer and surveyor, after reading accounts of the scene, brought out his development plan for Odsal, and its advantages can readily be seen from the photograph.

Finance is the big obstacle, but Mr. Wardley points out that his plan could be done in stages, and indeed, a small portion of the scheme has already been carried out on the new stand side.

Mr. Harry Hornby, Bradford Northern and speedway "chief," was delighted with crowd figure, and paid a compliment to the police for the way in which they handled the traffic.

But Mr. Hornby is not one who is of the opinion that Odsal is ready to stage the Rugby League Cup finals. "Wembley would still be my vote for the time being," he said. "Naturallyl, I hope the day will come when Odsal will be developed on a big scale, but until we have amenities similar to those at Wembley the Cup final must be considered out of the question. We can comfortably house the crowds for the League championship or internationals—but the final . . ."

HINT TO COMMITTEE

Then Mr. Hornby threw out a hint to the Rugby League Management Committee. "In the light of last night's experience I think the Rugby League should set aside their profits from the match and

then meet Bradford Corporation and Bradford Northern, with a view to Odsal's development," he said.

Mr. Hornby pointed out that Bradford Northern, helped by the money received from speedway when it was doing well a year or two ago, had effected a number of improvements at Odsal, but, with average crowds of 12,000 to 14,000 they could not be expected to tackle a big development scheme. He thought the time was due for a get-together on the possibilities of the stadium.

Ald. H. W. Semper, chairman of the Bradford Finance Committee, was at the match, and on the question of any development scheme for Odsal he had this to say today: "We are always open to consider reasonable suggestions, providing they do not put all the liability on the ratepayers."

From the number of passengers carried to Odsal last night by Bradford Corporation buses, Transport Department officials did not expect the record Cup final crowd was in excess of 102,500.

ALL-TICKET GAMES?

Mr. W. Fallowfield, Rugby League secretary, said that the game and the attendance had given satisfaction. He added that if more big games attracting such huge attendance were to be played at Odsal in the future, he thought that more crush barriers and the interfencing sections should be introduced.

The answer might be all-ticket games.

CUP WINNERS

A cup from an anonymous Leeds woman will be presented jointly to Mr. A. S. Dale (Bradford) and Mr. L. Hargreaves (Leeds), winners of the 1952 and 1953 area hymn tune competitions, at a convention of No. 2 (Northern) Area of the National Association of Brass Band Conductors to be held on 5 June at Hammond's Sauce Works, Shipley.

Speakers at the convention will include Mr. Phil Catalinet (a well-known brass band composer) and two officials of London No. 1 Area, Mr. A. V. Creasey and Mr. H. Gurney Doe.

THE RUGBY LEAGUE
CHALLENGE CUP COMPETITION
FINAL TIE
HALIFAX v. WARRINGTON

(Photo by courtesy of the Yorkshire Post)

ODSAL STADIUM, BRADFORD
WEDNESDAY, 5th MAY, 1954

Official Programme — Sixpence

THIS is the Odsal Stadium development plan, in model form—the "Wembley of the North"—visualised by Mr. S. G. Wardley, Bradford's City Engineer and Surveyor.

This scheme, the estimated cost of which is said to be in the region of £250,000, would provide for a crowd of 93,000, all of whom would be able to see easily, and, if needed, the limit could be extended to 100,000.

The plan would increase the size of the arena. There would be no lifting and re-setting of turf at the corners, as at present, to enable speedway racing to be held. The speedway track would be increased to 440yd., and would be wider on the bends.

The main stand (on left of picture) is moved back to give a better view of the field and track, with terracing between the front of the stand and the fence.

Behind the stand are the dressing rooms and refreshment rooms. A tunnel underneath the stand will lead from the dressing rooms to the field. Beyond the dressing rooms and refreshment rooms are lavatories.

The aim is to terrace all the ground. The speedway pits would be moved to the left of the picture, mid-way between the first and second bends.

One part of this plan has already been adapted, for when the old stand had to be pulled down, the new one (right of picture) fits in with the scheme. At the moment, however, seating is extended beyond the cover of this stand. In the plan, the front of this stand would be terracing.

Under the plan there would be under cover accommodation for 8,000.

(Aerial picture of Odsal during last night's game on Back Page).

❏ The evening of the epic replay still lives in my memory and, although the game itself was not a classic, the size of the crowd was amazing.

I, my sister and three brothers decided to visit Odsal on a pub trip from Otley. Everything seemed pretty normal as the bus approached the stadium on Rooley Lane but when the bus driver unloaded his passengers, that's when we met with the vast crowd trying to get through the turnstiles.

Each gate was jam-packed with folk squeezing and shoving and the mounted police were trying to ease the congestion which was nigh impossible. My sister and I finally entered the ground about three-quarters of an hour before kick-off and it was a hopeless cause trying to get down on the terraces which were full from the fence up to the highest rim of the Odsal bowl.

After walking right to the other end above the speedway pits, we found a small space from which only half the pitch could be seen. The big shock about the crowd size was that it had been a rainy day and nobody expected over 100,000. After the game it took us three-quarters of an hour to find our transport with there being bus after bus stretching for miles.

Harold Winterburn

❏ I'm 62 now and I have been going to Odsal since I was five. My dad used to take me as a child and I used to spend my time playing on the trellissing and running round and round. One day he made me stop playing and told me to watch a certain player who he said was the greatest full-back and kicker in the world. It was Jim Sullivan of Wigan.

Anyway to get back to the Odsal Replay, I lived in Bradford Moor then and I went by trolley bus to the game. They used to turn round at Laisterdyke for Odsal one way and at Bankfoot the other way and there used to be a special service on match days. That night there was so much congestion the trolleys could only get to Dudley Hill and we had to walk the rest of the way.

I am only short so when I saw the crowd I decided the only way to see the game was to climb a tree. There were some over by where the Northern Hospital adjoins the ground. There were about 20 or 30 of us up there in the trees. A lot of them were children whose parents passed them up. I saw everything up that tree, all the tries, all the action. I saw another match from the same tree when there were about 60,000 on the ground. Years later I went to watch Northern at Halifax and I met Dean and Kielty, the Halifax half-backs in the replay, in the bar. They were really nice chaps. I have always been glad to say that I was part of the Odsal Replay.

Frank Spencer

❏ At the time I worked as a wagon driver for Co-op Coal in Sowerby Bridge. I was determined to go to the game even though the boss said that any of us asking for time off and going would be sacked. So I

didn't ask! I went with my brother Peter and another bloke. Peter was friendly with a man who worked at the old sheds at Sowerby Bridge railway and he said we could go on the footplate on a shunting engine which went to Mirfield. It dropped us off at Low Moor and we walked to Odsal arriving about 20 minutes before the start. I remember seeing a mounted policeman trying to block a gap in the fencing but two kiddies just ducked under the horse's belly and walked straight in. I wished I'd been little enough to do that myself! We did not go through any turnstile but threw our money in a bucket which some chap was holding. He said the money would go to the after-match players' reception. It seemed a bit funny.

Inside the ground we managed to get a good view and saw everything. We were level with the try-line where Daniels scored as good a try as I have ever seen. I worked with him later at Mackintosh's and he said he scored. I'll swear until I die that it was a try. The referee wasn't up with the play.

After the game we went back to Low Moor and got another lift on a shunter and were back in the pub at Sowerby Bridge ages before anybody else. Our faces were black with the steam and dust when we got back. The landlord of the pub at Cunning Corner in Rishworth told me that the Warrington team called in with the Cup on the way home. Some of the customers told Gerry Helme that Halifax had been robbed. He replied *"Yes, but we've got the Cup"*.

Terence Rice

❏ My father went to the Replay. He brought back the local Bradford paper, *"The Observer"*, which I still have although it's a little worse for wear. When I was about twelve or thirteen in 1968-69 I went to watch a Rugby League and boxing roadshow film at a local club. During the show the 1954 Replay highlights were shown. As soon as the final whistle went I noticed two or three men run out to Gerry Helme and lift him up on to their shoulders. I was convinced one of them was my dad - two years before I was born.

When I got home I asked my father where he stood during the match and what did he do after the final whistle. He said he gradually made it to the front and stood close to the touch-line and as soon as the whistle went he and two of his mates, whose names I cannot now remember, picked Gerry Helme up on their shoulders. It was a weird experience seeing my father two years before I was born. I wonder if the other two men are still alive. My dad died in 1990. In all the years of watching rugby he said that, along with some of Bev's tries, the Fax v Wire replay was the most amazing experience he had ever had. Something that will probably, no certainly, never be matched. My father's name was Thomas Griffiths, the same as mine. To his army mates he was known as "Hovis" - after the bread. He ate two loaves a day.

T Griffiths

❑ In May 1954 I was 23 years old, a police constable on the Warrington Borough Force. Luckily, 5th May was my day off so I could go to Bradford for the match. However, a colleague was not so fortunate but he was determined to attend. He applied to the Chief Constable to change his day off. These requests were never granted without a very good reason. He must have given one - maybe to attend his grandma's funeral, I don't remember what - but it was granted.

Bank Quay railway station is very close to the police station so we had to take great care not to be observed when going to board one of the many trains heading over the Pennines. With hundreds of others we alighted from our compartment only to see, to our horror, Alex Jeffreys, the Chief Constable, in company with his friend Bob (Mr Rugby) Anderton. We ducked out of the way with relief and joined the snake-lines moving over the hills to enter Odsal expecting to be spotted at any moment by the Chief. I can't remember much about the game!

Gordon Hill

❑ I am 80 years of age and have been a keen supporter of Halifax RLFC since I was about 14. The first Challenge Cup final I ever went to was in 1931 when Halifax beat York. As you may imagine, it was a time of great elation to me. It was a great contrast to how I felt in 1954 when Halifax lost the Odsal Replay. It was an evening kick-off and I, along with my late wife Mary, decided to go early and left by train from Sowerby Bridge to Low Moor. We arrived at Low Moor at about 5 pm and quite casually walked up to the stadium and paid our entrance fee at the Low Moor end which had very few spectators in at about 5.30. We then wended our way round to the Rooley Lane end and picked a spot at the railings surrounding the playing area very near to the corner flag, the spot where Arthur Daniels scored a perfectly legitimate try. He was laid flat on the floor with the number two on his shirt clearly visible and hands and ball clearly visible. But Mr. Ron Gelder who was not up with the play was deceived by the Warrington players, who by the time Mr Gelder reached the spot had turned Arthur Daniels over on to his back. Ron Gelder spread his arms out to signify no try.

The try by Tommy Lynch at the Low Moor end was also disallowed but as I had not a clear view I could not comment. I was later informed that Ron Gelder had blown his whistle for a forward pass after Lynch had run over half the length of the pitch - why, oh why? In my opinion Halifax were beaten not by Warrington but by Mr. Ron Gelder. I left Odsal miserable and utterly dejected. To crown it all Mary and I walked back down to Low Moor station low in spirit and wet through for it was raining hard.

Douglas Rowlands

❑ I went to Odsal along with my father Mr. Jesse Horsfall and a friend of his, Mr. Les Armitage. There were lots of Warrington supporters around us and during the banter between us and them my father and Les each put a £1 note in the hands of a Warrington supporter and he covered it by two £1 notes, the winners to keep everything. Now here is the crunch. At the end of the match not only Halifax fans knew they had been cheated but the Warrington fans knew it too. The Warrington fan who made the bet refused to accept the winnings on principle.

Gordon Horsfall

❑ I went to the Odsal replay with my boy-friend, now my husband. It was the first and last match I ever went to. I was almost killed coming out at the end of the game. As we were leaving the ground we were suddenly confronted with some kind of metal barrier. It was all rusty and spikey and the pressure of the crowds behind us was pushing me onto it. My husband pulled me out of the way just in time. I remember breaking one of the heels on my shoes. I must have been mad going to a game in high heels! The whole affair petrified me. I go down to Wembley every year with my husband but I never go to the game. I go shopping with some other ladies. Actually, I tell a lie about not going to another game. I went to one at Parramatta last February when I was in Australia on holiday but that was something entirely different. I was just sitting in the sun enjoying myself!

Mildred Robshaw

❑ I went from Wakefield with my older brother Don to the game. He drove us there in an old shooting-brake. I remember it was two days before my thirteenth birthday. We parked in a field in Tong. There were loads more parked there. As it rained heavily we had to get some folk to help us get out of the mud at the end of the match. We saw Jim Challinor's try but we could only really see from one try-line to just over the "25" line. Where we were stood it was just like standing on old fire ash. There were people watching from the stand roofs. Lots of people came in and went straight out again. We came out before time and as we came away in the crush Don said, *"Don't put your head down. Keep it up"*. That was because people were passing out. We saw quite a few fainting cases on the way out.

Brian Taylor

❑ At that time we lived within five minutes walk of the ground. I went to Wyke School and I was about twelve. Me and my brother went straight to the ground from school at about 4.15 pm. We were both equipped with a pack of sandwiches. We were right down at the front behind the posts and near the bank of loud-speakers. I remember people sitting on top of the stand roof. At the end of the game we scrambled over the boards which were as tall as us and ran on to the pitch. A week later we went to the pictures and to our surprise saw ourselves on the newsreel. We sat through the whole programme again to see ourselves! There were a lot of folk who could not find their transport after the game so some of the local house-holders put them up for the night and they went to look for their transport the next morning. The whole thing was the main topic of conversation for the locals for weeks after.

Les Pyrah

❏ I have been involved in Rugby League all my life. I am 67 now and kit-man for Bradford Northern reserves. I was supposed to referee a junior match at Odsal before the 1954 replay but they decided not to have a curtain-raiser as the ground conditions were too heavy. Obviously I was on the ground very early. There was practically no one there when I walked all the way round the top of the stadium with Ralph Green, the ex-Wales RL international forward, who was a touch-judge then. It was amazing watching it fill up. Odsal was so big that it looked empty with crowds of 50,000. I saw the game from the ring-side seats with the lads who should have played the curtain-raiser. The referee, Ron Gelder, who I knew quite well, certainly upset one or two folk with his decisions, especially when Lynch ran over but had the try disallowed for a forward pass. Of course, the outstanding feature of the match was that great try by Gerry Helme.

Tommy Uttley

❏ I went to Odsal on a coach from Crosfields Chemical Factory in Liverpool Road. I remember most of the coaches were Frankie Yates' Coaches from Runcorn. Our party was all from the engineering department. We were diverted all over the place and the coach was stopped a couple of miles from Odsal. We walked through fields pushing through fences and hedges to get to the ground. I always say there were more like 150,000 than 102,000. I certainly did not see much. I don't think many did. I remember piling up sleepers in order to see more. The crush was so strong that the crowd walked through a six foot steel bar fence and pushed over a fence made of railway sleepers. I knew some of the Warrington players pretty well. I used to work with Ron Ryder and used to go to dances with Austin Heathwood and Gerry Lowe.

After the game we knocked on the door of a club - it was one of those great big battlement doors - and a head appeared at a little window and said, *"You belong to this crowd. They are all ready for you at the back"*. We were not with anyone really but we went in and there were tables all set up with refreshments. I had free beer all night and came out semi-drunk. I do remember we stopped at Oldham on the way home.

FW James

❏ I recall that at the time I was a thirteen-year-old pupil at St. Bede's Grammar school and already a fervent Rugby League, and in particular, Bradford Northern, fan. Some friends and I went straight to Odsal that Wednesday from school. We were very near the front of the queue for the boys entrance well over an hour before the turnstiles were due to open at 6 pm. I well remember the panic amongst us when, at about 6.20 pm, our gate was not yet open but many others were and through gaps in the fencing we could see hundreds of grown-ups streaming down the slopes inside the ground.

Eventually, of course, we did get in and managed to get to the front behind the posts at the Rooley Lane end. I also remember feeling a bit cheated when the winning try was scored at the far end, in the scoreboard corner. Overall, however, it was a tremendous occasion, especially for a young teenager in the fifties, and we thought nothing of the long walk afterwards down Manchester Road to the city centre to catch a bus home. It was certainly quicker than queueing for the "specials" into town. I am still very much a Northern supporter and have attended many big matches over the years but the 1954 replay was the first big occasion for me and Rugby League and will never be forgotten.

Jim Holroyd

❏ My experience at Odsal was one of sheer frustration. I was in a coach party travelling from Warrington and the journey became a long drawn-out affair with hundreds of cars and coaches proceeding at a snail's pace through Oldham, Halifax and on to Odsal Stadium - no motorways in those days. On the approach to Odsal we all left the coach and proceeded to walk to the match - some two miles - arriving at the ground at half-time! No one in the party had bothered to ask the driver where he would park the coach. He wouldn't have known where, anyway!

After the match we had to send out search parties for two hours before the coach was located and then organise further searches in the pubs, packed to the rafters, for other missing friends. We finally arrived back at Warrington at 1.30 next morning and I then had a three mile bike ride home in the wind and rain.

I only "saw" the second half and saw very little of the game, being swallowed up amongst the 102,000 spectators. Hundreds of fans returned to their cars and coaches to listen to the remainder of the game on radio. The sheer volume of traffic and the record attendance were something I will always remember. Bradford and district was just a vast car and coach park.

KJ Woods

❏ I and three mates travelled from home via Halifax, Denholme, Queensbury and Shelf. I always travelled this route to watch matches at Odsal although it was a longer way. On our way

*Wembley. Harry Bath misses
a penalty shot for Warrington*

from Shelf to Odsal I noticed that a few cars had parked on the wide grass verge near to Odsal. So I did the same and we walked from there. We got out of the ground all right and walked back to the car, got in and came home. On the way home we talked about the game and about the crowd. We talked that much about the game that I did not realise that we had come out of the Shelf road and across the Wibsey road and into the Queensbury road without stopping at the halt sign. I made no comment about it but thanked my lucky stars. Afterwards I knew I had made a good decision as to where we parked. Next day I was talking to a friend out of the village who had also been to the game. He had parked on the car park next to the ground and it was 10 pm before he got off the car park. We enjoyed the night and were lucky in more ways than one.

E Ralph, Giggleswick

❏ As a youth of sixteen I had been to Wembley and watched the drawn game. Consequently, very keen to see the replay, I left Warrington some six hours before kick-off with my father, brother-in-law and his wife (my sister) in an old van. Obviously this was before the advent of the M62 and the old route took at least four hours. The journey was uneventful until we approached Bradford and traffic was bumper to bumper. Some 3-4 miles from the stadium it was obvious we were not going any further. Having parked up, my father and brother-in-law decided they were going to listen to the match on radio in a public house. Mainly because I was under age, and they were stricter about this in those days, my elder sister and I decided to walk the rest of the way. Noting where the van was parked we set off. Finding Odsal was no problem as thousands of others had had the same idea.

On at last reaching the stadium, having tickets we were searching for the correct turnstile when a whole length of fencing just fell down. We and hundreds of others just walked in and obviously were not included in the official attendance. Forty years is a long time ago but, as I recall and I may be wrong, the fencing was railway sleepers and fell down just like dominoes. I am, however, absolutely sure that the official attendance of 102,000 was on the low side. After discussing it with friends over the years, I consider the number of people who attempted to attend, and would have if they could have got in, was nearer 150,000.

As to the match itself, my sister and I could only see about a quarter of the pitch but it was the quarter in which Gerry Helme scored the try that sent us home happy.

Elvin Meachin

❏ Having attended at the age of 21 years the drawn Cup Final at Wembley, I was looking forward to the replay at Bradford. I had thought that Warrington were just a little lucky to go to a replay. Although chances were few at Wembley Halifax could have won it on a single goal kick by Griffiths and, of course, Halifax had a fearsome pack with good half-backs in Kielty and Dean. So all was set for a mammoth replay. I remember that on the morning of the match the radio had been advised by the police to direct traffic away from the Halifax-Bradford road. The coach I went on decided to go via central Lancashire to arrive early at Odsal. Going the way we did we missed the traffic.

On entering Odsal I was able to move down near the wall. It transpired that spectators coming in later did not move down to allow further spectators to enter. I remember my father, who had gone by car, telling me that he was unable to get anywhere near Odsal and had to park up and listen to Eddie Waring's match report on the radio. Above me the wooden fence at the top was knocked down flat to allow many more spectators to enter. It is my view that at least 120,000 were inside Odsal with at least another 10,000 outside in cars and coaches unable to get anywhere near the ground.

As to the match, I remember Jim Challinor's try and Gerry Helme's clincher right in the corner where I stood. The following Saturday I again attended Halifax v Warrington at Maine Road, Manchester in the League Final which Warrington won. Save for Alex Murphy's time at Wilderspool, this was one of the best seasons for Warrington. Being in such a crowd at Bradford left me with vivid memories over all the years since. It was a joy to be there for a great, hard game, to see the struggle between two big, strong packs. The sorrow is that so many were kept out and missed such a momentous occasion.

M Darbyshire

❏ I did not attend the drawn final at Wembley the previous Saturday which, I gather, was probably the most boring ever! This makes the size of the crowd at the replay the more remarkable. I was fortunate in having two stand tickets for the replay and I went together with the late George Potts, who was then Sports Editor of the *"Pontefract & Castleford Express"*, and Everitt Hartley, a Castleford solicitor. I was teaching near Pontefract at the time and George picked me up from school at 4 pm together with my sandwiches. I thought it rather early to be setting off for Bradford for a 7 pm kick-off!

The M62 route to Bradford, of course, did not exist and our route lay through Wakefield and Tingley. We first met the traffic at Heath Common, not far from the Trinity ground at Belle Vue. At first we thought there had been an accident but soon realised that the queue was for real. We travelled nose to tail towards Bradford as the minutes ticked away. It would be about 6.40 pm when we reached the Odsal area. Every parking space nearby was filled. Our search for a parking area took us further away from the ground. Eventually we drove along an unmade road and through a farmyard. We got out of the car and ran in the direction of the noise of the crowd as we could not see the stadium. I can remember running through part of a golf course and we eventually found our seats in the stand at 7.10 pm. I have, on occasions, driven around the area to try to find our parking spot that night but without success.

I remember little of the game apart from Gerry Helme's curving run to the corner which brought Warrington a try, and the unlimited possession enjoyed by the Halifax forwards. I seemed to be more occupied with the amazing crowd scenes as spectators were still coming in at half-time. We eventually found our car and joined the queue for home. We decided to stop for a drink at the Half-Way House at Morley and just made it as the landlord called "time".

The journey to Odsal now takes me a comfortable thirty minutes. Whenever I go, I remember that night in May 1954.

R Gordon Jackson

❑ The draw at Wembley got very bad press reports and no one thought that the replay would create much interest outside of Warrington and Halifax. But by Monday every coach in South-West Lancashire had been booked. The thing you have to remember is that very few working class people had cars.

In 1954 I worked at J Crosfield & Co, one of the biggest firms in Warrington. It employed 4,000 people and, because of the number of requests for time off, they decided to close at 12 o'clock to allow everyone to go. The road outside the firm was packed with coaches. It was like the annual Walking Day in Warrington. I went to Bradford in a very old banger which I and four others dragged out of retirement. There was no MOT for cars then. It is being kind to say it should never have set out for Bradford but we could not get on a coach as they were all booked up. Every other company in Warrington was doing the same as Crosfield. I think the population of Warrington at that time was about 75,000 and it was estimated that 40-50,000 left Warrington en route for Bradford but hundreds never got there.

There was no motorway in 1954 so you either went via Oldham, down the East Lancs Road, via Rochdale or by secondary B roads. The stories that were told for days after the match were incredible, funny and sad.

We set off before the coaches because we realised we would have to go very slow so we did not overwork the old Ford Pop engine. We thought it best to go via Rochdale because a friend who was a wagon driver said the roads were not as steep as going via Oldham. We had our first breakdown on the East Lancashire Road about six miles from Warrington! The coaches passed us and our workmates were leaning out of the windows jeering at us but we were to have the last laugh as many of them never arrived at the match.

Three breakdowns later we arrived in Halifax. It was like a ghost town. It was incredible. We did not see anyone. We were lost at this point but just as we were becoming despondent a bloke came out of a pub. He was the landlord and he gave us a pint after we told him our story. He told us how to get to Odsal via some secondary roads. He was our saviour because we finally arrived at Odsal minutes before the kick-off. In those days we didn't even know what a traffic jam was! It was new to us. We just dumped the car and ran the last 2-3 miles to the ground. The landlord had told us that people had been in his pub since opening time and had started going to the ground hours before the kick-off.

As I said before, we broke down four times. We had a puncture, a fuel line blockage and leaking radiator. On top of that, when we came to steep hills, which seemed quite often, we all had to get out except the driver and we had to push. It took us four or five hours to get there but we were lucky because the coaches that went via Oldham were stuck miles from Bradford and some never got beyond Oldham because that's where the traffic jam started.

Our return journey was more eventful than the road to Odsal. We called at the pub in Halifax and, even though we were obviously Warrington supporters, the locals gave us a great time. When we left at closing time it was pouring down. The car had a fabric roof and it was like sitting in an open-top car. It rained in all the way home where we arrived at about three in the morning. I had left my push-bike at the security lodge and had five miles to pedal. I had to be back at work for 7.30 am but at least I had seen the match which was more than a lot of my work-mates did.

To go back to our arrival at Odsal, the chaos beggars description. All the fences had been pushed over and although the turnstiles were working everyone was walking in. The stewards were just asking them to pay but not many did. That's why everyone realised the figure of 102,000 was well short. It was many more than that. Thousands never got near the ground but turned back on police advice.

By the way, none of the five of us were Warrington supporters. Fred Taylor, the owner of the old banger, was a Saints supporter, Jack Shaw followed Salford and Ernie Rudd and myself were born and bred Wigan fans, who both moved to Warrington after we married but still support Wigan. The fifth bloke, Sammy Wilson, was a soccer fan but because of the crazy mood that took over everyone in Warrington, he could not resist coming with us.

Harry Shirley

❑ I worked in Halifax and I was 18 at the time. I went to Odsal on the supporters coach with my mother. We had been life-long Halifax fans. Mother had been taken to follow Halifax as a girl by her father. In those days gentlemen could take ladies in to see the match at Thrum Hall free of charge. However, on the replay day we treated ourselves to ring-side seats. Our seats were near the touch-line where the players used to leave the field to return to the dressing rooms. Our menfolk both worked in Bradford and made their way to the game separately.

It was so exciting. At every key move everyone jumped up and our slatted bench fell over as it was on a slight slope. We seemed to spend the whole game bending down and picking our bench up. I did not seem to notice the bangs and knocks my ankles received from the ever-toppling bench. My view was not too good as there was a row of benches in front of us and from a position level with the field the aspect of the game is completely different.

Halifax fans used to wait calmly until Tommy Lynch got the ball because in almost every key game once he received the ball, he would accelerate and burst through and almost certainly score a match-winning try. Then the fans would go mad. We were bitterly disappointed when we lost the replay and believed we had been robbed by the ref. The teams were so well matched, however, that it was hard for either team to score a try.

After the game we toiled our way up the Odsal slope. We saw a group of supporters scramble up a muddy grass bank and a lady fell full length and got her yellow raincoat covered in mud. I remember thinking, *"I hope she's a Warrington supporter"*. Incidentally, I am now a Bradford Northern season ticket-holder but my husband and nephew go to Thrum Hall. Ideally, I wish home games at Northern and Halifax did not clash and I could follow my two favourite teams at home every week.

June Sharp

❏ I used to go to Odsal a lot. As a lad I followed Bradford Northern in the days of Ernest Ward and Trevor Foster. Later I started watching Leeds but stopped when they finished playing on Saturdays. At the time of the Odsal Replay I was just short of 18. I was an apprentice in the mill and I went on a coach from the Royal Hotel, Pudsey. I remember I did not have time to go home after work and took sandwiches. We parked in a field off Rooley Lane. There are houses there now. I think we were about three-quarters of a mile from the ground. We stood opposite the main stand just off to the side about ten yards from the last of the sleeper terracing. We were standing on muck really. I remember a chap found an old tin lid and began to dig steps to stand in. I borrowed it off him and did the same. Hundreds of people used that tin lid to dig a firm foothold! Although I am only about 5' 6" tall I had a good view and saw everything. I remember we just got back in time for a last drink at the pub. There were probably nearer 130,000 there. It was a

hell of an experience. No one had ever seen anything like it before and they certainly won't again.

Neville Atkinson

❏ I am 80 now. 102,000 was well below the actual gate as thousands climbed over the fences and walls at the far end of the ground. I saw them myself. Four of us were working on maintainance down Sticker Lane at the time and got permission off the boss to go to the match. We clocked off around 4 o'clock. All the buses and trolleys were ram-jam full, all the cars too. After a while a rag-and-bone man with a horse and cart stopped and gave us a lift to Odsal. We gave him a couple of bob each. We managed to get in for the start. Daniels and Lynch scored two good tries for Halifax which were disallowed. Halifax were robbed by the referee.

James A Lockwood

❏ For the Wembley Final we booked a coach from Castleford. On the way down we had a half-crown sweep on the combined score. I drew number eight and jokingly said it must be a 4-4 draw. I little realised how true that would be!

For the replay we hired another coach and arrived with a good hour before kick-off time. There was plenty of room where we were standing behind the sticks at the far end. As the crowds streamed in the tannoy appealed for fans to move down to the front as there were thousands trying to get in. We were standing half-way up with enough room to play cards and there was no way we were going to move after standing there for a good hour.

We all enjoyed the match although it was nothing special. Gerry Helme deserved the Lance Todd Trophy but I have no great recollections of the match itself. I recall the fans in front all spilling on to the field and the fight to get out after the match. I have never seen anything like it. We were being funnelled out of a big gate and in the process of moving out I looked down on the ground. I could see a lady's shoe, a glove and a man's cap. We were that jammed together that you could not bend down to retrieve anything. If you had lifted your feet you would have been carried out. People were being crushed against the side of the gate unable to move. Women were crying and children being lifted up above the crowd. It was very frightening. Being in a crowd of 102,569 was one experience I would not have missed. I was 26 years of age at the time.

W Birdsall

❏ I was at that time a 14-year old attending Warrington Grammar School. After the drawn game we were warned by the headmaster that absentees from school who attended the replay would face severe punishment. Most of us decided to ignore this and I boarded a coach with my father on the afternoon of the game for the journey to Bradford.

After several hours travelling we were stopped from proceeding further by the police and the

Wembley. Des Clarkson runs into Stan McCormick. On the right Jim Challinor shapes to block any attempt by Clarkson to pass.

Wembley. Stan McCormick pops up in mid-field to pass to Jim Challinor. Peter Todd shapes to tackle and Derrick Schofield races to cover.

coach parked in a side street, where we were able to listen to the game on the radio. My father made sure that I was safe and then he left the coach to walk to the ground with others - a distance of ten miles. After the Warrington win the coach returned to Warrington arriving after midnight and dropped me at home. Mother was terribly relieved to see her son but furious that I had been abandoned.

My father arrived home for breakfast the next morning. He had walked several miles from Bradford and hitched a lift on another coach back to Warrington. I clearly remember that Mother refused to make him any breakfast and scolded him for days. Happy times!

My father discussed the occasion and reminisced with me only hours before he died aged 74 in 1979. It was his final memory.

Ron Jones

❏ In 1954 I was working as a bus conductress based in Pontefract. My hobbies were horse-racing and watching Rugby League. My boss at the bus depot was Albert Dobson, the famous referee. We used to get winter leave in those days for working the holidays. I always fixed it so that I could go to London for the Rugby League Cup Final and a few days sightseeing. That Saturday, instead of going to the game as I had not got a ticket, I went to Sandown to see the Esher Cup. Imagine my delight when I got back into the digs to find out that the match was a draw. I was already making plans to go to the replay.

I got back from London earlier than usual and when I found out when the replay was and the venue, I set about organising. I went round all the staff who were on the day shift and asked if they were interested in going to the replay. I had a very good response and Albert Dobson very kindly let us have a bus free, providing one of the staff who was going to the game would drive.

The day came amid lots of excitement and we set off. On our way out of Pontefract we approached Pontefract Barracks and there at the bus stop were two soldiers thumbing a lift. We did not know where they were going to but we told them we were going to the Rugby League Final at Bradford and if they would like to come along, they were welcome. They did not hesitate and jumped aboard. As we were about a mile from Odsal the road was pretty congested on both sides with coaches all parked up. The place was heaving with people alighting from the coaches and police on motor cycles were very busy organising the traffic. We had a long haul up the hill to the stadium and when we got there the queues were very big. Police on horseback were there to control people and you could sense there was a hell of a crowd inside.

After about 20 minutes I managed to get through the turnstiles to be confronted with a solid mass of people on the rim of the bowl which was impenetrable. By then the match had kicked off and the hum and cheers of the crowd were deafening. I was going frantic. I could not even see a patch of the field let alone the ball. After just listening to the reactions of the crowd for about half an hour I decided to withdraw from the stadium. Then suddenly remembered that the second half of the match was being broadcast on the radio. I thought I would try to get into one of the coaches outside to see if there was a chance of listening - most coaches had radios and the drivers stayed on the buses. I must have tried about 30 coaches as most of them were full of people in the same mind as me, when I got lucky. The second half had already been kicked-off a few minutes when I settled down in my seat, grateful but whacked out.

When the match was over we all piled out of the coach and I started down the road to find my own bus. The traffic was phenomenal and was practically all coaches. Finally I found the bus and after half an hour everyone was on board apart from the two soldiers. We waited another half hour but they did not show up so we went without them.

I often reflect that I set out to see both finals but never saw one! I wrote to Harry Hornby, Chairman of Bradford Northern, to complain about letting people in who had no hope of seeing anything and he sent me a very sympathetic reply to say how sorry he was but that on the day they could not have expected the gate to exceed that of Wembley. This goes to show the enthusiasm for the game is strictly in the North. I was brought up as a Featherstone Rovers supporter from being a young girl, known as a flatcapper nowadays, and I have loved every moment of the game.

Brenda McNeill

❏ I watched the Halifax v Warrington match last Saturday (29 January, 1994) and I got that feeling of deja vu. A feeling of being cheated out of what had been duly earned, shortchanged by the referee and positively deserted by any luck or run of the ball whatsoever. Someone up there likes Warrington, especially when Halifax are involved. That was the feeling after the match in 1954.

I had been to the Wembley match and what a poor match it was, one Halifax should have won but didn't. The day of the replay was my day at Halifax Tech and I sneaked out of chemistry lectures with my friend Donald and off we went to catch a Hebble special to Odsal. I don't recall any delay getting to Odsal, so I suppose we must have set off in good enough time. I was, however, surprised at the numbers queueing at the turnstiles. Donald and I got to the far end of Odsal and stood behind the posts on some decent terracing - and there was little enough of that.

I am the sort of person who always needs to go to the Gents at half-time but it soon became apparent that there would be no question of that as we became packed shoulder-to-shoulder just like sardines. The match got underway and it soon became clear we would get no change out of Mr. Gelder. Excitement mounted as play swung from end to end and it disturbed me to see the tightly packed crowd on the Odsal Kop opposite, who were standing on banks of uneven clinker, swaying from side to side following the play. I also saw some misguided spectators climb on to the roof of one of the stands. That might have had unfortunate consequences, I thought, but mercifully I was wrong. I was not close enough to comment on the disallowed Halifax tries, though I think we were unfortunate not to get the one from the quickly taken free kick. So the end of the match came and nothing for all our efforts, just a souvenir programme and the memory of what might have been.

Donald and I made our way back to our coach and the extent of the traffic problem became apparent, so much so that our Hebble coach still had not turned a wheel two hours after the end of the match. How such an event could end without fatalities amazes me to this day - an opinion echoed by my late father, himself a long-time supporter who was among the swaying masses on the Kop that I mentioned earlier.

Dr. MH Milnes

❏ I remember the Wires v Halifax replay as if it were yesterday. I was a young man in my early twenties. My manager at work was going to the game and told me I could go with him. He was a very efficient man in every way but a bit pompous. Anyway, we travelled by coach and when we approached Odsal the traffic was just chaotic. We had to get out and walk a good three miles. Cars and coaches were stranded or abandoned all over the place. Mind you, there were no car thieves in those days. After struggling past thousands of people my boss said, *"Right lad, here's a spot on this wall"*. By the way, the game was half-way through by then. We had just got settled when to our amazement two mounted policemen came down on us, knocking us off and calling us hooligans! Imagine my boss's face! Him a manager and protesting to the police about his status! As for me, it did me a good turn. I was pushed nearer to the field just in time to see Gerry Helme sell that outrageous dummy to win the match. It was the first rugby match I had ever seen and I have watched the Wires ever since.

Jock, Warrington

❏ I worked at a hair-dressers in Runcorn and we hardly ever got to an away game in those days because we worked Saturdays. We could get to the home games by taking a few hours off in the afternoon though. The replay was on a Wednesday and that was our half-day so we had plenty of time to get to Bradford. Nearly every pub in Runcorn ran at least one coach to the game. It was my first ever trip to Yorkshire. I remember my father always used to say, *"Bloody awful, Yorkshire"*. Anyway,

four of us set out for Odsal - my mother and father, my fiancee and me. We went in my father's 1951 Morris Minor.

I always remember we went via Blubberhouses because it's such a funny name. I remember all the sheep were grey. I was used to seeing the sheep in North Wales which were white! I think we set off around 1 o'clock and were at Odsal for about 3.30. My father was very proud of his car and asked a garage owner if he could park it on his forecourt practically outside the stadium. He agreed and my father gave him a two shillings piece although he did think it was a bit dear for the privilege!

We had lots of time so we walked down to Bradford for something to eat and I recall we had a meal at an upstairs tea-room somewhere. We got back to the stadium early and entered the ground. I was amazed when I saw the size of the bowl. We were amongst the first three or four hundred into the ground and went to stand behind the posts at the main road end. There was no crushing around us at all but we did see some at the other end. Once or twice the crowd seemed to fall forward at that end.

At the end of the game we just got into the car and drove away. What sticks in my mind is the number of coaches. We were still passing stationary coaches seven miles from the ground - we clocked the distance on the mileometer. They were all full of blokes waiting for other blokes to find their way back and I imagine many of them never actually went to the game. There seemed to be a policeman every hundred yards all the way to Oldham all waving us on as if to say, *"Get a move on, there's thousands behind you"*. We got back about mid-night after stopping for fish and chips in Oldham. The following day at the hair-dressers I remember lots of blokes coming in tired out with tales of arriving home at three, four or five o'clock in the morning. I have still got two programmes for the game.

It was the last match I saw before being conscripted into the Navy a fortnight later. I had never been back to Odsal again until this season when Warrington played Northern - nearly 40 years.

Keith Gilbert

❏ I was teaching at St. Mary's School in Warrington in 1954 but I was still a winger on Oldham's books. I did not like taking time off from school for the Odsal game even though the PE Organiser for Warrington invited me to join a coach he had arranged to depart at 2.30. Instead I went for the 4.30 train from Bank Quay station which was practically empty. I got off at Low Moor, caught a double-decker bus to the ground and arrived with plenty of time to spare. I remember bumping into Ray Markham, the great Australian winger who played for Huddersfield before the war, and we went for a drink in the bar at the top of the ground. There were very few people in the ground at that point. Soon, however, I noticed the crowd begin to swell a bit and I left Ray to get to my seat at the ring-side. Upto that point I had had no difficulties at all. All of a sudden the place seemed to be filled with fans, almost like a plague of locusts. The entry system must have simply been swamped.

The return journey went just as well as the journey to Odsal. I travelled in comfort and got back home easily and in good time. The PE Organiser's party never got to the game! They ended up stuck near Nont Sarah's in a huge jam and had to listen to the game on the wireless. The moral is, I suppose, travel with British Rail.

Joe Warham

❏ I remember going by car and parking at Bankfoot before walking to the ground. Actually I am more of a soccer man, having been on the board at Bradford Park Avenue, but I have always been involved in Bradford sport. I still go to all Bradford Northern's home games. I was a neutral for the Odsal Replay and do not really remember anything of the match itself. I had a seat on the back row of the little old stand and even then I could not see everything.

Gordon Phillips

❏ I was a Police Inspector with the Huddersfield Borough Force in those days. I have been watching Rugby League since at least 1921. I remember my uncle taking me to see the Australians, Harold Horder and Cec Blinkhorn's lot, in a test at Headingley. England won 6-5, I think. We lived in Harrogate then and I used to watch the Australians train there. Anyway, on the day of the replay at 5.45 I was called to go to Bradley Bar. I remember someone telling me, *"You're lucky, Fred. The traffic is all blocked from here to Brighouse".* When I got down to Brighouse it was chaos. The Brighouse Inspector was in his shirt sleeves doing point duty!

There was a Hanson's coach there which had more or less given up hope of getting to the game. I jumped on and told the driver there was a way through Bradley and on the Leeds Road. I told him not to worry about how fast he went and loads more vehicles sped after him in a great caravan. They got there in time for the match. Quite a few of the drivers thanked me, which was nice.

Later on I was down Fixby Road - the match would have been over by then - when an old banger of a bus appeared making a hell of a noise. The engine was noisy and the passengers were even noisier. There was only one person on the bus who was not drunk and thankfully he was the driver. Naturally we stopped them. They were Warrington supporters who had not got to the game. We advised the driver to turn round but he said, *"I'll just go up the road a bit more. This lot will never know they didn't get to the game!"*

A lot of the chaos was caused by people from Halifax sneaking round Huddersfield way. Of course, they merged with a lot of the Warrington buses and cars and caused the traffic to pile up in Brighouse.

Fred Huddlestone

❏ My father was Tom Winnard, the old St. Helens and Bradford Northern centre. I had been going to Odsal since I was three. In fact my earliest memories are from watching Rugby League matches at Odsal. I remember standing on a seat at Odsal with my mother's arm round me. Excited people suddenly used to shout, *"Come on, Tom"*, and then all jump up. Of course, to a little girl everything then went dark. It was quite a while before I realised what was going off!

Sometimes I used to go training at Odsal with my dad - I was a 400 yard runner - so I literally got to know every inch of the ground. There was neither a nook nor a cranny of that place I had not been. I loved sport, especially Rugby League, and at the time of the Odsal Replay I was sixteen. I went to it with another girl but we arrived too late to get a decent view. We went the entire circuit of the rim trying to find somewhere to stand but we could not see a dashed thing. It was almost time for the kick-off and I was really desperate when a miracle happened. Just where the players started to come down we bumped into my dad. He had been waiting for a friend and he had two tickets for the best seats. He realised that he was never going to meet his mate and saw the state we were in. So he gave us the tickets. I was so pleased I just had to squeeze and kiss him.

The tickets were for just about the best spot in the stand, right at the front and bang in the middle. I remember we sat between two men who smoked big, fat cigars. I remember being thrilled to bits and I have still got the ticket to this day.

Ann Walsh

❏ I am 88 now and Halifax was the first team I followed. In the 1950s I used to watch Huddersfield and they were the best footballing team I ever saw with Lionel Cooper and Pat Devery the stars. They played rugby as it should be played. Later I followed Leeds but now for family reasons I tend to follow Otley Rugby Union.

In the 1954 replay I wanted Halifax to win but never mind. I went to the game from Yeadon with my daughter. We went by coach. We had a good view of the game from just to the side of the little stand. When we came out we could not find our coach anywhere and we looked for an hour. We were standing at Odsal Top and beginning to wonder just how we would ever get home when a police car pulled up. I had been a policeman at Hipperholme and Harry Kitching, who later became Chief Constable, was a passenger in the car. Harry was brother to Jack Kitching, the old Northern and Great Britain centre. He asked us if we wanted a lift and the driver took us into

"The Entry of the Gladiators." A sea of humanity greets the teams as they take to the field at Odsal.

Odsal preliminaries. Referee Ron Gelder oversees the meeting of Eric Frodsham and Alvin Ackerley.

Bradford where Harry got out and instructed the officer to take us all the way home to Yeadon. It certainly solved our problem.

John Roberts

❏ I was born in Halifax but left in about 1950. I had followed Halifax from the 1930s when they used to call the forwards "steam pigs". Scrums in those days were as flat as good Rugby Union scrums. I played amateur Rugby League for Albion Rangers but later played Rugby Union for Halifax. A friend and I went to play for Halifax RU simply because they had three teams and we thought it would be easier to get a game there than at Pellon Rugby League who only had one team. I eventually became President of the Yorkshire Rugby Union!

In 1954 I was unmarried and living in digs in Hull. When Halifax got to Wembley I decided to go down on the train to the game on the Friday. Just packed a bag and set off. I did not even have a ticket. I had no trouble getting bed and breakfast in King's Cross. The following day I went to Wembley, paid on the turnstiles, saw an amazingly boring game and on the Sunday went back to Hull. All this was accomplished without a hitch even though none of it had been planned.

I went to the replay but it is just a blur to me. I cannot remember whether I went with anyone, how I got there or what I did afterwards. It is strange but I found Wembley the more interesting experience!

Bernard Rafferty

❏ At the time of the Odsal Replay I was in my early thirties and living in Hull although I am a Halifax man. I remember that after work I had no time to get a meal so I just stuffed my pockets with chocolate flake bars. I went on the train from Hull to Leeds and then caught buses to Odsal. I got there in reasonable time but could only see three-quarters of the field and was at the other end to where Daniels had his try disallowed. I remember you had to be safely wedged in all that clinker otherwise you could slip. I remember some wag shouting we would still be scraping clinker out of our navels the following year! When I got home I found all the chocolate flakes, which in the excitement I had completely forgotten about, had broken and melted. My pockets were a real mess which took me ages to clean.

Actually I was in another massive crowd at Odsal in 1939 when Halifax beat Leeds in the Cup semi-final. Leeds' main man was Vic Hey and I think he may have been carrying an injury. Anyway, Jack Cox, the Halifax forward who came from Luddenden, the same village as me, tackled him hard early on and he never did anything after that. I was at Heath Grammar School, a real Rugby Union stronghold, in those days and we went to school on Saturday mornings. The headmaster, DJD Smith, announced at assembly that anyone taking Saturday off to go to Wembley would be expelled.

Of course, I went with a friend from Hebden Bridge. My mother was appalled at the thought of me being expelled but my father was a dyed-in-the-wool Thrum Haller. I don't mind admitting that the whole thing caused a crisis in the household for a while. None of us got expelled though and Halifax beat Salford in the Final!

Anon, Wakefield

❏ I live in Clacton-on-Sea now and when I talk about the Odsal replay the locals think I am bloody mad. I was born in Leeds and went to Leeds Grammar School but in 1954 I worked in Manchester for a firm of calico printers. I lived in Marple and my next-door neighbour was Tom Haigh who played Rugby League for Huddersfield before the war and Rugby Union for Sale during it. Tom, a master printer in Manchester, was pally with Michael Betts who was the Rugby League correspondent for BBC Radio. Michael did not drive so he used to pay Tom his expenses to take him to the matches. I used to tag along. Of course, the BBC used to send Michael to the best matches so it was great.

With Michael Betts being with the BBC we usually ended up in the directors' box being royally treated. On the day of the replay, I just happened to be in Bradford on business. I had come on the train as I did not get a company car until 1958! I finished the business at about 4 o'clock, had a drink and a bite to eat and caught a trolley bus. I had to walk the last mile and a half to the ground. No one ever dreamed that that many people would descend on Odsal so when I got in I realised I would never get anywhere near the directors box. There were a lot more than 102,000 there. I started worrying about how I was going to get back home.

When the crowd dispersed I decided to see if I could find Tom and Michael and sure enough I found them with the directors. At least I would have my lift home. We left Odsal at 10.15 to find the car in Low Moor. There it was, slap bang in the middle of the main road on its own. Everything must have driven round it to get away! It was a pre-war Morris snub-nose, solid steel with dash-boards you could stand on. We started out for Lancashire and soon got into a real jam. We went via Nont Sarah's and the place was heaving even though it was a long time after hours. There was a lot of illegal drinking in those days.

I don't remember a bloody thing about the game!

Gordon Kilburn

❏ I learned something that day which has stood me in good stead ever since. I had gone to Odsal with my brother-in-law. I lived in Silsden and remember travelling on a West Riding single-decker to the game. Anyway, we were at the South End of the ground fairly well back and packed like sardines. I know we had not got into position until Warrington scored the first try. This little chap came past us shouting, *"Scuse me, scuse me. There's plenty of room down there".* We all let him through and we could see him worming his way down all the way to the front! I subsequently copied his act at other big games at Odsal and I even managed to get good positions at lock-out soccer games at Burnley by doing it. You'll certainly always be able to get through a tin of sardines like that!

Coming out at the end I remember a woman nearly getting crushed. There was a toilet block sticking out near the exit and somehow she got turned round and faced up against the wall. We just managed to pull her away in time. We were funnelling out and the pressure just seemed to build up from nowhere. I know I always leaned backwards in such situations.

Jack Swales

❏ My father had a milk round in Skipton and we went to Odsal in the milk van. I was 14. We got there in plenty of time and parked in a little car park near the ground. We had a good view of the game standing up the slope near the corner where Daniels scored that disallowed try. When he touched down the crowd suddenly surged forward and I started to fall down the slope but my father just grabbed me in time otherwise I might have been badly injured. I remember it as if it was yesterday. We were shouting for Halifax but it's Harry Bath I remember most clearly. He was built like a brick toilet.

The police were not really ready for what happened. No one thought that that many folk would turn up. I have been at Hampden Park when there were 100,000 in and there were far more at Odsal. We had an awful job getting home. We could not get out of the car park for hours. Then it was a slow journey via Manningham, Bingley, Shipley and Keighley to Skipton. We did not get home until 3 am. Unbelievable!

Covey Whitham

❏ The first game at Wembley was a depressing draw. Halifax could have won it with a late penalty from Tuss Griffiths. It looked dead on target but curled away at the last second. I remember Wilkie tackled the great Harry Bath so hard in the first half it knocked all the wind out of him and quietened him down for a bit but he came back strong in the second half. Peter Todd seemed to spend most of the Wembley match hobbling about - no substitutes in those days.

I saw every minute of the Odsal game. We lived on Whitehall Road then and I went by car with a pal and my wife went too, which was a rarity. We got there early enough to get a spot on the "25" on some old railway sleepers. I remember the crowd making the odd little surge but there never seemed to be any real danger. If ever a team was robbed it was Halifax. They were a strange team when they came up against really good opposition like Warrington. They never seemed to gel until they

got ahead. When Gelder disallowed Lynch's try under the posts there was pandemonium. Everyone round us was screaming blue murder. It was a dead straight pass. Once in front I think we would have got on top.

I did not go to the Championship Final at Maine Road. It was in my hard-up days! A friend of mine had just got a television so we watched it on that although the reception was not too good. Lost again! It did grate that we scored the only try.

Alf Sharman

❏ I went to Odsal with my boy-friend - now my husband. At the time he was doing his National Service at Lindholme, Doncaster. It was not a prison then! Such was the interest in the final that it was decided a bus was to come over to Bradford bringing the boys to the match. My boy-friend picked me up outside work at 5 pm and even then it was not possible to get a bus to the ground so we walked from the centre of Bradford. We did not have much trouble getting into the ground but once inside it was already filling up. We found ourselves a place at the score-board end, sat down, ate our sandwiches and savoured the atmosphere. There was space by us but just before the match people seemed to be coming in in waves, such was the crowd. After the match it was impossible to get out through the gates so we, along with many others, climbed the wall into the grounds of Northern View Hospital, and then had to walk back into Bradford.

Sadly, some of the airmen didn't make it to the match. They fell by the wayside at the first pub in Manchester Road!

A Thorley

❏ I have vivid memories of the 1954 Cup Final Replay which I attended with my father and father-in-law.

After gaining admission to the stadium we found ourselves at first on the rim of the amphitheatre with no hope seemingly of getting through the dense crowd to a more advantageous position lower down. Eventually, however, we worked our way round to the speedway entrance end of the ground and gained a position a little behind the speedway hut. Terracing, as such, was practically non-existent and the standing largely consisted of intermittent railway sleepers and black ash.

Despite the precarious surface there was a huge crowd behind the posts and a short time after the commencement of the game it began to move like a sea breaker heading for the shore. My companions and I were irresistibly carried forward on this human wave and to our alarm found ourselves behind the speedway hut which was itself shaking ominously. Fortunately, we managed to avoid being crushed behind or carried with it. We were swept forward like flotsam onto the pitch in the in-goal area. The perimeter fence had gone down like matchwood. Police and stewards shepherded us, and about a hundred others, to the far touch-line where we were delighted to find ourselves directed to benches placed at the side of the pitch.

Thus, from originally being unable to see at all we finished up with an unrivalled view of the match in general and a close-up, in particular, of Gerry Helme scoring a spectacular try in the corner where we were seated. Truly, a memorable day.

FD Reynolds

❏ At that time I was at Grange School, Bradford and the Odsal Replay took place the day after my twelfth birthday. I was not a rugby fan but followed Bradford Park Avenue. There must have been some good publicity about the game though as I was keen to go. I arranged to meet a class-mate, Bobby Ham, who later became a professional soccer player, outside the ground. At some point, though, we got separated. I worked my way to the far end and I must have been wandering about looking a bit lost. Anyway, a lady who supported Halifax took pity on me and got me down to the fence at the front and looked after me. I am only 5' 5" now so I must have been a very wee lad then. I remember I could only just see over the top of the fence.

I remember wanting Halifax to win, largely because that lady was a Halifax supporter. If she had come from Warrington I would probably have cheered for them! I must admit I was oblivious to any danger, possibly because I was used to crowds at football matches and because my father had been taking me to the speedway at Odsal since I was a five-year-old. At the end of the game I got back to the top of the ground and some chap obviously thought I might be in danger of being crushed because he picked me up onto his shoulders and carried me 100 yards out of the ground. Then I toddled off home to Little Horton. I have three boys of my own now and I am always pleased to be able to tell them I was there.

Raymond Graves

❏ My late father, who was President of Yorkshire County in 1951, went every year to Wembley from 1946 on with a group of friends. In 1954 one member of the party dropped out at the last minute and, although I was still at school, my father took me. Obviously, I can well remember the excitement of the occasion but also the disappointment in not seeing the cup presented nor even any tries scored.

As soon as the replay details were known I asked my father if he would take me, to which he said, *"No"*. When I asked him why not, his reply that I was at school seemed somewhat surprising. When I pointed out that it was an evening kick-off he told me that he would be leaving well before my school finished at 4 pm, as there was going to be a very large crowd indeed!

I cannot remember exactly what time he did set off but recollect that it was between 2.30 and 3 pm.

Certainly he was correct and I was left at home to do my homework and wait until 1957 before I had another trip to Wembley and, on that occasion, saw the cup presented. I do still have, however, a reasonably good quality programme from the Replay as a reminder of what I missed.

EP Harrison

❏ The 1954 Replay is the only match I have ever been frightened at and I have been in crowds of 70,000 and also attended thirteen Wembley Finals. My workmate and I decided to go to Odsal straight from work to get a good view. We arrived at the ground to be confronted by the longest queue I have ever seen. We finally got in just before half-time. We couldn't even see the field - just the tops of the goal-posts.

We eventually made our way to the scoreboard end and somehow got wedged in a spot quite well forward behind the posts. We were both wedged in with our feet well off the ground - most uncomfortable. I remember the big stand being full even when we went past it and there were thousands of Warrington supporters who had tickets for the stands with absolutely no chance of gaining entry. There were fans up telegraph poles, fans sat on roofs outside the ground. There must have been thousands there who were never accounted for in the official attendance. I remember Gerry Helme's dummy as clear as if it happened yesterday. He really was a crafty half-back.

However, when the match was over my troubles really began. Trying to get towards the entrance was a nightmare. There were people fainting and falling down and people just trampling over them. We just couldn't help them as our arms were pinned to our sides. We could see the gate open where we had to get out but we were constantly pushed to one side. The police gave it up as a bad job. We arrived home at 11 pm tired and exhausted but with plenty to talk about for a long time.

Les Ambler

❏ I went to Odsal with a party of friends from Wakefield. Setting off as we thought in good time, events soon proved that wrong. Traffic began building up around Birkenshaw, slowly grinding to a halt upon entering the Wakefield-Bradford road. Could it be due to a serious accident?

Impatience began to grow, seconds, minutes passing by and Odsal seeming a long way off. Anybody any suggestions? Yes, look out for somewhere to park this vehicle. We can walk it quicker than this carry-on!

We were lucky. Such a place was found. So, everybody out. Let's use Shanks' pony. So off we set some mile and a half to two miles from the ground. Others had the same idea. We could not believe it. I was in the 1932 crowd at the Huddersfield Town v Arsenal match - 65,000 plus - but this was ridiculous.

An awful moment for Halifax at Odsal. 'Fax players throw up their arms in delight as Tommy Lynch crosses the line only to have his try disallowed.

A good moment for Halifax at Odsal. Tuss Griffiths pilots a penalty goal.

We eventually made it, got inside to get a bird's-eye view from the top of the bank. It was not very comfortable underfoot, like being on quicksand. By this time the quickest route into the ground appeared to be over the top of the boards surrounding the ground. Thousands must have entered this way. The crushing was becoming a bit frightening, especially as we had in our party two young ladies aged eighteen years or so who had asked if they could go to witness their first Rugby League match. Some initiation! One they will never forget! If they had not been squeezed before they certainly got squeezed that day, fortunately without injury.

An evening I shall never forget, and to think that next day Roger Bannister ran a mile in under four minutes - but not in this crowd.

CL Cass

❏ I am a life-long Wire fan and I am now ground announcer at Wilderspool - have been for many years. In 1954 I was in the RAF on National Service and stationed at Weeton, Blackpool. I went to Wembley with Warrington Supporters and then to the replay on a coach from Blackpool Borough. I was a stranger but they made me welcome.

We eventually got to Odsal and joined the thousands outside the ground. Eventually a large wooden gate crashed down and hundreds of us charged through. I got a place by the touch-line wall around the "25" yard-line. The game kicked off. A bloke next to me pointed out that there was a section of empty seats in the stand opposite.

"I'll bet them as got tickets are locked out", he said
"Are we going over?" I asked.
"Come on", he replied.

Over the wall we went. I remember sidestepping Eric Frodsham, the Wire full-back. Over the other wall and up the boards into the stand. We had an excellent view. I reckon about fifty of us made the break.

I vividly recall "Chall's" try and Gerry Helme ducking the tackles to score and win the Lance Todd Trophy yet again. I got back into camp in the early hours, happy that Wire had won the Cup but worried whether I could be court-martialled for being a football hooligan!

Peter Robinson

❏ As a member of staff at Odsal Stadium employed by Bradford Northern I was closely concerned with the organisation and preparation for the replay. It was certainly a momentous event which created history for our wonderful game. The huge crowds and amazing traffic scenes were sights I shall never forget. There was excitement in the air. People were so anxious to get into the ground that they pushed their way past the fragile wooden rails at the car park entrance to gain free entry. There was no panic or untoward trouble though.

As kick-off time approached there were still masses of people in colossal queues - so many, you

wondered where they had all come from. There were, however, still pockets of space in various parts of the ground. Unfortunately, the days of crowd stewarding had not yet arrived. The game was played with no quarter given by either side. That wonderful player Gerry Helme scored an excellent try to give the Cup to Warrington.

Harry Hornby

The sporting world woke up the following day to the news that over 102,000 people had attended Odsal for a Wednesday evening match. I remember after the game all the bars and social rooms were full of people speculating on the crowd figure. At about 10 o'clock Mr. Harry Hornby, the Managing Director of Bradford Northern and the person most responsible for the development of Odsal, came into the social rooms, his face full of pride and shedding a few happy tears, to announce that his dream had come true and a world record crowd had been set. Everyone gasped.

Next day there was great coverage of the event in the press and photographers started arriving to take pictures of the Odsal bowl. There were telephone calls from all over the world. Mr. Hornby later had thousands of aerial photos of the crowded stadium printed. It was a wonderful day in the history of Rugby League Football and a very proud day for the great City of Bradford.

Trevor Foster

❏ I think three of us went to the game. One of us was certainly Alan Thirkill because it was his car. We had been to the Wembley Final, the 4-4 bore, and decided we may as well see the finish.

We parked somewhere opposite the ground in a pathway-cum-road. There were huge queues and, to be quite honest, we just walked to the front and cheeked our way in. From the time I finished work I guess this must have been about three-quarters of an hour before the kick-off. There was already a huge crowd in the ground so we ran right round to the far side and stood near the top of the hill. There was no terracing up at the top and the stand obstructed part of our view. There was a pathway half-way down and I remember people wandering around there not being able to see a thing.

I do not remember much about the game, to be honest, but we saw Warrington get the Cup and ran out the same way, got to the car and drove back to Leeds very easily. We obviously got out before most of the traffic started to build up because I remember seeing hundreds of coaches by the roadside as we sped back to Leeds. We even managed to get back to the Nag's Head in Chapel Allerton in time for a pint - I think the pubs closed at 10 pm in those days. That shows how fast we got away from the ground.

I remember some of the tap-room customers asking about the match and the crowd. I think it had been broadcast and they had been listening on the wireless. I told them about the crowd being huge and that I thought it would have been over 80,000. I was laughed down but I bet there were some surprises the next morning when they saw the papers!

I still don't know how we were so cheeky to push in at the turnstiles. It's not really my nature at all.

Eric A Hill

❏ In 1954 I was Police Constable Frank Dickinson and a proud member of the long since defunct City of Bradford Police Force. On Wednesday, 5 May, I was warned that my tour of duty would be 5.30 pm to 1.30 am and ordered to parade at the old Odsal Police Office at 5.30 pm prior to working with the Police contingent at Odsal Stadium for the Rugby League Challenge Cup Final Replay between Halifax and Warrington.

A big crowd was expected, we were told, as we gathered for work details at the familiar Police Station - alas, now also defunct - that stood opposite "Mary Shaw's". Eighty-two thousand folk, give or take a few hundreds, had attended the final tie at Wembley. The score there was a 4-4 draw, so fate and a few old men had dictated that the mucky, scruffy Odsal tip would stage a Rugby League match that would be remembered for all time.

"We can expect a few more terneet", said the Sergeant in charge, *"seeing that both teams are on t'doorstep so to speak"*. But no one could have foreseen that a crowd of over 102,000 fans would assemble under the ancient stands or on the slippy-slidy, wooden sleepered, cindery slopes of the largest football stadium in the United Kingdom.

It had become obvious to me as I travelled from my home in West Bowling on the upper deck of a blue City of Bradford Transport bus - defunct also! - that something dramatic, drastic and unique was taking place   about the drizzly heights of South Bradford. Manchester Road - t'Manch, in the local vernacular - was chock-a-block with nose-to-tail traffic barely moving. Smiddles Lane and Sticker Lane were the same. Every minor road and side-street was an illegal car-park and   a   hurrying urgency was manifest throughout the chuntering crowds of Rugby League followers surging like the Grand Army of Napoleon towards higher ground. All roads, it seemed, led to Odsal Top.

On paper my duties were simple and straight forward. In immediate hindsight the exercise was traumatic. In the rosy afterglow of 40 years' retrospection I know now that I lived through an experience I would not have missed for all the world.

My "detail" for the duration of the match was to patrol the area around the Pearson Road car-park boundary fence - inside the ground or out, as the circumstances dictated. A wicket-gate allowed my colleagues and me egress and entry between car-park and stadium. For the paying public there were three, possibly four, turnstile entrances manned by the usual venerable gate-men - tried and trusted servants who worked within a rigid discipline that outlawed any form of urgency.

As the match kicked off, thousands of grumbling supporters were still outside the Pearson Road paling, queueing in the time-honoured sporting fashion, the restrictive movements across the cinder-strewn car-park being dictated apparently at the whim and fancy of the gate-men, whose intent was to avoid any suggestion of panic or urgency.

It was my unfortunate lot to have decided at a tense moment to be in a position just inside the ground and within a few feet of the flimsy, fragile fence that separated car-park from stadium. I always regretted that decision because from that moment I became a victim of inadequacy, Kismet and Sod's Law.

A shriek of portentous promise from those already in position around the pitch lent urgency to the incentive of the creeping throngs inching ever so slowly towards hallowed ground. With a sudden bellow of frustrated rage and pent-up emotions and anger at the wastage of precious time, they all surged forward, bypassing the benign gate-men, who were obviously strangers to exigency, and leapt over and through the already falling fence.

I was wearing the old-fashioned choker tunic, obsolete but retained until such time as the modern collar-and-tie jackets became available. I heard the shouting and bawling around me and saw to my horror the rickety fence coming rapidly to the end of its long life, crumbling and finally collapsing. I saw the thousands of sweating red faces and wild staring eyes rushing towards me, their owners intent on gaining a favourable viewing position within Northern's sacred precincts. There was no malice afore-thought, just a wild urge of primeval instinct that had cast out all rhyme or reason.

Rather to protect myself than to attempt to halt the advancing, baying, non-paying hordes that bounded with Zulu-like agility towards me, I raised my arms in a futile, ineffectual gesture. I was bowled over in an instant and in attempting to rise and perhaps seize someone, a plethora of grasping hands ripped the buttons from my proud tunic - every one of 'em! My helmet fell from my head and was flattened in the mud by the trampling feet. Gone was my helmet, my status symbol and swagger, in a welter of flat caps and boots.

Of the match itself I have no real recollection beyond a distant, hazy glimpse of vague running and stumbling figures, more unsubstantial than real, on a faraway muddy field. The steadily falling rain was an ally to chaos. The dark skies roofed an occasion that only poignant memory could favour; and such memory, so necessary, will always highlight the jewels from time's mirror and emphasise the finer moments from any experience.

Later I learnt that Warrington had beaten Halifax by eight points to four, which was news to me. Being a Northern fan I wasn't really bothered, though I would have preferred victory for the Yorkshire club. Later still, after being re-equipped with tunic and helmet, I accompanied some of the takings to a bank in the centre of Bradford - on Market Street, I believe. The vehicle used was a taxi-cab, piled high above the window levels with cloth bags crammed to bursting point with coins and bank-notes, with yours truly, suffering from cramp, sprawling inelegantly on top. No Securicor guard, no Police car escort with screaming siren - just me and a taxi-man carrying a fortune through the crowded streets of old Bradford. Perhaps we try too hard these days ....

The official attendance figure for the 1954 Challenge Cup final replay at Odsal Stadium was recorded as 102,000 but I reckon that another 2,000 or more crashed their way through the Pearson Road barriers and other boundary fences, entering the stadium free and unrecorded statistically. Such an assembly of people will never again gather together to celebrate a sporting occasion in such a way. An era had perhaps ended. Mass television viewing and motor cars for all would soon dictate future sporting habits. My own participation was unique. Such a personal involvement will not happen again. History was made on that damp May evening 40 years ago. A record was achieved that will not be broken.

Other personal memories of this anomalous event come to mind. I remember particularly the scores of lurching "ale-cans" urinating publicly among the bushes and about the grassy slopes behind the far stand. And the youngsters, hundreds of 'em, all clambering over the fence from the Northern View Hospital grounds. I was too knackered to do anything about them. A few were caught and thrown out but individuals continued to slide over this fence until the end of the match. Some comedian swapped the "Ladies" and "Gents" signs from the respective toilets but no one seemed to mind.

Mainly though, I recall the sheer exuberance of the crowds of people acting out their part of a graphic scenario that would live forever in the hearts and minds of those who were there; a scenario that would become singular and remarkable within the pages of Rugby League history. My life is quieter now. I perhaps could remember more but it all happened a long, long time ago ....

Frank Dickinson

❑ Originally I was a Dewsbury fan although my grandfather played for Batley in the first Challenge Cup Final back in 1897. Now I live in Doncaster and follow the Dons. Anyway, back in 1954 I was living in Pudsey and working for the corporation and three or four of us went to the Replay. We went in one of the lads' car. There weren't many about in those days. His granny lived near Odsal so he arranged to park at her house. She sat outside and waited for us to arrive. She must have shooed off hundreds who tried to park before us!

We got there fairly early, or so we thought. But, my God, when we got in, I had never seen anything like it. It was just the awesomeness of the crowd that sticks in my mind. We were at the Rooley Lane end just above half-way down and we had a very good view. Helme was brilliant that day, even though Halifax had really good half-backs in Dean and Kielty. I remember we had to dig into the ashes and lean back. We never thought there was any danger although I suppose if someone at the back had started pushing it could have been nasty. I remember someone yelling, *"There must be 130,000 in here!"* It was a good game with the wrong result.

Harold Bennett

❑ I was the assistant secretary at Bradford Northern at the time of the Odsal Replay. I remember being on duty at Odsal at the speedway on the evening of the Wembley Final. A telephone call came through from Eric England, the Northern secretary, who was down at the final, to say that Halifax and Warrington had drawn and that the replay was to be at Odsal. He asked me to arrange to have the tickets printed right away. I managed that all right.

On the night of the replay only Eric and I were on duty in the office and, of course, we never saw any of the match. The gate-men never used to come back to the office until they had cashed up. That night all the gates had been in operation and the gate-men were coming in with money stuffed all over the place. I was adding up the attendance figures from the gate-men and I could not believe what I was getting. The figures were coming to more than 100,000. I asked Eric to check the figures and he confirmed that the figures were right. It was amazing. Even then a lot more people got in for nothing so the attendance would be much higher really.

Odsal. Referee Gelder lays down the law as Des Clarkson hits the deck. Jack Wilkinson eyes up Wire second-rower Austin Heathwood.

Odsal. Frank Wright and Jim Challinor deal with an opponent.

I know we were tired out when we had finished. The money was taken to the bank after the match by taxi. We always used Norman Shaw's Taxis. He had the garage next to the fire station at the top of Huddersfield Road.

Doris Beard

❏ I was a spectator at the 1954 Challenge Cup Replay. I went with my husband, Ted White, who played second-row for Warrington. In the 1954 Challenge Cup he played in every round but he broke his leg - a cracked fibula - in the first ten minutes in the semi-final against Leeds at Swinton. He stayed on all the match because there were no substitutes then. His second-row mate Syd Phillips broke his shoulder a couple of games later so they both missed the final. They got the medals though. If I remember right Ted was the only forward to score a try for Warrington in any of the rounds. After the final they went to Ireland to play Halifax in Dublin and Belfast for a copper kettle! Halifax won.

D White

❏ I knew I had broken my leg straightaway in that semi-final but you knew if you went off your team would lose the match. I was only of nuisance value really. There was less than a month between the semi-final and the final but Warrington still tried to get me fit. I even had a fitness test on the morning of the Wembley match but it was no good. I could only run straight. I went on the Irish trip and played although I could still only run straight! I don't recall much about the Odsal Replay except that we were sat in the stand and that it was a heck of a long walk down to the pitch! I went to Halifax this season (1994) with a party of the Warrington Ex-Players and had a look at the trophies in the pavilion but I never saw that copper kettle!

Ted White

❏ I am a near sixty-year-old farmer who played Rugby Union for Selby. I was a great Rugby League fan in my young days but now only see it on TV. I have kept a diary since 1946 and thought I could go straight to the date for details of the Odsal Replay but I am disappointed at my offering - I think I have improved since.

We had travelled to the Wembley Final in a Ford Prefect, three big lads and a Drax schoolmaster, an ex-Hessle prop, who was the driver. My diary entries for that day read:

April 24th
Dinner in Leicester Square
To Wembley in car
HALIFAX 4 WARRINGTON 4
Dull but even game
Tea at Maxim's Chinese Restaurant
Then saw Arthur Askey - "Love Match"
Bed 12

I have to say I have had more hectic times since!

The match ticket (3/-) is stuck in as is the signed serviette from Maxim's (my first Chinese meal). We decided to go to the replay as we did not think there would be a big crowd. Times were hard then! My diary says:

May 5th
Zoz came on 4.10 bus
Tea and off by 5
Jim, Wilf Earless, Uncle Walter, Zoz, Kay and me
Terrible traffic and crowd
Very good game
HALIFAX 4 WARRINGTON 8
Rain after. Waited, then home OK

My father was away in France or he would have been with us and driven. So I must have driven. What a mixed bunch we were. Jim Bellwood was our foreman. Wilf Earless was the son-in-law of the lady who cleaned for my mother. He was a railwayman. Uncle Walter was the local butcher who stood about 5' 8" and did not see a thing. They hoisted him over the top of the turnstile to get him in so he was one who was not counted in the official attendance. He had been a marine in the First World War. Zoz (Peter Mumby) went to school with me and hooked for Old Draxonians before we amalgamated with Selby in 1954. He could dribble a rugby ball like a soccer player. Kay was my younger sister.

If my father had not promised me £1 for a full diary in 1946, I would have sworn black and blue that I never took Wilf Earless anywhere, never mind Odsal in 1954!

Don Bramley

❏ I come from the Pocklington area and I have been to 42 Challenge Cup Finals, including the Replays of 1954 and 1982. One of my great-uncles was one of the first players from this area to turn professional - with Batley. I always say I studied the Three Rs - Rugby League, Rugby Union and racing!

We went to Odsal by car and got there early. I remember I went with a chap called Renshaw, a coal merchant in Pocklington. We came in from the York direction so it was not too difficult. I remember there used to be about six fields with stone walls somewhere near Odsal and we parked in one of those. Someone charged for the use of the fields. The charge would probably be six pence or a shilling. When we got in it was really surprising. I reckon there were about 120,000, never mind 102,000. I do remember one of the hoardings crashing down at the top of the ground. It was not anything vicious. They were really flimsy things. It would be just the pressure of people pushing which knocked them down. I do recall that even though there were so many people there, you could walk about with ease. I always remember that on hot days at Odsal it was such a mucky place that everyone came out black!

Roland Hunter

❑ I now live in rural Lincolnshire but I originate from the Warrington area. My job as an Inspector of Taxes moved me here nearly twenty years ago. However, I still make the 360 mile round trip occasionally for the big match but normally see the Wires at Leeds or other Yorkshire venues. I cannot remember the date of the first match I saw but I do know it was Warrington v Hull KR some time in the late 1940s when I was nine or ten.

The season 1953-54 was, of course, a special "double" season for Warrington. I certainly saw all the home games and all the aways I could as well - subject to Saturday morning school rugby leaving me travelling time. I went to the second round Cup match at Watersheddings rather pessimistically, I suspect, because Oldham were a very, very good team at that time. The pitch was a quagmire and the terraces were covered in snow. The ground would have been considered unfit for the spectators' safety these days. Oldham, as expected, absolutely dominated the game. They led 4-2 and were camped on the Warrington line at the far end from me. Oldham created an overlap on their left wing and the centre, Davies, threw out a pass to his winger, O'Grady to go on and score. Unfortunately for Oldham, "Bev" did not even consider tackling either. He had his eye on the ball and one of his speciality interceptions resulted. Merely catching the ball left twelve of the Oldham team stranded behind him for they were never going to catch him, were they?

However, Ganley, the Oldham full-back, was yards behind them. I think he was round about his own "25" yard line. It seemed to take Bevan a lifetime to come towards us. He had to haul each boot out of the quagmire with every step he took and Ganley waited calmly and confidently to smother him. I was standing with my school friend Brian Rhodes and "Uncle" (no relation) Jack Taylor from the same road, a pensioner who was as avid a Wires fan as any excitable youngster. *"Bernard will get him"*, said a nearby Oldham fan, whether in confidence or hope, I do not know. Uncle Jack felt obliged to express the Warrington view - based entirely on confidence in view of the article carrying his hopes. *"I have a ten bob note 'ere as thah can 'ave if Ganley even touches 'im"*. "Bev" did his famous chin-up-stuttering side-step. Ganley went one way and he went the other. A try under the sticks, converted by Bath and roll on round three. Jack's ten bob note never felt threatened, if he ever had one, that is!

I think that was the crucial score of the entire Cup campaign and possibly the most important try "Bev" ever scored. It was the nearest to defeat Warrington came in crucial games that year.

Another memory comes from the semi-final. Delighted to draw Leeds, our passport to Wembley, we won rather more comfortably than the score (8-4) suggested. I remember when the final whistle went play was taking place right in front of us opposite the tunnel. After the usual jumps of joy, handshakes, etc Harry Bath searched out Arthur Clues and made him piggy-back Harry all the way back. I presume this was the result of some pre-match bet. Arthur certainly accepted his menial task without too much objection.

The Final was my first visit to Wembley. Unfortunately the game did not justify the pre-match build-up. After all, the top two teams were playing. I remember that there were hardly any breaks at all and recall reading a London evening newspaper and being incensed at the report. They suggested that no one was capable of beating his opposite number whereas current Rugby Union stars would have run riot. I knew better but have to admit they had a point based on the dross presented that afternoon. I think I was quite relieved to draw in the end and suspect that Halifax had marginally the better of a very flat contest.

At the time of the replay I was a fourteen-year-old attending the local grammar school at Newton-le-Willows, situated midway between the four Rugby League strongholds of Warrington, Wigan, St. Helens and Leigh. All these clubs were supported within the school. The replay was, of course, an evening game and there was no M62. This meant that travellers from Lancashire would have to leave early or mid-afternoon, which necessitated time off school. The headmaster was for some reason away from school and the deputy head had the authority. I can see him now, wearing his gown, bouncing a golf ball off the radiator to improve his catching on the cricket field. He said that time-off could not be given. He also added, unforgivably, *"If it had been a cricket match it might have been different"*. Perhaps he was joking but it still hurt.

I cannot remember whether he changed his decision or I just played truant together with dozens of others. Anyway, I went, once again with my school friend Brian Rhodes. I do not remember any swingeing punishment on return to school. Perhaps we did get permission after all, or perhaps the punishment was not noticed in the euphoria of victory.

Most people remember the clogged roads getting to Odsal but I cannot. I do recall being amazed at the number of people and coaches and thinking it would be a very big gate. The official attendance was a laugh. I now wonder in my professional capacity as a Tax Inspector if it was some kind of tax dodge! Actually, in reality I know better. I was one of goodness knows how many thousands who did not pay. We simply walked in over a wooden fence which had long been knocked to the ground. There was some hunting around for the best viewing spot. I recall we were very high on the banking - higher than the score-board which blotted out part of my view. Generally though I saw most of the action. When we went to Wembley we went on the ground very early and in those days there were massive uncovered concrete terraces behind the goals. I remember being gobsmacked at seeing this vast acreage of concrete. At Odsal it was the vast acreage of human heads that took my breath away.

The game was terribly close again and the crowd noise was louder than anything I have heard before or since. I remember the two Warrington tries well. The first one, scored by Jim Challinor, followed a passing move from the Warrington left towards the right wing and the ominous threat of Bevan getting the ball with a few yards to work in. This threat encouraged the Halifax centre to move towards Bevan and Challinor, using Bevan as a foil, - I don't recall an actual dummy - cut inside and then ran diagonally to the right corner. The second and winning try by Gerry Helme was scored in front of me. It followed one of his special jinking runs and he only just made it!

The ecstasy of winning soon turned to dismay, however. Streaming from the ground in the general direction we had come in earlier, we quickly realised we did not really know where we were going or where our coach was parked. I never fought in a battle, I am pleased to say, but I have read about plenty and the aftermath of Odsal was, I now realise, on a par with the chaos of a retreat. Lots of people and motor coaches. That is what I remember most of all - the number of motor coaches. I never knew there were so many in existence. From all over northern England they came and all clogged up in every street and thoroughfare. None moved, just thousands of supporters moving amongst them.

I cannot remember the time scale but I do know that Brian and I became utterly lost and were contemplating turning ourselves into the police, who could at least inform our parents that we were safe! However, we must have had our bearings right because one coach of the hundreds we had passed suddenly opened the door and welcomed us back. We had long since given up hope and had not even noticed it. Yes, it was our coach from Newton-le-Willows. Eaves was the name of the firm and I think they are still in existence.

I have no memories of the journey home. I probably slept most of the way. Getting back to Newton was not the end of the matter. I lived in Collins Green, a little hamlet, two or so miles away and Brian a mile further on in Burtonwood. We reached home walking in the early hours of the morning with anxious parents very relieved having heard about the enormity of the day.

The newspapers in the following days were full of aerial photographs of the vast crowd and tried to estimate the real attendance. A figure of about 120,000 seemed to be most popular. Another theme was that the event proved that the final should be held in the north.

Friends who had not made the trip rued the fact that they were not there. One of my friends went to school in Liverpool (fee-paying) and consequently his parents, who were doing the paying, would not

countenance his absence. I remember that he felt he had missed out on history and had to suffer what he said was a very Halifax-biased radio commentary by Harry Sunderland.

Whilst obviously remembering with great affection a wonderful season for Warrington and being part of an historic occasion, really my main memory of the year is surprisingly of Halifax. They were redoubtable opponents. All three games could have ended in their favour. There was never more than a gnat's whisker between two great sides. Warrington won out and went into the record books but it could so easily have been Halifax who did the double. They were good enough and I still feel a touch of sorrow for them and their supporters to this day.

Dave Roberts

❏ My tale is merely what happened - nothing exciting. In my teens I went with Dad every week-end to a Rugby League match, mid-week too when convenient. I lived half a mile from where I live now in Liversedge. We left home early, parking in our pre-determined "big match" place to the right on the right hand bend just past Allied Colloids.

We walked up and I have no special memory of crowds and queues but we were inside in ample time to go to our pre-determined "big match" spot. In those big crowds we used to stand in the ashes near the top to the left (viewed from the pitch) of the main stand above what then were the speedway pits. The terrain there was so steep that we could pick our spot, use our feet to create a level area and, having taken yesterday's newspaper, we could, and did, sit down, untroubled by neighbours on any side and with a clear view of the pitch. Others did the same but we never had need to jump up because we could not see.

I remember Gerry Helme's wonderful try with some clarity. I have only once seen a re-run on TV but I don't particularly remember the Daniels' was-it-wasn't-it try in the dying moments of the game.

It was our practice to leave a busy match about two minutes from the end to beat the crowds and I do remember clearly arriving home - about five or six miles - within 30 minutes of the final whistle. As I said, nothing exciting but happy memories!

Peter Sampson

❏ At the time I was sixteen years old and I went with my friend Yvonne Merchant, also sixteen, my brother John Hitchen and his friend Malcolm Rawnsley, both aged eleven. We set off early in the afternoon in order to get a good place. If it was not in the school holidays (Crossley & Porter for us girls and Haugh Shaw Juniors for the boys), then we must have taken the afternoon off!

We caught the bus to Odsal and were amongst the very first to get into the ground. We had taken sandwiches and sat on the cinders half-way up behind the posts where the car-park/roadway now

Odsal. Another view of the disputed Tommy Lynch try. Ron Ryder, Harry Bath and Arthur Daniels are the onlookers.

Odsal. Confusion at the corner flag.

is. Looking at the famous aerial photo we would be on the top right hand corner. We picked our spot carefully but as the ground filled up and became so crowded, the two boys had great difficulty in seeing although Yvonne and I had a good view throughout.

I had been to Wembley with my grandfather, Mr. Irvine Hitchen, a past treasurer of Halifax RLFC in the '30s and '40s, because my father had just been diagnosed as having angina and did not go to Wembley. However, my father got a place in a wheel-chair on the perimeter of Odsal! He got better and is still alive aged 87!

I can remember little of the actual match except the heartache at the disallowed tries. At the age of sixteen we could see no reason why the tries were disallowed. Obviously it was a biased ref and ridiculous decisions!

What I remember very clearly was the journey home. There were so many people waiting for buses and no sign of any that we decided to walk. We walked in the middle of the road all the way back to Halifax, through Buttershaw, Shelf, Northowram and up Godley. My mother was waiting on Northgate and saw the stream of people walking down New Bank. Every time this occasion is mentioned - on Sky TV when we played Warrington recently, for example - I, like Max Boyce, say proudly, *"I was there!"*

Margaret A Wilson

❏ I have lived in Marrickville, New South Wales since 1964 but I'm really a Yorkie who was born in Todmorden, moved to Hebden Bridge aged two weeks and to Bradford when I was fourteen. I worked on the railways for eight years and at the time of the Odsal Replay was working at Low Moor. That night we had carriages all over Low Moor and had to send some empty trains to the goods yard down in Bradford.

Our station master that particular night was a Scot. Our regular station master was a Welsh tee-total Baptist. It was so hectic that the Scotsman told us to get rid of all the trains properly and that he would buy all the drinkers a couple of pints, which he did. At the day's end all the special trains were away as well as the regular trains. We used to get trains every hour from Liverpool, divide them into two sections and send one to Bradford and one to Leeds.

We used to close Low Moor station at 11.30 every night. After we finished four of us were walking up Cleckheaton Road towards Odsal when we came across a fellow wearing a peaked cap and a white coat followed by a crowd of other men. It was a coach driver who had lost his bus. He had completely forgotten where he had left it! We hadn't seen it either!

Incidentally, another strange thing happened after the drawn final at Wembley. It was the Sunday morning and I hopped on a train of empty carriages

going through Low Moor from Halifax to Laisterdyke where I lived. I walked through the train to the guard's van and when I got there I saw this lad with his head in his hands. He stank to high heaven! I asked the guard what was up and he asked me if I had smelled that kid. He thought he had filled his pants. When we got to Laisterdyke the guard told the lad that I would show him how to get home.

The lad could hardly walk. He was falling over the signal wires, the signal rods and the train lines. I said, *"What have you done to yourself?"* He said, *"I don't know. My mother bought me a new suit and a new rain-coat to go to Wembley with my mate. My mate left me in London to go off with some girl. If he has my rain-coat I'll love him but if he hasn't, I'll thump him".* I left him in a bus shelter waiting for the red Hebble bus back to Halifax. He would have had to wait two hours for it but I certainly was not taking him home with me!

Roy Broadbent JP

❏ I am 64 now and I have been a long-time follower of Huddersfield. I had been to Wembley the year before when Fartown beat St. Helens but in 1954 I could not get there. So I was delighted when there was a replay.

We got a bus from Huddersfield at 4 o'clock. Usually it only took about quarter of an hour from where I lived at Bradley to get to Odsal. It was a good job we left early. By the time we got to Bailiff Bridge the traffic had ground to a complete standstill so we got off the bus and walked to Odsal. When we got there the crowds were amazing. We queued for three-quarters of an hour and thought we would never get in. When I say queued, there was not really a queue - just a massive crowd. It was a hell of a sight. All of a sudden the fencing, maybe a hundred feet of it, fell down through the pressure of the crowd. There was a mad rush. Thousands got in free. I know I didn't pay. The police could not do anything about it. There was nothing malicious about it though. Rugby League fans aren't like that.

When we got in, we stood to the left of the old stand and could only see half the pitch, the end that Helme scored at. When play moved into the half we couldn't see, folk in the stand shouted to us what was happening. At least we knew who had the ball even if we could not see it.

We walked all the way back to Bradley. There was just no point in waiting for a bus. I'll always remember it as a great evening.

Jack Beaumont

❏ I have been going to Thrum Hall since I was ten years old. I watched Luddenden Open age team before that. When I got to ten my dad allowed me to watch Halifax and I am still a season-ticket holder and pleased to say that I have weaned my husband from football to Rugby League.

Because I was only thirteen in 1954 my dad said I was too young to go to Wembley and took my older brother and sister but not me. I was really upset but bit my fingers listening to the radio commentary with my mum. I was really pleased it was a draw as I said nothing was going to stop me going to the replay.

My father, brother and sister went to Odsal straight from work and were late getting there. I went with three friends from school (Sowerby Bridge Grammar). At home time we all ran down to Sowerby Bridge railway station with sandwiches in our satchels instead of homework and caught the train to Bradford. We got off at the nearest station to Odsal and walked up to the ground. It seemed to take ages but when we got there I remember how empty the stadium looked.

We were there ages before kick-off time and got a place right against the wall at the front by the "25" line. We ate our packed food and watched the crowds come in. We were wearing the team colours over our school uniforms. I cannot remember very much about the game itself. I know I shouted a lot! I did in those days. I vaguely remember Warrington scoring the winning try which came from a blatant forward pass. I know - I was standing just where it happened! I remember shouting abuse at Mr. Gelder, the referee. I thought we had been robbed. Things don't change - I have seen it happen this season!

The atmosphere was really something special - all those people, supporters from both sides all together, the banter, the friendly arguments and not a bit of bother. It was magic just being there but, of course, upsetting that we lost. I cannot remember much about the return journey except that the train we caught back was packed to the seams.

Two years later I was allowed to go to Wembley at last which again was a marvellous experience but very disappointing because we lost to Saints. It was nice to go there twice in the '80s and I hope we can go there again before too long.

Kath Brooke

❏ Until the last couple of years I have been a season-ticket holder at Thrum Hall - ever since I was twelve and that's over 60 years. My wife and daughters are still one hundred percent Thrum Hallers. They would go in fifteen foot of snow, never mind one foot.

I went to Odsal with my father-in-law by car. I picked him up outside the Automatic Screw Company which is down below where Sainsburys now stands. I lived up near Thrum Hall - still do - and crossed King Cross and went down the side of Skircoat Moor and past the Shay to pick him up. It was obvious from the amount of traffic coming through King Cross from Lancashire that it would be a waste of time going that way. This would be about five o'clock. We went via Southowram, Brighouse, Baliff Bridge and Bradford Road and

must have got through before the bottleneck formed at Baliff Bridge. We parked near the caravan site, our usual place, and walked to the ground.

I'll bet there were 120,000 there. A lot got in for nowt. I remember the gate-men were so hard pressed that some were taking money in buckets, the old two gallon metal ones. People threw their half-crowns into them. Some went in the buckets and some went in the gate-men's pockets. Those buckets were overflowing. The buckets were on the floor as they were too heavy to hold. I know they brought some of the gate-men from Halifax for the replay. I bet if they put the money in their right pockets they would have walked cock-eyed!

We had a good view from ring-side seats at the Rooley Lane end. I had got our tickets from one of the Halifax directors who was a coal merchant. We were at the opposite end to where the winning try was scored but lots of folk said it came from a forward pass. Of course, that was only hearsay. We couldn't tell. We could tell that Arthur Daniels scored though. It was definitely a try. I used to be a painter and decorator. In fact I painted all the seats in the main stand at Thrum Hall blue about thirty years ago. Arthur Daniels used to be a groundsman there and my son, who is 45 now, used to sit in Arthur's wheelbarrow!

After the match we were in no hurry to get back to Halifax. We knew there wasn't much point in rushing!

Albert Lomas

❏ Apart from playing second-row for Leeds I had a sports shop in 1954 and I supplied the balls for the replay. The traffic was so bad from Leeds to Bradford that the police had to give me an escort all the way from Headingley to Odsal Top otherwise those balls would never have got there! I had a real struggle to get the balls down to Bill Fallowfield in the dressing-rooms. He had given me tickets for the stand but when I tried to get down to it there were so many people that I gave it up as a bad job. I watched from right at the back of the crowd and couldn't see a bloody thing beyond the "25". After the match it took me hours to get away from the car park.

Arthur Clues

❏ As I began watching Warrington in 1945 I have seen many great occasions but none remotely to compare with the Odsal Replay. I saw Brian Bevan's first match. I saw his last. In between I must have witnessed about 500 of his near 800 tries, including the day he went past the Great Britain full-back, Jimmy Ledgard, seven times! Like, I am sure, many of my generation, I often despair of current references to "super" this and "mega" that, whilst previous world-beaters are rarely, if ever, mentioned. Who now thinks of Lionel Cooper, Billy Ivison, Ike Owens, Trevor Foster, Neil Fox and many, many others of their class?

Anyway, back to Odsal. It was my first visit and I was stunned as I left the turnstile at the sheer vastness of the place. I was early and there were only a few thousand in who could hardly be noticed. I had been to Wembley, of course, eleven days previously and was at Maine Road on the following Saturday. Both were big attendances but I only remember them vaguely in comparison to Odsal.

I was lucky enough to be half-way up the terrace at the end where Gerry Helme scored his try and that try is my most abiding memory of the event. Don't forget, Halifax finished top of the League and they conceded only 219 points in 36 matches. Their defence, obviously, was phenomenal. On that 40 yard curving run Gerry Helme gave the dummy to five players in succession. Leaving Bevan apart, it was simply the greatest try I have ever seen, considering the opposition and the occasion. Don't forget either, we were without the great Albert Naughton and the best uncapped second row pair in the League, Sid Phillips and Ted White.

Bernard Cain

❏ Having been to all the matches leading to the Wembley Final and unable to afford the outing to the original final, I and two street pals, Brian Slater and Billy Thomas, decided to attend the Replay at Odsal. I was the oldest at thirteen, the others both being twelve. We all came from Platt Street, Warrington. We booked our seats with Lancashire United Coaches and, came the day, set off. Being children and still at school, time didn't seem to matter. I believe some of the coaches never even made it to the ground, including the Warrington board's coach, but we duly arrived.

I can't remember the match in great detail but the one thing that has always stuck out in my mind is that during the after-match celebrations Billy Thomas somehow got lost in the mêlée. Brian Slater and I set off to find our coach and wait for him. To our dismay it became clear that he must be completely lost. After about half an hour or so we told the coach driver that we would go and look for him. He said he would wait and we set off to find a policeman. Having found one, he put us in his vehicle to drive round the area to find Billy as we were the only persons who could identify him. There was a loud-speaker on the car and the driver was repeating over it, *"Is Billy Thomas in the area?"*

Well, as you can imagine, even at this late stage there was a large crowd outside the stadium and it was like looking for a needle in a haystack. We returned to our coach empty-handed. I don't know what was arranged between the coach driver and the policeman but we set off for home. Little did we know but at our moment of departure Billy Thomas was somewhere crossing the Pennines as he had reported himself lost to the police and could not find his coach. So he was duly seated in the aisle of another coach on a biscuit tin and was homeward bound.

At least we had seen our team win the Cup which is more than can be said of some of the Warrington directors whose coach never got anywhere near the ground.

William G Rowland

❏ We left the Town Hall and went via Irlam to Manchester. In Manchester we went up to Oldham Road and after about two miles we ran into the traffic going to the match. It was bumper to bumper all the way to Bradford - about 20 miles per hour. We got to Bradford and all at once the traffic stopped. We got out of the bus and they said we could not go any further. Every street was full of cars and buses and we were at least two miles from the ground. We all set off and walked the rest of the way. When we got to the ground we managed to get to the turnstiles but the police were all around and there must have been at least a thousand people waiting. They said the ground was full and nobody else was allowed to go in. By now it was five minutes to half-time and nobody knew what the score was. The ground was like a giant basin. We eventually managed to clamber up the hillside and all we could see was the very far end of the pitch. The only time we saw the ball was when it went up in the air during the kicking duels. It wasn't long before we decided to go back to the bus and we heard the finish of the match on the radio.

Stanley Gregory

❏ In 1954 I was eight and still at Boothtown Junior School in Halifax. I had no interest in Rugby League at all then but within two years I was a fanatical Thrum Hall supporter. It is strange though what you remember as a child. As I said, Thrum Hall did not mean anything to me at the time and the fact that Halifax were at Wembley did not register with me. What I do remember is that on the Friday evening before Wembley there was a magazine programme on television previewing the Cup Final. It showed both the Halifax and Warrington goal-kickers having a pot shot from the touch-line at Wembley. They were dressed in their civvies although I suppose that they must have worn boots. Anyway, I remember that Tuss Griffiths missed his shot and Harry Bath kicked his. It must have been an omen.

The following day, the day of the Wembley Final, I remember about four of us, including my brother, went to the pictures at the Gaumont, which is now a night-club. I distinctly remember the half-time score being flashed on the screen - Halifax 4 Warrington 0 - and, of course, the final score too. When we came out I remember folk being unable to believe that we could know the score. News travelled slower in those days! They thought we were having them on.

We lived up Claremount Road and could see right down into Halifax. I remember looking out of

the window and watching the traffic at a standstill across North Bridge on the evening of the Odsal Replay. I remember that all the family sat in one room and listened to the radio broadcast. I can still see my father twiddling with the knobs on that old wireless to get the reception right. It did not upset me that Halifax lost as I did not even know who the players were. Two years later it did upset me when we lost to St. Helens and by then there was nothing I didn't know about the players.

Stuart Smith

❏ I remember it all quite vividly. I was in the Hull City Police Force at the time and had played for the Hull Police Rugby League team. When we realised there was going to be a replay we hired a Danby's coach and filled it with hairy-arsed coppers and set off for Odsal. The coach ground to a halt three or four miles from the ground and the driver gave us some instructions about meeting us after the match but I am sure we never found the coach until about mid-night. We half-ran and half-walked to the game.

I remember seing the game all right although we were so high up that the players looked about an inch tall. Halifax were the muckiest team God ever let live. We hated them in Hull. In fact I am sure they were so unpopular that even the Yorkshire folk were shouting for Warrington.

Getting out of the ground at the end was a problem. With the score being so tight and it being a Cup Final everyone was hanging on to the final whistle. I was fourteen or fifteen stone and even I was carried along with my feet off the ground at times. There could have been some nasty accidents in the crush but the crowds were good in those days. There was no bother or fighting.

Words cannot describe the electric atmosphere of that night. It was superb. The traffic though was practically unimaginable. The only thing I can compare it to would be to think of a coach trying to drive up Wembley Way when the Cup Final crowds are going up it. I imagine a lot of folk would be left in Bradford that night.

I am 65 now and I have been going to the Boulevard since I was eight. I am black and white through and through but I was proud to have been at Odsal as part of the biggest crowd in history. Perhaps I am unique as I was also at the Boulevard for Hull's lowest ever crowd. I was doing the PA that day.

Albert Walker

❏ We were coming out champion. Admittedly there were a lot of people but they were were civilised and sensible. Then somebody started pushing. I don't know who. People were tumbling about all over the place and grabbing on each other.

I had my handbag at the side of me and I thought, *"This might easily get pinched".* So I held it up in front of me. It was the worst thing I could have done. All the pushing had caused a crush and I got the handbag, a hard framed one, squashed on to my heart. I couldn't get my breath and started to panic. Nora Morby, who worked with me at Town Tailors in Castleford, was against me. She must have realised my predicament and shouted to Eddie, *"She's getting crushed!"*

Eddie managed to get across to me and put his arms around me in a circle to hold everybody back. He had all on to hold them back to protect me. They were like loonies trying to get out. He was a big lad was Eddie. He had been a boxer in the army and he played rugby for George Street in Featherstone but he was frightened. I could see it in his face. He ended up walking backwards all the way out. When I come to study it, he had a lot on his shoulders protecting me and walking backwards.

It didn't half knock the stuffing out of me. I thought I was a goner that day.

Hilda Fletcher

❏ One hundred thousand converging on Odsal created great traffic chaos. Late-comers told amazing stories of the difficulty they had in getting there. Getting away was probably worse. I did not leave the ground until 40 minutes after the end of the game, and even then there was a huge traffic jam at Odsal Top. The vehicle in which I travelled took a quarter of an hour to get from Odsal Top to Low Moor Working Men's Club. Coaches from Lancashire were parked all down the road as far as Wyke, and at 10.15 I counted 35 coaches that had paused on the journey home parked between Bradley Bar and Northgate.

"Autolycus", "Huddersfield Examiner",
6 May, 1954

ODSAL OR WEMBLEY?
Elland, 6 May, 1954
❏ Sir - I have derived no small amusement from the remarks made by Frank Williams and other sports reporters on the claims of Odsal as the venue for the Cup Final. One hundred and two thousand spectators "saw" the final they say. What a joke! It is obviously a good view from the press box but what about the thousands of people who paid to get in and never even saw the ball? I was one of them.

After a halt in a traffic jam and walking for twenty minutes from the bus parking place, we were late getting in, and there were thousands behind us. We had not a hope of seeing anything. Even a bus load of Warrington supporters who all held a 6/6 ticket were unable to get down to the seats they had paid for. By half-time there would be at least 10,000 people outside the ground who had been in the ground and were three shillings plus bus fare down the drain.

If the Rugby League Council decides against Wembley, they want their heads seeing to.
Yours, etc. DISAPPOINTED SUPPORTER
The above is a letter which appeared in
"The Halifax Courier & Guardian"

❏ As thousands poured into Odsal's stadium about an hour before the start of the big match last night a woman of large proportions was seen standing her ground and shouting: *"I'm 14 stones and I've been here since three o'clock. I'm not moving for anyone".*

But she did! There was a sudden surge forward of several hundred people, and she was swept away.

Another spectator displayed a battered pair of shoes after the match. *"They were standing so close to each other that everyone was on someone else's toes",* he said, adding with a smile: *"If there were any pickpockets about they couldn't have done very well. It would have taken 'em ten minutes to get their hand out of someone's pocket again in such a crush".*

From *"City Topics"* column, Bradford
"Telegraph & Argus"

WHO'LL TAKE THE LEAD AT ODSAL?
❏ The moment appears to be opportune for a few words on the grand Odsal spectacle. A Cup Final in the North at last, and a hundred thousand reasons why every Bradford Northern supporter should be proud, or should they?

The majority of the spectators - were they comfortable? Several thousands stood ankle deep in ashes, others on clay. There must have been thousands who could see very little of the game.

Is this good enough, Bradford? Cannot we do better than this? What is to be done about that terracing so conspicuous by its absence? Who is responsible, the club or the Corporation? Is it a shortage of money, or shortage of labour?

Money - surely it is a good investment for any city to have a ground capable of holding 100,000. Labour - I suggest that a hint to the Bradford Northern Saturday-afternooners and they will be there in hundreds, skilled and otherwise, to offer their time.

Come along, Bradford. Who's going to take the lead for us? We are known for our wool, why not for our Wembley?

"I'm Willing", Bankfoot

❏ SAW NOTHING
I was a victim of the complete lack of organisation at Odsal Stadium. I went to watch the Rugby League Cup Final, but was unable to see anything of the game. I have written to the secretary of the Bradford Northern club, inquiring as to the possible return of my entrance fee. Can nothing be done to ensure that there is no recurrence of this fiasco?

FA Walker, Menston

❏ ODSAL - ACT NOW, CITY COUNCIL

Surely the Bradford City Council will now do something to make Odsal Stadium the well-equipped place it ought to be.

I was only able to read about the exciting events at the Rugby League Cup replay but to have got the largest crowd of all time into a ground built out of Bradford's dustbins seems to me to be a direct hint to the city planners to finish the job properly.

The initial cost may be heavy but it will be covered easily if those responsible have the courage and imagination to go forward now with plans for what would, indeed, be a "Greater Wembley".

Anonymous

The above three letters appeared in the Bradford press shortly after the Odsal Replay

❏ I went to Odsal with Chief Inspector Cyril Payne and a couple of other Halifax Borough police officers in a car. How I found them after the match, since I sat in the press box, is beyond me. But I did, and they got me back to the *"Yorkshire Post"* office in Horton Street, Halifax, in time for a shock.

As the reporter regularly covering Halifax, I had not been asked to go to Wembley. This was a great disappointment. So when there was a replay at Odsal, I applied for a press ticket. This apparently denied some big-wig, who was intending to go, a seat in the box. So when I got back to Halifax I was asked to write 350 words of impressions immediately to fill the space. I felt they were making a point rather than really wanting me to write a report.

You can imagine my amazement the following morning when I found that the sports editor had given me my very first by-line in *"The Yorkshire Post"*. Indeed my very first by-line anywhere: *"By Bernard Ingham,* of our Halifax staff" (see next column). It's a funny old world, as someone said.

My impressions are contained in this, for me, memorable report. I have few other recollections other than the massive crowds; the congestion which must have been less than we have got used to in the late 20th century because I got back to Halifax remarkably quickly; the inability of many to see into the Odsal bowl; and the feeling of let down in Halifax who were second best on this occasion.

I suspect that such a crowd, digging a foothold in the shifting cinders at the southern end, would never be allowed today. It is amazing there was no disaster.

Sir Bernard Ingham

❏ I was sixteen at the time and lived in Bradford Road, Wakefield. I was a pupil at Wakefield Grammar School and we went to school on Saturday mornings. The head was a bit snotty about me going to Wembley but my parents took me anyway. It was a rotten game.

Few chances for Halifax

By BERNARD INGHAM, of our Halifax staff

Odsal Stadium lacked the splendour of Wembley but none of its excitement. Cup final replays are so very rare and the Odsal scene was unique.

As thousands poured into the bowl, cramming every vantage point, one wondered how many would not see the match. Many did not and hundreds must have caught only fleeting glimpses as they strained to peep. Some did not even bother and one elderly woman made herself comfortable on the bank and calmly read a newspaper.

As the players strode down the hillside on to the turf, Halifax people, jovial and confident, made their greater numbers heard. The Warrington supporters were more serious in this predominantly Yorkshire crowd, but it may have been an indication of Lancastrian purpose.

Try as Kielty and Clarkson did to carve an opening in the initial assault, Warrington, looking formidable even in defence, weathered the storm. Too many dropped passes lost Halifax ground and then, in a flash, the Lancastrians were jubilant and Halifax stunned by Challinor's early try. In only eight minutes Warrington had succeeded in doing what they failed to do in 80 minutes at Wembley.

Brilliant Helme

Now the blue and white rosetted Halifax people were in a doubting mood. But they die hard at Thrum Hall and back they came, the forwards taking hold of the game. Warrington always had the measure, however, and were superior at half back. Helme was a dangerous and brilliant tactician and Price a valiant partner.

Halifax hearts dropped a beat on each of the four occasions Bath had penalty shots at goal and the nearness of his efforts left Halifax uncomfortable. They were set roaring when Daniels crossed the line for his disallowed try and they were heartened when Griffiths made the score 3-2.

At the interval Halifax wondered if their pack could wrest supremacy in the second half, but it was not to be. As Mr W. Hughes, the Halifax secretary, later conceded: "We were disappointing and there is no doubt the better team won on the day."

At 4.15 on the afternoon of the replay I was still in Wakefield Bull Ring umming and aahing about going. I was wondering whether it was worth the money after Wembley and also contemplating the prospect of riding up Westgate Hill on my Raleigh Lenton bike. I decided to go, dashed home, had a quick tea and set off through the traffic. Traffic jams were already piling up in Wakefield and it was like that all the way to Odsal although I got there quite easily weaving in and out on my bike.

I got there ten minutes before the kick-off, paid fourpence to park my bike in the official car park and went through the schoolboys entrance without any problems. I made my way to the far end down to the old loudspeakers somewhere near where they used to have an old tram which acted as a scoreboard. I was not a big lad but, miracle of miracles, I got a great view and saw all the game uninterrupted. Heaven knows how I got down there. I suppose as I squirmed my way through people were probably thinking, *"Cheeky young puppy!"*

I remember there was a hell of a crush getting out at the end. I got home easily enough though. It was nearly all downhill back from Odsal and I was home in about an hour. That is more than can be said for my dad who got home after midnight. He had gone by car and got stuck in the car park. My uncle, Jack Crosland, the old Hunslet forward, had never got further than Heath Common. He was going by bus and had to listen to the wireless commentary.

Mike Dews

❏ My husband John played prop for Halifax in the 1954 games. I remember the wives went to Wembley separately from the players. We went by train and stayed at different hotels. We went down the day before Wembley, I think, but I remember we wore our Wembley outfits even so. The *"Courier"* came and took our photograph at the railway station. We felt like film stars! Actually I had come back from South Wales after taking our son Daniel to stay with relatives.

I was six months pregnant with our daughter Anna at the time so she "accompanied" me to Odsal. I cannot remember how we got to Odsal but we must have got there early as I do not recall any hassle. I remember sitting on my own in a good seat and felt perfectly safe. However, I think that if you put me into a crowd like that today I would be terrified. It's funny, but I remember it was wet and I was wearing a Dannimac with small blue and white checks. Halifax used to win lots of games by small margins in those days and I used to shout a lot. I used to get quite worked up about losing and I was always worried that Albert Fearnley would give away penalties!

I remember that the wives got back to the reception at Halifax Town Hall a long time before the players.

Avona Thorley

Telegraph & Argus

HALL INGS, BRADFORD, 1
Telephone: Bradford 29511

Thursday, 6 May, 1954.

ODSAL

BRADFORD is proud of Odsal. It is proud of the fact that it has a ground that last night accommodated a crowd of more than 102,000. It is proud of the men who had the vision and the enthusiasm to make a stadium from a tip.

Although everyone is sorry that since it was first opened as a stadium the Corporation and the Bradford Northern Club have not shown as much enterprise as the originators had and have not developed it as they might have done, it would be unfair to be too critical.

It is easy to say now what should have been done, and how much money should have been spent in terracing, stands, refreshment rooms, lavatories, etc., which would be required to make Odsal the Wembley of the North, but when Odsal was opened—in 1934—there wasn't much money to spare. (Read the argument which is going on in our correspondence columns about the unemployment of the thirties.)

Not many years afterwards came the war, and since the war the demands on public funds have been so great that a big development programme for Odsal would hardly have obtained Ministerial approval even if it received public approval. It wasn't easy indeed to obtain sanction for the much lesser task of making St. George's Hall up to date.

But we live in hopes. The City Engineer, Mr. S. G. Wardley, has a plan ready for when funds are available and circumstances permit. Then we may be prouder still. In the meantime, whatever faults the stadium may have, Bradford will justifiably boast about last night.

It is true that a considerable number of would-be spectators didn't get an adequate viewpoint and went into their motor-cars, if they had wireless sets, or home to listen to the broadcast. Whether that was their own fault or Odsal's is a matter of argument, for the great majority present were, we are sure, well satisfied.

Bradford Northern, the Rugby League, the Chief Constable, and Mr. C. T. Humpidge, the City Transport Manager, deserve a tribute. There was no serious mishap. Bearing in mind all the difficulties their administration and organisation was admirable.

93

DAI BEVAN
(HALIFAX LEFT WINGER)

Before we got to Wembley the directors told us that as long as we stayed in the Cup we would be treated to steak meals at Far Flat Head Farm which was a local restaurant. So every Tuesday and Thursday in the Cup run that's what we got. I was always a poor eater so there used to be a scramble to sit next to me among the big forwards like Wilkie and John Thorley. I enjoyed the sweets but couldn't manage the steaks so they would have mine. When we went down to Wembley we stayed at the Selsdon Park Hotel in Surrey. The head-waiter told us proudly that it was the finest hotel in Europe bar none and that if the foreign residents ever left England the country would be a hell of a lot poorer if they took their money with them. The meals there were amazing, seven or eight course affairs. He said they usually had enough butter to feed an army but our forwards practically ate the place empty. I remember Dolly Dawson saying that if the Battle of Waterloo was won on the playing fields of Eton then Wembley was only drawn by Halifax in the dining room of Selsdon Park!

I remember that on the Friday evening before Wembley Les Pearce, myself and another Halifax player together with three Warrington players went to Wembley to be interviewed on the pitch by Eddie Waring for some programme or other. He asked me something about how I thought the game would go and I said it was in the lap of the gods. He obviously wanted something a bit more meaty than that so he said, *"They say that Halifax are a dirty side"*. I told him that there was no way we were dirty, just hard and fit. When we were moving away Les Pearce, I think it was, noticed that Eddie had pulled Brian Bevan to one side and was slipping him some pound notes. We were not getting anything so we went over and tackled him about it. Anyway, in the end we all came away with a fiver!

Talking of Brian Bevan, people often ask how I managed to keep him from scoring in those three games in 1954. I just did what I normally did. I always kept inside him so that he would be forced wide. The Australians call it sliding defence now. It's not new! Brian was really tricky so it was no good trying to tackle him head-on because he would be somewhere else when you thought you had him so I always kept him on the touch-line. I would not do that to Martin Offiah though. He is probably faster than Bevan was.

At Odsal we were robbed. Both Arthur Daniels and Tommy Lynch scored perfectly good tries. What I remember was going home after the match. It was late when we got to the reception in Halifax and even later when Derrick Schofield and I were taken home to Lancashire in a taxi. Going over Blackstone Edge we came across a parked coach which was returning from the match. Unfortunately, our taxi headlights picked out quite clearly two rather robust ladies who had been caught short and were relieving themselves behind the coach! They were certainly covered in confusion if not much else!

We were robbed even worse at Maine Road in the Championship Final. We were winning 7-6, I think, when Ken Dean, or was it Stan Kielty, was penalised in front of the posts but it was a con trick by Ray Price who was all over him which should have been penalised.

We were so confident of beating Warrington that we took a crate of champagne to Wembley for the celebrations. We took it to Odsal and we took it to Maine Road but it never did get opened.

Dai and Brian Bevan meet at Wembley before the Cup Final.

ARTHUR DANIELS
(HALIFAX RIGHT WINGER)

Oddly enough I do not remember very much at all about the Replay. As for the disallowed try I took quite a bump in the incident and can only remember seeing a few stars! It is no good arguing about referee's decisions. They see what they see. It wouldn't matter if the referee had been in Leeds!

I must admit I was disappointed that we had lost after all the effort the team put in. You would have thought we had won the Cup when we came back to Halifax we had such good treatment. I think we would have been in the Queen's honours list if we had won.

It's funny but I remember more about the trip to Ireland. We thrashed Warrington in both games there. I have still got a miniature copper kettle for winning in Ireland. Cyril Stacey, the old Halifax winger, was one of the Halifax trainers then. He used to wear his rugby medals on his watch chain. When we came home I remember Jack Wilkinson showing his miniature kettle to Cyril and saying, *"You haven't got one of these, have you?"* Cyril said, *"How do you know?"* Jack replied, *"'Cos if you had, it would be hanging round your neck!"*

I remember we had an invitation to go round a brewery. As we were coming away Frank Dawson, our coach, said, *"Whatever they call this place I'll be back tonight. All the beer's free!"*

I remember there was a machine at Manchester airport offering tickets for two shillings to insure passengers for £1,000. Perhaps Frank bought one and must must have been expecting an accident as when we landed he said, "I knew the odds were too high!"

KEN DEAN
(HALIFAX STAND-OFF)

The game at Wembley was a bit of a let-down. At the end no one seemed to know what to do. Some players started to go towards the royal box but were told not to. Even the officials had no idea. It was a poor ending. I'll tell you what, Tuss Griffiths could have saved us all a lot of bother if he had kicked that goal at the end.

We had no idea that the crowd at Odsal would be that big. Someone had said it was a big crowd while we were in the dressing room but when we came out it was unbelievable. Usually at Odsal even in big crowds you came to flat bits where there were no spectators. That night you never left the crowd all the way down to the pitch. Running around before the game I remember looking at the crowd and it took your breath away.

We always seemed to be unlucky in finals in those days. I don't know what it was about us. If we had got in front we would probably have won particularly in cup-tie football. Dolly Dawson had us really well trained defensively. I think Warrington would have known that too but somehow we never got in front.

Ron Gelder, the referee, got a bad name in Halifax that season. Folk said he disallowed about thirteen Halifax tries in five games that year. I don't know if it's true. A few years later I went to a sportsman's do at Featherstone and one of the Odsal touch-judges came up and said that Arthur Daniels scored that try at the end. He said he told the referee that it was a fair try but he was waved away. Touch-judges had no power in those days. I seem to remember chasing Gerry Helme a lot of the

Wembley. Arthur Daniels is dragged into touch by Ray Price and Stan McCormick.

way when he scored the winning try but never got near him.

I think we got £20 all in for both games. The official rate for losing at Odsal was going to be £5 but they doubled it because of the crowd we had attracted. Before the first round one of the directors had said if we got to Wembley they would buy us blazers and slacks. Do you know, we had to pay for them ourselves to be made up at Neville Reed's. They just bought the material. They only gave us the badges. Des Clarkson never paid though. We had a good laugh for months. Neville Reed kept coming up to training nights for about six months and Des would disappear down to the dark side of the ground where he could not be seen. There were only training lights on the top stand. I'm sure Neville never got his money and gave up in the end.

Losing at Maine Road was rough especially as we scored the only try. Harry Bath should never have been given the penalty which won the match. Stan Kielty just picked up a Warrington loose ball but the referee was not watching. Stan had a reputation for stealing the ball and when the referee saw it was Stan he gave a penalty. Anybody else and it would have been OK. I remember Dolly Dawson asking, *"What have we got to do to win?"*

There was a lot of bother before Wembley started by the newspapers saying we were a rough team. Joe Humphreys started it after we beat Bradford Northern in a rough match. That was in a national paper. He let it drop though and it was Roland Tinker in one of the Bradford papers who kept it going. Whenever we went away the crowds used to yell all sorts at us and I think it rubbed off on some of the referees who would penalise us for nothing. I think some other teams became wary of us and their packs were dead before they even got to Thrum Hall.

When we went to Ireland we beat Warrington twice - thrashed them. There was probably a bit of the revenge element in it. They could always turn round and say they had won the ones that mattered though! Half-a-dozen top Rugby Union officials came to our hotel (Drury's) in Dublin one morning. They had seen the game at Belfast, were impressed and wanted to know more about the game. The directors told them that Dolly Dawson would tell them all they needed to know. Dolly liked his drink and he started by asking them, *"Who's buying?"* *"You can have what you like, Mr. Dawson"*, they said. So he started with a bottle of whisky. At teatime he was still in the bar, drunk as a lord, holding court to those Rugby Union officials. But about eleven o'clock he turned up to a dance we were attending sober as a judge. He must have literally drunk himself sober!

ALBERT FEARNLEY (HALIFAX SECOND-ROW FORWARD)

I remember about a month before the Cup Final Joe Humphreys wrote an article in *"The Daily Mirror"* criticising Halifax's style of play, more or less saying it was a shame Halifax were at Wembley. Our coach, Dolly Dawson, the best coach I ever played under, called a players meeting in the Thrum Hall pavilion. He was blazing mad and expressed the view that perhaps we should not play at Wembley unless an apology was forthcoming. I thought to myself, *"Well, I'm certainly playing at Wembley. It's everyone's ambition to play there"*. A few more felt like that too. It all blew over in the end. There was no way the club would not play at Wembley. I don't recall that the article made us play any less hard but subconsciously I suppose it could have had an effect on our play.

Whenever I think about the replay, I also remember the confusion that followed the 4-4 draw at Wembley. It was the first final at that venue that ended in a tie and nobody seemed to know whether extra time would be played or not. After a delay we were informed that there would be a replay.

When I learned that the game would take place at Odsal Stadium I was pleased. It had a special significance for me for I was the only Bradford-born player in either of the two teams and I still lived in Bradford.

On the day of the game the first indication that something special was happening was when I received a telephone call from a friend in the Bradford Police Force informing me of the vast number of people assembling at Odsal. He offered to pick me up in a police car and transport my family and me to the stadium. This he did and I remember my surprise on seeing so many people present. Once inside the stadium I took my wife and two sons, aged seven and four, to their seats which were wooden benches placed around the speedway track. I understood the shortage of seating accommodation at Odsal but felt that our closest family could have been provided with better facilities. As I saw the vast crowd assembling I also felt concern for their safety.

Although we felt there was room for improvement on our Wembley performance training had followed the usual pattern and as we gathered in the dressing-room at Odsal we were quietly confident and determined to go one better and return to Thrum Hall with the Cup. During the pre-match preparation we had looked out of the dressing-room window and were amazed at the size of the crowd.

Dolly Dawson

I arrived on the field and, looking around, realised that something special was occurring. It brought back memories of the days when I had played as a schoolboy in front of a handful of people.

As at Wembley the game was a close one. It took a spark of genius from Gerry Helme to win the game for Warrington although it would have been a different story had referee Gelder not disallowed Arthur Daniels' try which he definitely did score - I was pretty close by. Earlier in the game, if my memory serves me right, another touchdown had been disallowed. A pattern of similar decisions followed which always seemed to go against us when this official was in charge.

However, it was no use in crying over spilt milk and Warrington had to be congratulated. I felt very disappointed with the result and have very little recollection of the events after the match. I would, of course, have been even more disappointed if I had known that Warrington would again defeat us in the Championship Final, this time by 8-7, John Thorley being the only try-scorer of the game.

Although it was very much a second prize, we did manage to salvage a little pride from our encounters in Belfast and Dublin where we were the victors on both occasions. I don't know about Warrington but we certainly went there to win.

As time passes I have become even more aware of the significance of a gate of that magnitude being attracted to Rugby League. I feel very proud to have taken part in that historic occasion.

ERIC FRODSHAM (WARRINGTON FULL-BACK AND CAPTAIN)

The favourite holiday destination of my wife and myself is Tenerife. One night we went for a drink in this hotel and another couple came and sat at our table. We got into conversation and my wife said she thought they must come from near us in England and we said we came from near St. Helens. The man said he knew St. Helens well as they came from Warrington and he had played rugby at St. Helens.

It came out that we had played against each other - the last time being the replay at Odsal. It turned out he was Billy Mather, the Halifax centre, who was reserve at Wembley but played at Odsal. So, of course, we had a few drinks together that night. That was 1991 so we hadn't seen each other for 37 years!

Something I have sometimes been asked about the replay was, did Arthur Daniels score?

Well, this move was discussed before the match in team talks when we were alerted to Kielty putting in a kick from the base of the scrum. This happened at a scrum close to Daniels' wing. The kick was a good one and Daniels did catch the ball over our try-line but both myself and Stan McCormick held him and the ball on his back. He was unable to ground the ball, we being underneath him.

After the Cup had been presented to me as captain high up in the stands, I remember the players had to virtually fight their way back to the dressing rooms. I remember Austin Heathwood telling me he was going to make sure he got his picture in the papers. He hoisted me on his shoulders complete with the Cup and carried me all the way back to the sanctuary of the dressing-room. Do you know, we didn't meet a single photographer all the way up!

Before the Championship Final at Maine Road we discussed the ploy that Stan Kielty had perfected. As he went into tackle, Stan would bring his elbow up into his opponents' midriff, winding them and causing them to spill the ball. It worked a treat that day when early in the game I was tackled by him near the line. I dropped the ball and John Thorley scored the Halifax try.

RON GELDER (WEMBLEY AND ODSAL REPLAY REFEREE)

The week before the Wembley match I was contacted by the Rugby League who had obviously been affected by some of the publicity about the Halifax forwards being too rough. Halifax certainly had a fearsome pack and no doubt some referees were frightened of them. Anyway, the Rugby League Council intimated that I should go into both dressing-rooms to let the teams know there was to be no nonsense. Now that was something I absolutely never did. As far as I was concerned everyone always started with a clean sheet at kick-off time. I decided to speak to both clubs' chairmen at the top of the tunnel. I said to them, *"Look, I have been instructed by the Rugby League to go into the dressing-rooms. You will notice I have not done that. As far as I am concerned, it's a fresh start."* Both chairmen were obviously delighted.

The Wembley game was hard fought but no classic. I remember that the Halifax forwards were noted for *"growling"* - verbally intimidating the opposition but that hurt no one. Anyway, the first scrum went down right in front of the royal box. Gerry Helme dummied to put the ball in and I said sharply, *"Get that ball in, Gerry"*. He replied, *"Do you really want it in or shall I wait for the raw meat?"*

The climax came at the last scrum of the game. I used to referee by deterrence. In other words I warned players off doing things before they did them. I did not like too much whistle. Some things warranted automatic penalising though. Gerry Helme failed to retire and I immediately penalised him. He admitted he had not retired but he was almost in tears as he realised the enormity of what he had done. It was 4-4 and the penalty was very kickable - not too far out and about fifteen yards to the side of the sticks. I must admit it also suddenly hit me that I could have decided the destination of the Cup on a minor infringement. I was quite relieved when Tuss Griffiths missed! Tuss should have kicked that goal and if he had there would have been no Odsal Replay. The Replay was really the game-that-never-should-have-been.

The end of the game was sheer anti-climax. Everybody missed not going up the steps for the medals. We all just walked off.

So it was all off to Odsal. I was lucky in that I lived in Wakefield near the Bradford Road so I could drive in without hitting the traffic from the west. I arrived a couple of hours before the kick-off which meant quite a bit of hanging about. Around 6.45 Eddie Waring, who was reporting for the BBC, came to my dressing-room. He said, *"We have a bit of a problem, Ron. Can you kick off a bit early? If there is any injury time we will get cut off for the news at nine o'clock"*. I said, *"Sorry, I can't do that, Eddie. The only man who can tell me to do that would be Bill Fallowfield"*. Anyway, a few minutes later back comes Eddie in the company of the Chief Constable and Bill Fallowfield. The Chief Constable said, *"Look, Mr. Gelder, I estimate there are around 100,000 in the ground and probably another 100,000 outside. If you could start early it would help quieten things down"*. I told him that Bill Fallowfield was the man to ask. Bill then said, *"Ron, on behalf of the police it would be appreciated if you would kick off early"*. So we did.

I took the teams down and we kicked off four minutes early. The crowd behaved perfectly all the way down. However, what really got my goat was

Eddie Waring. The following week in his column for *"The Sunday Pictorial"* he wrote, *"Brickbat - to referee Ron Gelder for kicking off early at Odsal when there were still thousands outside trying to get in"*. We never spoke for a year! We made it up later though.

Eddie Waring

I remember at half-time I was standing on the pitch with my touch-judges. There was no orange juice or tea for us. You just stayed on the field at Odsal in those days. All of a sudden thousands of folk decided to occupy the speedway track to get a better view. One of the touch-judges said, *"What are you going to do about them?"* I asked him what he thought I should do about them and he said, *"Well, can't you go and blow your whistle and tell them to stop?"* He must have thought I was mad. There were thousands of them. I told him he must be joking and I would rather be a live coward than a dead hero! To their credit, the crowd never encroached on the field in the game.

Gerry Helme's winning try was a great one. He fell over, though, a yard from the line and sort of rolled over. No one tackled him. The most controversial incident, however, was the Arthur Daniels try which I disallowed with the score at 4-8. The main point of that was that it did not, as is often stated, cost Halifax the match. Even if the try had been awarded Halifax would probably not have won. What you have to remember is that the kick would have been six inches from touch on a very muddy surface. The way Tuss Griffiths was kicking it would have been a miracle if he were to kick the goal. I believe the whole episode was blown out of all proportion and that the decision did not lose the match for Halifax. To be fair, Arthur said he scored. He was an honest lad and he might have been right. Equally, he said that it all happened so quickly and he knew that I only saw the end of the incident with him on his back. You have to remember that my priority was to get to the goal-line. Unfortunately there were three or four players between me and the incident and a referee can only give what he sees and what I saw was Arthur on his back and the ball off the ground.

At the end of the game I had to climb the hill to the dressing-room. Considering the Daniels incident it was quite amazing that no one even touched me as I went up. I had no problem at all getting to the top. I had a problem when I got changed though. I never even got a cup of tea, nor did the touch-judges! The security people on the tea-room doors would not let us in! I decided not to bother and go home. As I went to find my car a Police Superintendant or Inspector asked me how I was going to manage as the traffic was horrendous. He told me to hang on for five minutes after which he provided me with a motor-cycle escort right down to the Wakefield Road. I remember the officer on the motor-bike saluting me good-bye. I thought it was a charming thing to do. I was home in Wakefield half an hour later.

You certainly did not get rich refereeing in the 1950s. I remember I got £20 for the two games - less £4.50 in tax!

AUSTIN HEATHWOOD (WARRINGTON SECOND-ROWER)

I find recalling details of what happened 40 years ago a bit difficult but what I do remember is carrying Eric Frodsham on my shoulders from the ground all the way up to the changing rooms. Now I would find it difficult just to walk up that Bradford slope myself.

I also recall the state of the ground's so-called boundary fences, large gaps in the railway sleepers and so-called turnstiles made out of 3" x 2" timber, all of which had been flattened by eager fans trying to get in. An American friend of mine came down from the stands at half-time to see me. I knew that I had given him a ringside seat ticket!

Travelling to the ground in itself was an experience. We must have covered miles on the wrong side of the road escorted by police to avoid moving and parked coaches. Even after the match, again with police help, we had travelled some way when we noticed the coach carrying the wives going the opposite way. However, we did eventually meet up in Rochdale where a celebratory meal had been arranged.

STAN KIELTY (HALIFAX SCRUM-HALF)

I get annoyed when people say the games with Warrington were terrible. They should remember that Warrington and Halifax were great teams. They just cancelled each other out.

We always seemed to have unbelievably bad luck in big games. All that fuss kicked up by Roland Tinker about "Halifax thugs" didn't help either. The away crowds used to boo us like mad. Mind you, I always felt real running out after our forwards. Some teams seemed frightened when they played us. The crowds used to gasp when our forwards went in three at a time. I was glad I was playing for us! I remember I used to go around the opposition saying, *"Watch out. Wilkie's coming, Thorley's coming"*. It used to wind them up. I remember doing it to Tommy Harris at Hull.

At Wembley it was stalemate. Neither side deserved to win. I think we only had one chance really to win and that was when Tuss Griffiths missed the penalty.

We could have won at Odsal. Arthur Daniels certainly scored when he took my kick from a scrum. If he had let go of the ball when he grounded it I think the referee would have given the try. Tommy Lynch scored too although I can understand that the way Arthur and Tommy worked the switch could have confused the referee. I should have had a try as well. We got a penalty 25 yards out and the ball was at my feet. Alvin Ackerley was going to call up Tuss to kick but we had an understanding that if I saw something was on I should take the chance. So I tapped the ball and ran for the line. There was no one ready to stop me but Ron Gelder called me back. I suppose we were just unlucky.

Although the crowd was so massive I don't think it affected the players at all. I do know it was a struggle to get back up that hill at the end though. I suppose it would have felt much easier if we had won! The crowd was pretty sympathetic as we went through it. It would have been grand if we had won. We hadn't half trained hard.

When we went to Ireland we knocked seven bells out of each other for a copper kettle! I don't remember much about Ireland as I have never had so much Guinness.

Actually I have been trying to forget the events of 1954 for 40 years but people keep reminding me!

TOMMY LYNCH (HALIFAX RIGHT CENTRE THREE-QUARTER)

We had to have a police escort most of the way to Bradford or else we would have been a day late for the match! One police official assessed the attendance at 125,000. As we approached the ground we saw one enterprising pair who had removed a couple of sheets of iron from the fence and were doing very well having collected a bucket full of money and a fast depleting roll of tickets. They moved on quickly when the police appeared.

As to the match itself, my only memories are of the size of the crowd and the two disallowed tries. One by Arthur Daniels from a kick by Stan Kielty was at the town end but he had been turned on his back by the time the referee arrived. The other, at the opposite end of the ground, was when I scored from a pass from Arthur Daniels. Unfortunately, the referee belatedly blew for a forward pass at the "25" yard line. I believe the Warrington section of the crowd got to the man in control. I have, until this day, had the conviction that on this occasion the oft quoted saying "we was robbed" was indeed justified. I still have the blue and white jersey I wore on that day.

Later that May we went to Ireland to play a couple of games against Warrington. The game in Belfast was a great advertisement for Rugby League. It was after this match that I met Noel Henderson, the great Irish centre, whom I had seen play for the 1950 British Isles in New Zealand.

The Dublin fixture had some pre-match tension. Warrington wanted Halifax to let them win so there could be a victory each! Halifax refused this suggestion and "play to win" was the order of the day. Another strange thing was that when it became apparent that there was to be a very large crowd Warrington wanted more money or they would not play! I remember telling Dolly Dawson, our coach, that I was prepared to play for nothing and, from memory, the other players supported me. As the game was played, the matter must have been resolved.

One of the most pleasant memories of that trip was our visit to the Guinness Brewery. The guide told us that the best brew was made in vats of Kauri wood from New Zealand.

BILLY MATHER
(HALIFAX LEFT CENTRE
THREE-QUARTER)

I was the back reserve for Wembley. I think Les Pearce was the forward reserve. There was no chance of us being used, of course, as there were no substitutes then. It was just a matter of rubbing down players' legs and wishing them good luck.

I played in the replay though as Peter Todd was injured and unable to play. I am a Warrington lad and have always lived there. I played for Warrington and Lancashire Schoolboys. It was Dai Davies, the old Warrington half-back, who took me and Frankie Broadhurst to Halifax. We were as green as grass in those days and I think Dai did it to get one back on Warrington who had done the dirty on him. I was seventeen when I signed for Halifax in 1950. I stayed until 1957 and I really enjoyed my rugby there. I had supported Warrington as a boy and with me playing for Halifax I got ribbed a bit.

I remember Frank and I used to train one night a week at Halifax and one night in Warrington at Ryland Recs. I don't recall any special training for the Odsal replay. I travelled to Halifax on the day of the game to join the coach. I remember the police escort, of course. The crowd was breathtaking, the pitch was flooded with folk and it was a bit off-putting. Once the game got started you didn't notice it though. Really and truly, I did not have a very good game although I do not remember too much. I do remember late in the game coming through with Arthur Daniels outside me. The Warrington cover was streaming across and both of us would have been taken into touch so I tried to kick in-field with my left foot but sliced the ball and I think it went dead. I got a bit of stick for that but if you don't try anything .... You have got to have luck. Halifax did not seem to have it in those big games.

I went into the army to do my National Service a couple of weeks later. I think that helped to erase my memories of the game! It meant I missed the Irish trip but I went to France with Halifax two years later to play against Carcassonne and Albi.

They often say that a team is as good as its reserves. Halifax had good reserves and we won a lot of trophies. I remember five days before the Wembley Final Halifax had to play at Hull in a league match and we fielded the entire Halifax reserve team. Hull were a good team then but we only lost 7-15. I remember getting the losing pay. So did the first team and they were sitting in the stand!

I had a tape of the Odsal Replay with most of the game on it but my wife went and taped over it!

STAN McCORMICK
(WARRINGTON LEFT-WINGER)

There never would have been an Odsal Replay if Bob Ryan had not dropped the ball late on at Wembley. It was one of the most expensive knock-ons in history. We had stayed at a hotel in Buckinghamshire prior to Wembley and in training we had decided that if it was tight at the end of the match I would come infield and try to drop a goal. I used to do that at St. Helens. Anyway, late on it was close and I set myself up near the Halifax posts and waited for Bob to give me the pass from the play-the-ball. I was pretty certain I could have dropped the goal but Bob knocked on and that was that.

The Wembley game was probably the dullest ever. There were so many great players out there that they all cancelled each other out, stuck like glue to each other. Later we went to the Cafe Royal in London. You'd have thought we had gone to a funeral! If I could have come home straight away I would have.

The Odsal game was unbelievable. The atmosphere was totally different to Wembley with the

Maine Road. Stan McCormick struggles to hold the ball as Arthur Daniels tackles.

crowd practically on top of us. When I think about it now it's just like a dream. When we came to the ground from Ilkley there was just field after field after field full of cars. I have never seen as many cars. Talk about thousands of people. It seemed more like millions. I remember at half-time we assembled on the half-way line and my brother came over. He had a ring-side seat and even then he complained that he could hardly see anything.

While you are playing your mind is transfixed and I don't remember too much of the game. What I do know is that Arthur Daniels never, ever scored that disallowed try. I remember the incident as plain as day. I think it was little Stan Kielty who put the little kick up. Arthur was taller than I was so I knew he would get the ball and he was strong so I knew we had to stop him getting the ball down. He caught it all right in both arms and turned in the air but I was on his left and Eric Frodsham was on his right and as Arthur came down we sort of enveloped him and brought him down on his back. It was like we were all three welded together. You could not have got a lettuce leaf between us and

there was no way he could have grounded that ball. I know there will be blokes in Halifax who'll go to their graves swearing Daniels scored but I know he did not.

Another thing people sometimes get confused about is Gerry Helme's try. They often say that when he threw his dummy it was towards Brian Bevan. Well, it wasn't. It was towards me. Remember, he scored out towards our left wing. Bev was on the right wing.

The games in Ireland later on were much tougher affairs than the Cup Finals and the Championship Final. I don't know why they were so rough in Dublin and Belfast. We thought we were going for friendly fixtures, to put on an exhibition. There was an exhibition all right - of Kung Fu, karate and all sorts. There was stick given out all over. I remember Harry Bath, big, tough Harry, saying, "they've all gone crazy". I remember telling him that I didn't want the ball. Bev said he didn't want it either! They used to call me a flying winger. It was men like Albert Fearnley and Jack Wilkinson who put ten yards on my pace!

Afternoon delight. Gerry Helme and Ces Mountford celebrate. Stan McCormick and a photographer look on.

CES MOUNTFORD (WARRINGTON MANAGER)

My memory is not so good these days but this is what I do remember. I live in Queensland now but was reminded of the replayed final just recently. Prior to the second State of Origin game held in Melbourne the record attendance at Odsal was mentioned several times on radio and in the press. At Odsal, of course, there were many gate-crashers making the attendance much higher than the official estimate. I remember the stories of gates being broken down.

The return journey was, as you can imagine, chaotic. Coaches were rolling into Warrington early in the morning and the coach carrying wives and relatives never reached the place they were to have dinner.

There was one episode in the game I will never forget. That was when Gerry Helme scored. At half-time I spoke to him telling him to run when the opportunity arose. He scored the winning try doing that. Gerry was a brilliant half-back when he ran with the ball. If he wasn't running, the tempo slowed down.

Our preparation for big games was fairly simple compared with today. Usually for important games we would spend a few days at Blackpool's North Shore but for the replay we went to Ilkley. There was not much emphasis placed on diet in those days. Each player had his own preference for what to eat on match days. We did, however, place emphasis on sprint training and laid our own cinder track at Wilderspool. Spiked shoes were a must at each training session. Speed for the first forty yards was important.

In retrospect the game was vastly different in those days, money-wise, promotion-wise and in so many ways. However, I feel we did produce results. Brian Bevan was the best winger in the world in those days and we had many Internationals in the team but the main interest was for Warrington to get results. We had a wonderful group of players with tremendous team spirit.

Thanks to the visit to Ireland and all the games played in the Cup and Championship Finals we were able to make a friendly relationship with the Halifax players.

BOB RYAN (WARRINGTON LOOSE-FORWARD) - In conversation with Ernie Day

In any analysis of the past the words "if only" are bound to crop up but those two little words were never more applicable to Bob Ryan and his team in 1954. In the later stages of the game at Wembley with the scores locked at 4-4 Bob dropped a simple pass within reach of the Halifax try-line and along-side the posts. Tuss Griffiths too, the Halifax full-back, must have muttered the same two words as his last ditch attempt at goal failed whilst the Warrington team stood with fingers crossed willing the ball to pass outside the uprights.

These two incidents did happen but if either Bob had held the pass or Tuss had landed the goal .... Well, that fantastic night at Odsal would never have materialised. Perhaps we should be grateful that that dreary non-event at Wembley gave us the opportunity to participate in those historic scenes at Odsal.

Prior to the game the Warrington squad had spent a few days at Ilkley, a favourite place for past touring sides to relax. Its location helped the team coach to miss a lot of the traffic that converged on Odsal although a police escort really ensured that they arrived at the ground in fairly good time. From their dressing room window high up in that famous bowl they could see part of the crowd assembling. Bob Ryan remembers Trevor Foster, the Bradford Northern stalwart, calling in to wish them luck and remarking that the attendance could be 40,000. Eric Frodsham also recalls having a quiet bet with Gerry Helme for a couple of pints that there would not be more than 50,000 present.

Bob also recalls with a smile how throughout the game the Warrington forwards continually wound up Des Clarkson, the Halifax loose-forward, who they remembered had been sent off as a Leeds player when Warrington won the Odsal semi-final of 1950.

Some of the wives of the Warrington side travelled together with girl-friends and "A" teamers in a coach and Bob's wife remembers the frustrating journey which ended abruptly with the vehicle breaking down and leaving the occupants with a half hour's walk to reach the stadium. They then faced a mini-assault course to reach their seats in the stands by scrambling over a partially demolished wall only to hear the half-time whistle blow as they slid into their seats. She remembers too that Brian Bevan's wife had only been discharged from hospital a few days earlier after an operation and still had the stitches in.

The victorious team had a late meal before returning home to Warrington and arrived back well before their wives who reached home, tired and bedraggled, at 2 am.

Both Bob Ryan and Eric Frodsham feel that the Irish venture was ill-conceived. Both sides must have been sick of the sight of each other. The Warrington players, however, approached the trip in a carnival spirit and as a chance to let their hair down a bit, whilst the Halifax lads were in a more serious mood seeing an opportunity to redress the balance a little and settle a few not very old scores, which they certainly did. The plane they flew in seemed a mite fragile. In fact one joker suggested that they all get behind it and push! Most of the party had never flown before and poor Danny

Siamese Twins? Gerry Lowe and Derrick Schofield

Naughton, a giant of a man on the rugby field, was literally shaking in his boots at the thought of flying.

Talking of Danny Naughton, Eric Frodsham recalls an amusing tale. Prior to the 1954 Challenge Cup Semi-final against Leeds at Swinton the Wire squad stayed at Cleveleys on the Fylde coast. When the arrangements regarding room-mates were being made it became a matter of interest when Ally Naughton refused to share a room with his big brother. What Ally knew was that Danny was an habitual sleep-walker. He kept that knowledge to himself, however, and Syd Phillips found himself as roomy to Dan. After a late night talk from Ces Mountford they went to bed. You can imagine the state of Syd when in the middle of the night he was rudely awakened by someone pulling him up and down by the shoulders. It was Danny kneeling across him and shouting, *"Come on, Cluesy, play that bloody ball!"*

The trophies won by Warrington that season, mainly at the expense of Halifax, were on display at both Belfast and Dublin and were the subject of a lot of ribaldry between the two sides. In one game Albert Fearnley had run through a paper-thin Warrington defence to score a try and as Bob Ryan picked him up from the turf he recalls saying, *"Nice try, Albert. Remind me to show you my medals one day"*.

The patience of Ces Mountford, the Wire manager, was stretched to breaking point too one night in a sea front bar in Bangor where the locals most generously entertained his team all too well until long after closing time.

The players received £4 for the trip to Ireland.

DERRICK SCHOFIELD (HALIFAX SECOND-ROWER)

I was the only Lancastrian in the Halifax team. That didn't help me at the mill I worked in at Rochdale. They all supported Warrington in the Cup Final so you can imagine the fun they had at my expense! I used to get picked up by taxi with Dai Bevan for the games at Halifax and we would go to away games in Dai's sports car.

I remember the fuss about our so-called rough tactics but really I think it was just the press stirring things up. It never affected our approach to the game, in my opinion. We played just as hard whatever was said. I think it all blew up after our game with Bradford Northern. They were a good side and the atmosphere was a bit charged.

Halifax always used to make sure we got well fed after training and I remember the steak meals they treated us to in the run-up to Wembley. It was wonderful as was all the pre-Wembley training under Dolly Dawson.

I remember coming back to Halifax on the Monday after Wembley. We were going to play Keighley that evening in a league match at Thrum Hall. I remember Mr. Horsfall stopping the coach on the way into Halifax and making us all put on our blazers for the entry into the town. Just like we were kids! I remember during the half-time against Keighley all the Halifax players spent the time collecting for Arthur Daniels' testimonial.

We were not pampered like modern players. I remember on the day of the Odsal game I went to work as usual, had a great big canteen dinner and was picked up by the taxi at 4 o'clock. When we saw the crowd gathering it was unbelievable. A party of my supporters got up a coach trip from the Gale Inn in Rochdale but they never got near the ground. They had to listen to the match in a pub somewhere.

Obviously I was very disappointed by the result at Odsal. I thought we were the better team. The referee gave us nothing. I always felt he was told to keep a tight grip on Halifax. Warrington seemed to get away with a lot more, not that they were dirty or anything. Tommy Lynch's try was a good one but then again I'm bloody biased! Arthur Daniels' try looked all right to me too. He was a good player, Arthur, but not showy. He and Tommy Lynch were marvellous with that merry-go-round move of theirs. I remember Gerry Helme's try. It was a good one. I think Albert Fearnley and I tracked him all the way and if Tuss Griffiths had forced him inside we might have got him but he ducked under Tuss's tackle.

I remember when Dai and I went home in the taxi that night we kept stopping at pubs over the moors to get a drink but never managed to get one as by that time they were all packed by fans travelling back to Lancashire.

I always used to take an umbrella to games in those days. Thinking back we always seemed to play well on soft grounds. It didn't help us at Odsal that night!

ARNOLD STEVENS (WARRINGTON CENTRE THREE-QUARTER)

In 1954 I was a reserve for Warrington but when Ally Naughton was ruled out I was lucky enough to be picked to play in the centre at Wembley. The first I knew of it was on the Thursday morning before the game. We were down at Gerrard's Cross and I was rooming with Ike Fishwick, the reserve hooker. The officials moved me out of the annex and into a room with Stan McCormick. I think Stan got less sleep than me and he was an experienced International!

It was my first visit to Wembley. In fact I had already booked to go down on a coach. My mother and father had already gone down to London before I had been picked. Dad was "Hookey" Stevens. He had played for Widnes at Wembley in 1930 when they beat St. Helens. When he heard I was going down as a reserve, I remember he said, *"The experience will do you good"*. My father was one of those blokes who seemed to get caught short whenever something exciting happened. Apparently he and my mother were in London and he bought a newspaper. All of a sudden my mother found herself all alone wondering where he was. He had had to dash off to the toilet because there in the paper was a picture of me staring at him and a story of how I was playing in the Cup Final! I remember

when we got back to Warrington Bank Quay station on the Monday they were both waiting. My dad was in tears!

My most vivid memory of Wembley was coming out before the kick-off. I was only 19 - just a bit of a kid really. I am not surprised that even seasoned players get nervous there. You walk out of the dressing-room up a little slope and you can see the sky in the distance. I can still see it to this day, coming out of the tunnel into a sea of faces, walking into a cauldron of noise. It is all a bit like a dream really.

I can't remember much about the game although people complained that it was boring. I know I did not get my medal until weeks after the game. I have still got my jersey after all these years. I have never washed it and it is sealed in plastic now.

For the Odsal game I was back at reserve. A lot of people said I should have played at Odsal as I had not had a bad game at Wembley. Ronnie Ryder replaced me. I wasn't peevish about not being included though because I was just pleased to be part of the squad. The Warrington lads were a great set to be with. It was all a bit strange to me really as Wembley was only my eleventh first team game - I had only made my debut in January against St. Helens marking Duggie Greenall! I always felt that club officials did not want to play me because I was due a £500 contract fee after I played twelve games. In fact I did not play for the first team again until 24 September, 1955 when we played Halifax again at Wilderspool!

What struck me most about the Odsal game was the journey from Ilkley to Bradford. There were amazing numbers of cars. When we got to Odsal and started walking down from the top the crowd was just amazing. I never saw anything like it and the atmosphere was unbelievable. I think it was a great game and seemed to be over in a flash. It was certainly as good as anything you'd see today. The teams were well matched and it took a piece of brilliance by Gerry Helme to break the stalemate.

I know that it was about four o'clock before I got home to Widnes. Even though we left Odsal late it was so busy that the coach more or less crawled home. I remember it was certainly getting light by the time I arrived home.

The trip to Ireland was just an excuse to have a good time as far as we were concerned. It was the first time I ever tasted Irish Draught Guinness - lovely! All the heat was off and there was no animosity between the teams as far as I remember. The games were just two friendly exhibition type games. In fact all our games with Halifax that season were played in good spirit.

Maine Road. John Thorley scores the only try of the Championship Final.

JOHN THORLEY
(HALIFAX OPEN-SIDE PROP)

There is a lot to remember about 1954 when I come to think of it. Apart from all the big Halifax games, I played in the first World Cup competition in France later that year when Great Britain won the trophy.

I remember all the bother before Wembley when Joe Humphreys and Roland Tinker wrote those articles about Halifax being a set of thugs. It was Roland who really kept the thing going. The Halifax forwards were certainly hard, rough and robust but dirty - never! We had a good disciplinary record. Actually we were incensed about the business and talked about suing Roland at one point. Even when Roland became the reporter for *"The Courier"* a few years later those of us who were still at Thrum Hall had not forgiven him. Psychologically I honestly think all the bad press had an effect on our play and we were never quite as good as we could have been.

Halifax were a bit mean in those days. We were given material for blazers and slacks but had to pay ourselves to have them made up. Halifax did give us the badges though! Mind you, the Warrington lads did not have club blazers and slacks. After the draw at Wembley Bill Hughes wanted to give us losing pay but in the end I think we got £20. I know we only got £4/10/0 for Odsal and Maine Road.

On that Wembley trip Alvin Ackerley, Jack Wilkinson and I, together with our wives, went to the BBC studios at Shepherd's Bush on the Sunday evening to see *"What's My Line?"*. I remember Alec and Eric Bedser were also guests that evening.

We had taken a load of champagne down to Wembley. We took it to Odsal and Maine Road too but it never got opened! We did not return to Halifax until the Monday when we were due to play Keighley in the final league match of the season. I remember Alvin Ackerley taking a bite out of a pork pie that day and the club chairman, Mr. Horsfall, knocked it out of his mouth telling him we were in training and he should not be eating pork pies when we had to play Keighley!

I am pretty sure I worked the day of the Odsal Replay. I remember the trip to the match with the police escort. I remember a chap followed us in a car all the way from Shay Lane to very near Odsal - on the wrong side of the road, of course - before a police car stopped him. We were unlucky not to win the game. Daniels and Lynch certainly scored and Stan Kielty did too when he took a quick tap penalty but was brought back by the referee. The Warrington front row had a problem getting the ball in those games. Our captain, Alvin Ackerley, was a great hooker and I know that they used three players opposite me to try to get the ball - Dan Naughton, Gerry Lowe and even Harry Bath.

We were very late getting back to Halifax after the game but there were still a lot of folk to greet us. We did not get an escort back - just came back in the queues of traffic - and by the time we arrived at the Town Hall all the councillors had scoffed the sandwiches. We just got a glass of beer and a wave.

We enjoyed the trip to Ireland. It was a great three days. Everybody enjoyed the Guinness factory! Some of the players who did not play in the Cup and Championship Finals got to play in Belfast and Dublin. I know Ray Illingworth would remember Dublin. He and Les Pearce went to tackle Brian Bevan. Les was one for always trying to get a dig in and he had a go on this occasion but instead of getting Bevan he split open Ray's mouth!

JACK WILKINSON (HALIFAX BLIND-SIDE PROP)

You have to remember that in 1954 nobody had actually considered a draw as a possible result and when the final whistle went it was like somebody had pulled the plug out. Nobody knew what to say or what to think. We trooped off the field with the Warrington players and they told us that it felt just the same to them - frustrating.

When we reached the dressing room our coach, Dolly Dawson, went through the match pointing out where we had missed our chances and I remember him saying, *"Come on, lads. We've not lost yet. We're still in this game".* It must have been as frustrating to the fans as it was to us. We and Warrington were the top two teams in the League and as a spectacle the Wembley match was a complete failure. Our celebrations in central London were very subdued that night.

I well remember the day of the replay. We set off for Odsal in late afternoon and I recall being very surprised by the number of cars making their way from Lancashire to Bradford. The route in those days took them through Halifax and they were queueing for the match even when we set off. I thought we would never reach Odsal. We had a police escort and we drove on the right hand side of the road all the way to Odsal.

I thought we would never be able to reach the pitch, never mind play a game. People were just pouring in to Odsal from every direction and as we dropped down the steps from the dressing room it was a sheer test of strength. All they wanted to do was slap us on the back and wish us luck. As far as I recall, the crowd behaved themselves and there was no trouble.

When we got down to the pitch it was an incredible sight - faces as far as you could see in any direction. The noise was simply amazing. Most of the men in those days wore hats and every time somebody scored it was like a coloured snowfall, as up they went into the air. For Halifax it was not the happiest of occasions. We lost 8-4 and nobody could persuade us that was the right result. We always consider that a Warrington try was doubtful and that we had a perfectly good try turned down by Mr. Gelder.

As losers it was a long trek back up the Odsal slopes. People were very pleasant to us on the way back but the bottom had fallen out of our world because we had lost the Cup Final. There was a civic reception for us in Halifax after the match and we were very late making our arrival there. People were still trying to reach Odsal even after the match and the traffic outside the stadium was jam-packed.

Gerry Helme was fantastic at Odsal that evening. He played well at Wembley but he was brilliant in the replay. He won the Lance Todd Trophy and the people who voted for him certainly got it right. Harry Bath also caused us problems in both matches but we did manage to keep Brian Bevan relatively quiet. We put Dai Bevan to watch him because he was a great tackler. Our pack was a bit special in those days with players like Derrick Schofield, Albert Fearnley and Alvin Ackerley but we never got it together and did not give our backs the supply of ball they needed to deal with Warrington. Tommy Lynch, our New Zealand centre, was a great player and had he been given a better service, who knows what may have happened?

Note - Jack Wilkinson died in 1992. The above is taken from an interview Jack gave to John Huxley in 1982.

Jack Wilkinson

Halifax Captain,
Alvin Ackerley

Halifax
Vice-captain,
Stan Kielty

Evening Post

TELEPHONES:
LEEDS .... 32701 (18 lines)
LONDON Central ...... 9693 (8 lines)
DONCASTER .... 4001 (6 lines)

Odsal

THERE was the strongest possible witness at Odsal Stadium last night to the strength and popularity of the Rugby League code in the North. There was also the strongest possible warning that something drastic must be done about the amenities.

That crowd of 102,000, of course, raises once more the question whether the R.L. Final should be played at Wembley or at Odsal. Mr. W. Fallowfield, secretary of the League, says: "Not yet," which seems to imply that the Final ultimately may be in the North. We are not so sure about that.

The Wembley touch is not to be despised. The R.L. Final can fill Wembley, and a London Final certainly advertises the game in the apparently reluctant South. But anybody seeing the vast crowd at Odsal last night must have been struck by the thought that the R.L. code, if properly put across in other regions, might easily succeed. The Odsal crowd was a cross-section of humanity, not just of the North.

But even if Wembley were retained as the setting of the Final that would not weaken the case for a swift and drastic overhaul of the Odsal amenities. There were perilous moments at the exits. We are afraid the Odsal authorities will have to meet many complaints from those who paid to go in but were not able to see the game. The flat terraces at either end harboured many unsighted persons.

The stadium authorities deserve some sympathy, for they were overwhelmed. Probably they do not know the capacity of the ground. But on another such occasion they must know, and to know they must have the ground properly surveyed. What is wanted is a survey and a plan, which would include a traffic plan as a by-product, for there was understandable chaos last night.

Here surely is a challenge to enterprise. The Bradford Northern club is only the tenant of the Corporation. Let the Corporation, the Rugby League, and any other body with constructive ideas, get together. Odsal last night was an augury.

Wire Scrum-half,
Gerry Helme

Halifax Prop, John Thorley

Wire Stand-off,
Ray Price

MISCELLANY

* If the Odsal Replay had ended in a draw there was to be a two minute interval before extra time was played, some of which would have had to be under floodlights.

* Scores of taxis were chartered by Halifax fans to take them from work to Odsal. *"We are rushed out,"* reported one taxi-cab proprietor.

* Although full-back Eric Frodsham captained Warrington in their victories at Odsal and Maine Road, it was the absent-through-injury Ally Naughton's name which was inscribed on both the Challenge Cup and the Championship Cup.

* Stan McCormick earned a unique distinction by gaining winners' medals for all four cups in 1953-54 with different clubs. Warrington won the Challenge Cup, the Championship and the Lancashire League Championship. Stan joined Warrington after helping St. Helens to defeat Wigan in the Lancashire Cup Final earlier in the season, thus winning medals for all four cups.

* A Salford man, James Mather, a former Powderhall sprinter, was reported to have been the last man admitted to the ground at Odsal - ten minutes from the end of the game!

* Local licensing courts had a busy time with applications for extensions of licensing hours on the day of the Odsal Replay. West Riding Magistrates refused Arthur W Home's application for an extension from 10 to 11 pm at his pub, Nont Sarah's, at Scammonden. Arthur had correctly surmised that the traffic after the game would be terrific.

* Halifax Borough Licensing Court had been more generous in allowing L Hilton of the William IV in King Cross Road to extend his afternoon opening from 4.30 to 5.30. However, Alderman A Pickles, OBE, JP (presiding) had told the licensee of the Wellington Inn, New Bank, Mr HM Hemmings, that the Bench was very generous in granting extensions for later hours but they were only granted for special or annual events. *"This is not such an event"*, said Alderman Pickles in one of the great miscalculations in sporting history.

* The Earl of Derby was to have presented the Challenge Cup at Wembley. In his absence at Odsal the Cup was presented by the Chairman of the Rugby League Council, CW Robinson, MC. Lord Derby did, however, present the Championship Cup at Maine Road.

* There was no live television coverage of either Wembley or Odsal. The BBC had offered £350 to televise the Wembley match but the RL Council had said they would accept no less than £500.

The BBC then agreed to pay £500 but required agreement by noon on 7 April. As the Cup & Rules Revision Committee's next meeting was not until 8 April there developed an *impasse*. Consequently no agreement was made and the game went untelevised. The owner of Wembley Stadium, Sir Arthur Elvin said that the BBC should pay a fee of £500 with an additional payment of £500 for unsold tickets. The BBC were allowed to make a telefilm, however, to be shown on any convenient programme.

* The Championship Final was televised live by the BBC who had agreed to pay £150 after originally offering only £100. The Rugby League's minute book recorded, *"It was agreed that the BBC be informed that in the opinion of the Committee the fee was disappointingly small for a match of this nature."*

* The main counter-attraction to the Odsal Replay for Bradford residents was the appearance of Laurel and Hardy at the Alhambra. They were performing in a new comedy sketch entitled *"Birds Of A Feather"*. Tickets ranged from one shilling to 4/6.

* All the games at Wembley, Odsal and Maine Road were transmitted on BBC Radio. The Odsal Replay went out on the North Home Service (434 and 261 metres) and the second half only was covered. Alan Clarke and Alan Dixon were the usual commentators with summaries supplied by Eddie Waring and Harry Sunderland.

* The gates at Odsal were opened at 5 pm. At 5.30 there was to be a curtain raiser between Low Moor and Sedbergh Under 18s. It was not played, however, as the state of the pitch was too heavy. At 6.30 the Black Dyke Mills Band began to perform.

* For the Replay there was an 8,000 seating capacity comprising 1,000 Old Stand tickets at 25 shillings, 4,500 New Stand tickets at 10/6 and 3,000 ringside tickets at six shillings. There was reported to be standing room for 100,000 at three shillings. The Halifax and Warrington clubs were each allotted one-third of the seating tickets.

* A couple of years before the Odsal replay, the Bradford City Engineer and Surveyor, SG Wardley produced a plan for Odsal to accommodate 95,000 *"quite easily"*. His plan allowed for 10,000 under cover, 64,000 on concrete terracing, 18,000 on sleeper terracing and 3,000 around the speedway track. The scheme would have cost around £200,000. Forty years later schemes are still being floated for the development of Odsal Stadium but the projected costs now range from £100 million to at least twice that figure!

* During the 1953-54 season five Warrington players appeared in international fixtures - Ally Naughton (England), Ray Price (Wales), Gerry Helme (International Selection in France), and Harry Bath and Brian Bevan (Other Nationalities). Additionally Stan McCormick had played for England whilst a St. Helens player. Six Halifax men had played in internationals - Alvin Ackerley, Stan Kielty and Jack Wilkinson (England), Arthur Daniels and John Thorley (Wales) and Tommy Lynch (Other Nationalities) whilst Dai Bevan had represented Wales as a Wigan player. Amazingly, no Wire players won county honours during the season. From Halifax Ackerley played for Cumberland whilst Yorkshire caps were won by Kielty, Ken Dean and Albert Fearnley.

* In the Australasian Tour Trials the selectors called on Ackerley, Daniels, Kielty and Wilkinson from Halifax and on Helme, Ally Naughton, Danny Naughton and Price from Warrington. Staggeringly, only Wilkinson, Helme and Price were selected to tour.

* Tragedy accompanied Halifax in the final months of the season. No fewer than three deaths occurred at games involving the Thrum Hallers. Before the Cup Semi-final against Hunslet at Odsal John Moore (42) of Sowerby Bridge died outside the ground. The following week, again at Odsal, during the League fixture against Bradford Northern, Mr. Harold Jones (50) of Bradford collapsed and died. Finally, at Maine Road 65 year-old John Lynskey of Bewsey also collapsed and died at the Championship Final.

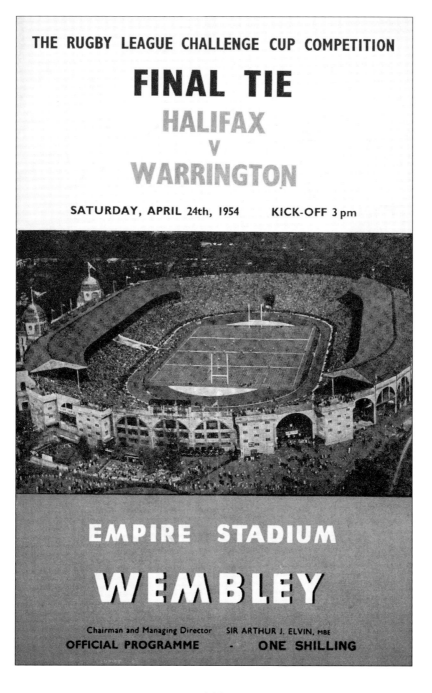

Wembley. Halifax centre Peter Todd breaks through leaving Ray Price and Jim Challinor in his wake.

Halifax coach, "Dolly" Dawson has an audience for a pre-Wembley session at the Selsdon Park Hotel.

STATISTICS

THE NORTHERN RUGBY FOOTBALL LEAGUE
FINAL TABLE, SEASON 1953-54

Our Exclusive Comprehensive Guide to the Performances of Clubs during Season 1953-54 specially compiled by the Editor (Stanley Chadwick) for the use of " Rugby League Review " readers

Figures in parenthesis denote final position last season.	HOME			For G.	T.	Pts.	Against G.	T.	Pts.	Total Attend.	AWAY W.	L.	D.	For G.	T.	Pts.	Against G.	T.	Pts.	Total Attend.	League Pts. Last	S'son	* Cty.
	Pl.	W.	L.D.																				
1 Halifax (2)	36	18	0 0	65	57	301	14	19	85	200,707	12	4	2	48	47	237	34	22	134	203,753	62	(60)	Y
2 Warrington (9)	36	18	0 0	80	92	436	34	21	131	247,036	12	5	1	49	43	227	42	32	180	204,472	61	(41)	L
3 St. Helens (1)	36	16	1 1	68	85	391	39	15	123	301,000	12	5	1	58	55	281	45	28	174	220,156	58	(66)	L
4 Work'ton T. (16)	36	15	3 0	60	73	339	33	27	147	162,536	14	4	0	56	51	265	39	36	186	146,384	58	(34)	C
5 Hull (15)	36	17	1 0	83	94	448	21	24	114	173,000	8	10	0	51	45	237	53	43	235	133,363	50	(36)	Y
6 Huddersfield (4)	36	15	3 0	75	103	459	38	42	202	209,199	9	9	0	46	46	230	40	45	215	187,305	48	(56)	Y
7 Wigan (11)	36	15	3 0	77	104	466	38	25	151	267,073	8	9	1	42	46	222	56	43	241	184,296	47	(40)	L
8 Barrow (5)	36	15	3 0	57	75	339	23	32	142	185,683	8	10	0	47	47	235	38	53	235	134,745	46	(55)	L
9 Bradford N. (3)	36	12	6 0	69	74	360	31	35	167	211,500	10	8	0	50	56	268	53	47	247	165,161	44	(56)	Y
10 Leeds (6)	36	13	5 0	101	97	493	57	51	267	263,300	9	9	0	54	55	273	59	44	250	193,974	44	(48)	Y
11 Wakefield T. (18)	36	12	6 0	57	95	399	47	50	244	95,663	7	10	1	55	54	272	66	44	264	115,308	39	(32)	Y
12 Oldham (8)	36	13	3 2	65	68	334	36	22	138	181,805	4	12	2	37	32	170	57	38	228	198,315	38	(46)	L
13 Leigh (7)	36	11	7 0	51	65	297	45	42	216	165,000	8	10	0	56	46	250	54	45	243	180,613	38	(48)	L
14 F'stone R. (24)	36	12	4 2	52	63	293	41	39	199	77,000	6	12	0	40	35	185	50	44	232	100,589	38	(25)	Y
15 Hunslet (12)	36	15	3 0	55	54	272	35	26	148	134,572	4	14	0	39	35	183	63	59	303	131,960	38	(40)	Y
16 Widnes (23)	36	12	5 1	56	59	289	29	28	142	101,370	4	12	2	28	25	131	59	57	289	106,628	35	(28)	L
17 York (25)	36	12	6 0	45	53	249	33	35	171	119,302	5	13	0	32	33	163	37	52	230	99,803	34	(20)	Y
18 Keighley (17)	36	12	6 0	70	44	272	41	38	196	98,819	3	12	3	45	37	201	68	67	337	134,772	33	(33)	Y
19 Rochdale H. (22)	36	9	7 2	55	54	272	41	38	196	154,154	5	12	1	27	26	132	48	55	261	117,724	31	(29)	L
20 Dewsbury (19)	36	11	5 2	46	48	236	37	42	200	90,500	3	14	1	32	44	196	58	64	308	108,636	31	(31)	Y
21 Whitehaven (10)	36	11	6 1	52	33	203	31	33	161	102,321	3	15	0	39	27	159	70	81	383	108,882	29	(40)	C
22 Salford (13)	36	11	6 1	40	60	260	34	32	164	120,000	2	15	1	19	24	110	53	56	274	124,261	28	(40)	L
23 Swinton (14)	36	8	10 0	36	34	174	49	35	203	111,000	5	12	1	34	33	167	56	66	310	120,871	27	(36)	L
24 Batley (21)	36	9	8 1	42	41	207	57	52	270	81,872	4	14	0	32	32	160	62	88	388	119,380	27	(30)	Y
25 Bramley (29)	36	9	6 3	54	42	234	51	52	258	59,600	2	16	0	43	39	203	82	108	488	117,099	25	(12)	Y
26 Castleford (20)	36	7	11 0	61	35	227	64	65	323	79,084	4	13	1	45	40	210	78	83	405	121,106	23	(30)	Y
27 Man. B.V.R. (27)	36	7	10 1	45	34	192	56	40	232	53,428	0	17	1	26	21	115	79	108	482	115,688	16	(20)	L
28 Hull K.R. (28)	36	3	13 2	43	27	167	57	44	246	84,720	2	16	0	19	31	131	88	105	491	104,895	12	(19)	Y
29 Doncaster (26)	36	4	13 1	43	33	185	62	75	349	27,650	1	16	1	43	23	155	76	113	491	95,399	12	(20)	Y
30 Liverpool C. (30)	36	4	14 0	36	30	162	56	71	325	24,250	0	18	0	38	22	142	76	100	452	87,676	8	(8)	L

* Denotes County. C—Cumberland, L—Lancashire, Y—Yorkshire.

NOTE.—Hunslet v. Hull K.R., August 24th, abandoned after seventy-five minutes, with Hunslet leading 12—0. Rochdale H. v. Manchester Belle Vue R., December 26th, abandoned after seventy-six minutes, with Rochdale H. leading, 15—0. Results of both matches allowed to stand. Fixtures between Hull K.R. and Hull, September 21st, played on Hull City ground, and Rochdale H. v. Keighley, March 23rd, played on Rochdale A.F. Club ground (both under floodlight). Bradford N. home fixtures with Wakefield T. and Hunslet, and Leigh home fixture with Bramley, played under floodlight. B.B.C. Television of whole of match between Hunslet and Barrow, on January 16th. French referees in charge of four matches during Easter. All-Ticket Match, Wigan v. Leigh, April 16th Free admission at match between Liverpool C. and Whitehaven, November 21st.
Halifax and Warrington won all their home matches. Liverpool C. lost all their away matches.

PLAY-OFF FOR NORTHERN RUGBY FOOTBALL LEAGUE CHAMPIONSHIP

SEMI-FINALS

	G.	T.Pts.			G.	T.Pts.	Attend.
Halifax (1)	3	4 18	Workington T. (4)		2	1 7	14,300
Warr'ton (2)	4	1 11	St. Helens ... (3)		0	0 0	23,798

FINAL

	G.	T.Pts.			G.	T.Pts.	Attend.
Warr'ton (2)	4	0 8	Halifax ...	(1)	2	1 7	36,519

Played at Maine Road, Manchester. B.B.C. Television of the whole match.

Kiwis Sudden Death. Clarence Alfred Hurndell, New Zealand second-row forward, died on his way to work. Hurndell was a member of the 1947-48 New Zealand team to tour England and France but was taken ill at Panama and returned home. Aged twenty-seven years and had announced his retirement from representative football this season.—Sunday, August 1st.

Devery Presentation. The Huddersfield Cricket and Athletic Supporters' Club presented P. C. Devery with an illuminated address. Devery retired from football last season, and is returning to Australia.—Monday, August 2nd.

For Transfer. William McGowan, Swinton front-row forward, placed on transfer list at his own request (fee £1,250). The club has removed the names of F. Osmond (hooker), R. Thomas (scrum-half), and Holder (forward) from the transfer list.—Wednesday, August 4th.

Swinton Loss. £343 on season 1953-54 (loss of £1,568 season 1952-53 and £1,098 season 1951-52). Drop of £1,880 in gate receipts of £12,762. Wages, bonuses, and transfer fees amounted to £6,304, with £1,878 paid in entertainments duty.—August 4th.

Warrington Signing. Peter O'Toole, 22-year-old prop or second-row forward, from Orford Tannery. Weight 14 st.—August 4th.

Blackpool Follies ? Blackpool R.L. club to make an addition to their title but final decision not reached.—August 6th.

RUGBY LEAGUE REVIEW, AUGUST 12th, 1954—351

THE RUGBY LEAGUE CHALLENGE CUP COMPETITION 1953-1954

FIRST ROUND, FIRST LEG	Belle Vue Rangers	15	Huddersfield	20	2,000
	Castleford	8	Doncaster	5	3,000
	HALIFAX	19	Dewsbury	0	12,000
	Hull	24	Widnes	0	14,000
	Keighley	12	Barrow	11	6,600
	Latchford Albion (At Warrington)	20	Wigan	40	9,032
	Leeds	13	Batley	20	16,500
	Liverpool City	5	Oldham	15	1,000
	Rochdale Hornets	9	Bradford Northern	9	10,879
	St. Helens	26	Featherstone Rovers	7	16,000
	Salford	3	Hunslet	18	3,500
	Swinton	2	Leigh	17	6,000
	Wakefield Trinity	24	Whitehaven	13	10,000
	WARRINGTON	17	Bramley	0	10,789
	Workington Town	50	Wheldale Colliery	2	5,575
	York	18	Hull Kingston Rovers	0	8,380
FIRST ROUND, SECOND LEG	Barrow	6	Keighley	10	12,352
	Batley	6	Leeds	23	15,000
	Bradford Northern	11	Rochdale Hornets	2	20,014
	Bramley	5	WARRINGTON	30	2,048
	Dewsbury	9	HALIFAX	15	3,500
	Doncaster	7	Castleford	2	1,274
	Featherstone Rovers	16	St. Helens	27	6,000
	Huddersfield	31	Belle Vue Rangers	6	4,958
	Hull Kingston Rovers	0	York	0	2,400
	Hunslet	20	Salford	5	5,170
	Leigh	13	Swinton	4	13,000
	Oldham	18	Liverpool City	11	7,492
	Wheldale Colliery (At Castleford)	6	Workington Town	32	750
	Whitehaven	15	Wakefield Trinity	3	6,000
	Widnes	2	Hull	5	5,000
	Wigan	41	Latchford Albion	2	8,139
SECOND ROUND	HALIFAX	24	Keighley	5	16,128
	Huddersfield	12	St. Helens	5	31,172
	Hull	5	Workington Town	5	20,000
	Hunslet	10	Whitehaven	2	8,334
	Leeds	12	Leigh	3	22,600
	Oldham	4	WARRINGTON	7	21,000
	Wigan	15	Bradford Northern	10	26,120
	York	11	Doncaster	2	9,952
REPLAY	Workington Town	17	Hull	14	16,000
THIRD ROUND	Hunslet	16	Huddersfield	7	20,136
	Leeds	31	Workington Town	11	33,341
	WARRINGTON	26	York	5	19,118
	Wigan	0	HALIFAX	2	43,953
SEMI-FINALS	HALIFAX (at Odsal)	18	Hunslet	3	46,961
	Leeds (at Swinton)	4	WARRINGTON	8	36,993
FINAL (at Wembley)	HALIFAX	4	WARRINGTON	4	81,841
REPLAY (at Odsal)	HALIFAX	4	WARRINGTON	8	102,569

WARRINGTON'S TRIPLE CUP WINNERS

Back Row: E. White, S. Phillips, R. Ryan, G. Lowe, J. Challinor, A. Stevens, A. Humphreys, B. Bevan,
   H. Fishwick.
Sitting: W. Sheridan, A. Heathwood, D. Naughton, S. McCormick, A. Naughton, C. Mountford, E. Frodsham,
   R. Ryder, H. Bath, F. Wright.
Front: R. Price, G. Helme.
Trophies: R.L. CHAMPIONSHIP CUP, R.L. CHALLENGE CUP, LANCASHIRE LEAGUE CHAMPIONSHIP CUP.

HALIFAX AT MAINE ROAD

Standing: A. Fearnley, D. Clarkson, J. Wilkinson, J. Thorley, A. Ackerley, P. Todd, T. Lynch, D. Bevan.
Kneeling: K. Dean, S. Kielty, T. Griffiths, A. Daniels, D. Schofield.

HALIFAX'S RECORD 1953-54
(Played 48, Won 38, Drawn 3, Lost 7)

		R	T	G	P	T	G	P	CROWD	
Aug	15 DONCASTER	W	8	8	40	1	2	7	8698	
	22 Batley	W	9	8	43	0	0	0	6000	
	24 LEIGH	W	5	3	21	1	1	5	11069	
	29 BARROW	W	1	0	3	0	1	2	10159	
Sep	2 Featherstone Rov	W	2	4	14	1	0	3	6100	
	5 Castleford	W	3	1	11	0	0	0	6000	YC
	7 CASTLEFORD	W	3	0	9	1	0	3	10537	YC
	12 HULL	W	3	3	15	3	1	11	11073	
	19 Hunslet	L	1	2	7	2	5	16	11200	
	26 ST. HELENS	W	2	4	14	1	0	3	17468	
	28 Hull	L	0	2	4	4	2	16	14000	YC
Oct	3 CASTLEFORD	W	1	7	17	2	3	12	10352	
	10 Leeds	W	8	8	40	2	2	10	22944	
	17 WAKEFIELD TRINITY	W	3	4	17	2	1	8	11111	
	31 SWINTON	W	7	4	29	1	1	5	8893	
Nov	7 Doncaster	W	3	2	13	0	1	2	984	
	14 BATLEY	W	4	2	16	2	0	6	7200	
	21 Dewsbury	D	2	3	12	2	3	12	5121	
	28 LEEDS	W	2	6	18	3	2	13	15015	
Dec	5 Leigh	L	2	1	8	6	2	22	9777	
	12 YORK	W	2	4	14	1	0	3	12057	
	19 HUNSLET	W	3	0	9	0	0	0	10003	
	25 Huddersfield	W	4	0	12	0	1	2	20417	
	26 HUDDERSFIELD	W	2	2	10	0	0	0	16438	
	28 Swinton	W	2	2	10	0	0	0	8000	
Jan	2 Barrow	L	0	0	0	2	2	10	13005	
	9 York	W	1	1	5	0	1	2	8493	
	16 DEWSBURY	W	2	4	14	0	0	0	8583	
	23 Keighley	W	1	0	3	0	1	2	7096	
Feb	6 DEWSBURY	W	5	2	19	0	0	0	12000	CUP
	16 Dewsbury	W	3	3	15	1	3	9	3500	CUP
	20 St. Helens	D	1	1	5	1	1	5	22813	
	27 HULL KR	W	4	6	24	0	1	2	8797	
Mar	6 KEIGHLEY	W	6	3	24	1	1	5	16128	CUP
	13 FEATHERSTONE ROV	W	2	1	8	1	0	3	8959	
	20 Wigan	W	0	1	2	0	0	0	43953	CUP
	27 Castleford	W	3	4	17	1	4	11	4942	
Apr	3 Hunslet (1)	W	4	3	18	1	0	3	46961	CUP SF
	5 BRADFORD NORTHERN	W	3	3	15	0	1	2	11313	
	10 Bradford Northern	W	3	3	15	1	2	7	19370	
	14 Wakefield Trinity	W	1	3	9	1	2	7	7502	
	17 Hull KR	W	3	4	17	0	4	8	7354	
	19 Hull	L	1	2	7	3	3	15	15000	
	24 Warrington (2)	D	0	2	4	0	2	4	81841	CUP F
	26 KEIGHLEY	W	3	4	17	1	0	3	13026	
May	1 WORKINGTON TOWN	W	4	3	18	1	2	7	14300	CH'P SF
	5 Warrington (1)	L	0	2	4	2	1	8	102569	CUP FRe
	8 Warrington (3)	L	1	2	7	0	4	8	36519	CH'P F
	TOTALS		133	137	673	52	63	282		

Neutral venues: (1) Odsal (2) Wembley (3) Maine Road

WARRINGTON'S RECORD 1953-54
(Played 49, Won 41, Drawn 2, Lost 6)

		R	T	G	P	T	G	P	CROWD	
Aug	15 SALFORD	W	3	4	17	0	2	4	12290	
	19 BARROW	W	2	3	12	1	2	7	10023	
	22 Hull KR	L	1	1	5	3	4	17	5597	
	29 ROCHDALE HORNETS	W	4	2	16	0	2	4	10256	
Sep	3 Barrow	W	1	1	5	0	0	0	11869	
	5 BELLE VUE RANGERS	W	6	5	28	1	2	7	11400	LC
	8 Belle Vue Rangers	W	3	4	17	2	4	14	3000	LC
	12 Leeds	L	2	4	14	9	8	43	19240	
	19 WIGAN	W	1	5	13	3	0	9	18046	
	24 OLDHAM	W	2	3	12	1	4	11	15524	LC
	26 Whitehaven	W	3	5	19	1	1	5	6678	
	30 St. Helens	L	2	2	10	3	4	17	23184	LCSF
Oct	3 HULL KR	W	8	9	42	3	2	13	12590	
	10 Castleford	W	6	5	28	3	2	13	6416	
	17 SWINTON	W	5	4	23	2	1	8	14350	
	24 Workington Town	L	1	2	7	1	3	9	12285	
	31 LEEDS	W	3	3	15	1	3	9	16109	
Nov	7 Belle Vue Rangers	W	1	3	9	0	1	2	1082	
	14 HULL	W	1	3	9	0	1	2	10132	
	21 Salford	W	2	2	10	2	1	8	7252	
	28 LIVERPOOL CITY	W	8	3	30	0	3	6	7424	
Dec	5 CASTLEFORD	W	8	6	36	2	3	12	9479	
	12 Bramley	W	3	5	19	0	3	6	2953	
	25 WIDNES	W	5	4	23	1	2	7	10599	
	26 Leigh	W	3	2	13	2	0	6	12360	
Jan	1 Wigan	W	3	4	17	2	3	12	22048	
	2 St. Helens	W	1	2	7	0	1	2	18000	
	9 WORKINGTON TOWN	W	3	3	15	1	2	7	16115	
	16 BRAMLEY	W	11	10	53	1	1	5	9556	
	23 Rochdale Hornets	W	5	2	19	1	2	7	14200	
	30 Hull	L	2	2	10	4	6	24	16000	
Feb	13 BRAMLEY	W	5	1	17	0	0	0	10789	CUP
	17 Bramley	W	8	3	30	1	1	5	2048	CUP
	20 OLDHAM	W	2	4	14	0	1	2	17271	
	27 ST. HELENS	W	2	3	12	0	4	8	29107	
Mar	6 Oldham	W	1	2	7	0	2	4	21000	CUP
	13 Liverpool City	L	0	1	2	1	1	5	2748	
	20 YORK	W	6	4	26	1	1	5	19118	CUP
	27 Swinton	W	3	3	15	1	3	9	7800	
Apr	3 Leeds (1)	W	2	1	8	0	2	4	36993	CUP SF
	8 Oldham	D	1	2	7	1	2	7	7257	
	10 BELLE VUE RANGERS	W	10	6	42	2	0	6	12387	
	16 Widnes	W	5	3	21	1	1	5	15527	
	17 WHITEHAVEN	W	11	5	43	1	2	7	14726	
	19 LEIGH	W	5	3	21	3	3	15	22658	
	24 Halifax (2)	D	0	2	4	0	2	4	81841	CUP F
May	1 ST. HELENS	W	1	4	11	0	0	0	23888	CH'P SF
	5 Halifax (3)	W	2	1	8	0	2	4	102569	CUP FRe
	8 Halifax (4)	W	0	4	8	1	2	7	36519	CH'P F
	TOTALS		173	165	849	63	102	393		

Neutral venues: (1) Swinton (2) Wembley (3) Odsal (4) Maine Road

CHALLENGE CUP FINAL ACCOUNTS
WEMBLEY, 24 APRIL, 1954

RECEIPTS

PAYMENTS

	£ s d		£ s d
Gate	29,706/ 7/3	Wembley - 25% gate & BBC	5,254/ 8/ 1
Tax	8,724/16/3	Cup Pool 10%	2,098/ 3/ 1
	20,981/11/0	British Playing Fields Soc 2½%	524/ 5/ 9
		Halifax 8%	1,678/10/ 5
BBC	52/10/0	Warrington 8%	1,678/10/ 5
		Hire of coaches	16/16/ 0
		Agents commission - paid by Wembley	16/ 8/ 9
		Band, refreshments, press advertising, paid by Wembley	371/ 2/ 0
		Match expenses - officials, travelling, gratuities	80/ 7/ 0
		Badges for officials	9/17/ 3
		Film	3/ 3/ 0
		Medals	170/ 6/ 0
		Balance being net profit on match	9,132/ 3/ 3
	£21,034/ 1/0		**£21,034/ 1/ 0**

CHALLENGE CUP FINAL REPLAY ACCOUNTS
ODSAL, 5 MAY, 1954

RECEIPTS

PAYMENTS

	£ s d		£ s d
Gate	18,623/ 7/0	Bradford Northern 10%	1,390/13/ 8
Tax	4,716/10/0	Cup Pool 10%	1,390/13/ 8
	13,906/17/0	British Playing Fields Soc 2½%	347/13/ 5
		Gateman & Stewards	93/ 7/ 9
BBC	21/ 0/0	Police	68/11/ 9
		Posting & Advertising	35/13/ 7
		Printing tickets	38/ 7/ 6
		Refreshments	55/ 0/ 2
		Erection of and repairs to track seats	56/19/10
		Black Dyke Mills Band	25/ 0/ 0
		Bank Charges	21/ 0/ 0
		Referees and Touch-judges	23/ 6/10
		Halifax - 8% net gate plus 8% grant	2,225/ 1/10
		Warrington - as Halifax above	2,225/ 1/10
		Film (sound)	3/ 3/ 0
		Balance being net profit on match	5,928/ 2/ 2
	£13,927/17/ 0		**£13,927/17/ 0**

STILL AVAILABLE -
FROM THE AUTHOR OF "THERE WERE
A LOT MORE THAN THAT"

"GONE NORTH: WELSHMEN IN RUGBY LEAGUE" (Volume 1)

184 pages, fully illustrated. Price £6.50 – The story of Wales' greatest Rugby League players. This volume features, amongst others, Billy Boston, Wattie Davies, Trevor Foster, Roy Francis, Jim Sullivan, Jim Mills, Tommy Harris, Emlyn Jenkins, John Mantle, Colin Dixon, Kel Coslett.

"An unusual and compelling history" - **Paul Fitzpatrick, "The Guardian"**
"A thoroughly readable book" - **John Kennedy, "South Wales Echo"**
"Compelling reading for followers of both codes" - **Raymond Fletcher, "Yorkshire Post"**

"GONE NORTH: WELSHMEN IN RUGBY LEAGUE" (Volume 2)

182 pages, fully illustrated. Price £9.99 – More great Welsh Rugby League players including Gus Risman, Johnny Freeman, Garfield Owen, Lewis Jones, Clive Sullivan, Johnny Ring, Ben Gronow, David Watkins, Maurice Richards, Alan Edwards, Joe Thompson, Danny Hurcombe, Johnny Rogers

"Scrupulously researched, incisively perceptive and admirably readable" - **Huw Richards, "City Limits"**
"Once taken up I could not put it down" - **Ray French, "Rugby Leaguer"**
"Overflowing with superlatives" - **Trevor Delaney, "Code 13"**

********* NOTE: Both volumes of "Gone North" may be obtained for £13.50 the pair (post free) **********

"THE STRUGGLE FOR THE ASHES"

208 pages, fully illustrated. Price £8.00 – The history of Anglo-Australian Rugby League test matches 1908-84. Match by match accounts of every Great Britain-Australia test match.

"Not only a statistician's dream but a darned, good read" - **Brian Smith, "Telegraph & Argus"**
"Quite simply the best book on Rugby League, ever" - **"Leeds Other Paper"**
"One of the game's most ambitious writing projects has turned out a winner" - **David Middleton,**
"Rugby League Week"
"If points are awarded for this book, Mr. Gate scores ten out of ten" - **John Billot, "The Western Mail"**

"CHAMPIONS: A CELEBRATION OF THE RUGBY LEAGUE CHAMPIONSHIP 1895-1987"

192 pages, fully illustrated. Price £12.00 – A pictorial and statistical record of Rugby League's most important competition featuring all Rugby League's champion teams.

"Nostalgia drips from the pages" - **Harry Egar, "Open Rugby"**
"The photographs alone were worth the price" - **Ray French, "Rugby Leaguer"**
"Deserves a place on the bookshelf of anyone with an eye for the history of the game" - **Phil Lyon, "Halifax Evening Courier"**

ALSO BY THE AUTHOR IN ASSOCIATION WITH MICHAEL LATHAM

"THEY PLAYED FOR WIGAN"

78 pages, fully illustrated. Price £5.99 – A complete statistical record of all the players who have appeared in the cherry and white of Wigan between 1895 and 1992.

All the above books are available post free from

Robert Gate, Mount Pleasant Cottage,
Ripponden Bank,
Ripponden,
Sowerby Bridge HX6 4JL

Please make cheques payable to RE Gate